A Morning in June

To Mac David
1/9 2050
The best every

[signature]

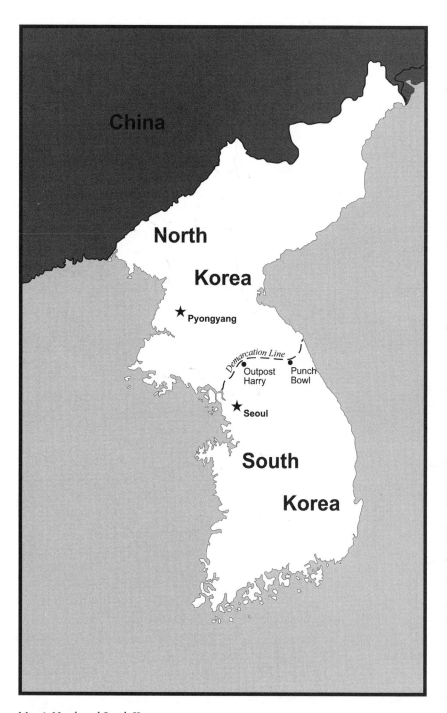

Map 1. North and South Korea.

A Morning in June

Defending Outpost Harry

JAMES W. EVANS

With a Foreword by John S. D. Eisenhower

THE UNIVERSITY OF ALABAMA PRESS

Tuscaloosa

Typeface: Bembo

∞

The paper on which this book is printed meets the minimum requirements of American National Standard for Information Sciences-Permanence of Paper for Printed Library Materials, ANSI Z39.48-1984.

Library of Congress Cataloging-in-Publication Data

Evans, James W. (James William), 1929–
   A morning in June : defending Outpost Harry / James W. Evans.
        p.   cm.
   Includes bibliographical references and index.
ISBN 978-0-8173-1669-3 (cloth : alk. paper)
ISBN 978-0-8173-8181-3 (electronic) 1. Evans, James W. (James William),
1929– 2. Korean War, 1950–1953—Personal narratives, American. 3. Outpost Harry
(Korea : Military base) 4. Korean War, 1950–1953—Campaigns—Korea—Ch'orwon-gun.
5. Soldiers—United States—Biography. 6. United States. Army. Infantry Division, 3rd—
Biography I. Title.
   DS921.6.E945 2010
   951.904'242—dc22

                                                                      2009035172

To all who participated in the defense of Outpost Harry,
Chorwon Valley, Korea, 10–18 June 1953

Contents

List of Illustrations

Figures

Table

Maps

Foreword

Through a long career in the Regular Army, the Army Reserve, and as a writer on military subjects, I have always carried the memory of a military action fought in the last days of the Korean War that to me epitomizes the valor and dedication of the American soldier. The action was the defense of Outpost Harry by the 3rd Infantry Division and its attached units in June 1953.

It was a small operation by strategic standards, involving eight to ten infantry companies. But to the foot soldier there is no such thing as a small action; all actions are essentially the same, fraught with danger, fatigue, and the trauma that goes with the unnatural act of killing fellow human beings. And the killing is not a distant, impersonal thing; it is personal indeed: the killer sees the eyes of his victim. Though the act is necessary to the preservation of one's own life, the later recollections can be traumatic indeed.

The defense of Outpost Harry had all of these elements, but it included one more. The participant, both officer and private, knew before he trudged up the hill that he was facing almost certain death, wounding, or capture. For Harry was a small piece of ground, a knob in the no-man's-land between the American and Chinese lines. By all logic it should have been the property of the enemy. Nevertheless, the American high command was determined to hold it at all costs. The fact that the American soldiers of the 3rd Division and the attached 5th Infantry Regiment, 5th Regimental Combat Team (of which James Evans was a member) went up the hill without reservation and fought a superior enemy to a standstill continues to engender in me a feeling of awe.

The Outpost Harry action took place late in the Korean War; the truce between the U.S.-led United Nations forces and the Chinese–North Korean forces was signed at Panmunjom only about six weeks after the battle's close. It is fair to wonder, then, if the action had been in vain—whether the American high command could have afforded to give up this sole surviving outpost, thus sparing the lives of so many brave soldiers. Possibly so. All of the other outposts, to the best of my recollection, had been given up. Their names are better known than Harry, possibly because they are more colorful and likely because they were lost at times when there were no other momentous events to deflect public attention. Some, such as Pork Chop Hill, Heartbreak Ridge, Arrowhead, and others still live in the memories of the Korean generation. But of all this line of outposts, Harry was the only one that remained in American hands when the peace agreement was signed. I like to think the successful defense of Outpost Harry had a psychological effect on both friend and foe. It demonstrated that Americans, when necessary, could hold any terrain despite the odds. Being on the spot myself, I noticed that after the action on Harry, the Chinese never hit American units again; in fact, from then on the enemy seemed particularly careful to avoid hitting American (in contrast to Republic of Korea, or ROK) forces.

I was associated, though remotely, with the Outpost Harry defense, as the G-2 (Intelligence) officer of the 3rd Division at the time. I ran the G-2/G-3 operations desk for half of every night. During those four crucial days, the drama of OP Harry riveted our attention. We never knew if Outpost Harry would survive the night or not. It should come as no surprise, therefore, that I feel a keen interest in seeing that it receives its due as one of the outstanding feats of arms in America's military history.

It is also important, however, for the public to be reminded that actions such as OP Harry take their toll on the young men who fight them. We justifiably mourn the dead, but we tend to overlook the price paid by the survivors for the rest of their lives. James Evans has taken on the worthy cause of explaining both the military action and the aftermath on its participants. He has my sincere congratulations on his effort.

John S. D. Eisenhower
15 April 2008

Preface

After North Korea invaded South Korea in July 1950, the fighting to free South Korea was on a fluid battlefield for nearly a year. Both the North Korea People's Army (NKPA) and the Chinese People's Volunteer Army (CPVA) fought the United Nations (UN) forces up and down the Korean peninsula.

The early years of the Korean War generated interest and produced numerous documents by military historians, including tales of the Pusan Perimeter, the Chosin (Changjin) Reservoir, and the Inchon Invasion, to list just a few well-documented battles. Because of the peace negotiations at Kaesong, Korea, on 10 July 1951 the fighting came to a stalemate and military historians lost interest, ignoring the Korean War from then until the fighting stopped on 27 July 1953.

This was unfortunate, since nearly as many Americans were killed after the line stabilized on 10 July 1951 as were killed while the battle lines were still fluid. The battles of Heartbreak Ridge (September–October 1951), Hill Eerie (March 1952), Pork Chop Hill (March–July 1953), the Hook (May 1953), and Outpost Harry (10–18 June 1953) resulted in heavy American casualties. According to the U.S. Headquarters IX Corps Combat Operations Command Report for the month of June 1953, the number of personnel killed in action was 1,056; wounded in action, 3,030; and missing in action, 89. The majority of the casualties were from the Republic of Korea 9th Capital Division. This IX Corps report was only for the final month of fighting before the signing of the truce agreement!

The stalemated war from July 1951 until July 1953 became a trench war, in contrast to World War II, which was a maneuvering war both in Europe and in the Far East. Internet searches for information regarding "trench war" focus their responses on descriptions of World War I battlefields. For instance, the Wikipedia entry for "trench warfare" includes an acknowledgment that trench war existed in Korea and that there was occasional use of trenches in Vietnam, primarily during the defense of Dien Bien Phu, but that is the entire offering about post–World War I trenches. The lack of documentation regarding Korean trench warfare is very disappointing, since thousands of American service members died in the trenches.

During the period of 10 June through 18 June 1953, the Chorwon Valley of Korea was the site of a very important trench war battle. This engagement was about a combat outpost named Harry. The mission of American forces was to "hold [the outpost] at all costs." Most Korean War historians ignored the successful effort to stop the Chinese from taking the outpost. Historians overlooked information as reported in the Headquarters IX Corps Combat Operations Command Report, June 1953, GEN R. E. Jenkins, Commanding, that during the twenty-four-hour period from 1800 12 June until 1800 13 June 1953, artillery units within the IX Corps fired 88,184 artillery rounds. This represented the largest volume of fire by the IX Corps for any like period since the start of the Korean War, and the majority of the artillery support was for the defense of Outpost Harry.

One of the reasons I wrote this book is to explain to service members who are now, or soon to be, in the civilian world how I survived in civilian life after participating in the most terrible form of infantry combat: hand-to-hand trench warfare. Knowing how I survived may be of benefit to both service members and their families. However, I realized that before I could suggest a survival technique, I must validate my credentials as having experienced war.

In describing the war in Korea, in which I participated for a year, I present certain historical information along with my combat experiences. In addition, I review the battles fought in Korean trenches, the trench construction, the success of racial integration within the U.S. Army, and the difficulty of commanding an infantry company in combat. Most important, I report on my transition from a bloody combat environment to a civilian world.

A Morning in June: Defending Outpost Harry is a history of the last days of the Korean War and a historically correct accounting of Able Company, 5th Regimental Combat Team's participation in the battle for Outpost Harry. Thanks to the declassification of many official military records, one of which provides an official timeline of the combat, this is a factual and documented history of the events that took place on the outpost. Throughout the book, quoted unit reports verify the narrative. One of several military documents referenced is a time log of radio messages between Outpost Harry and rear echelons. The portion of the log relating to those hours that Able Company, 5th Regimental Combat Team (RCT), defended Outpost Harry was particularly useful.

The defense of Outpost Harry was one of the last major battles ever conducted in the trenches by American forces. Being one of the last trench battles, what happened at Outpost Harry is significant and therefore makes *A Morning in June* unique. Future combat leaders can read about problems that an infantry company commander confronts and realize that in combat there are no preconceived solutions available. The combat situation is often chaotic. A combat leader must analyze and solve each problem with individual initiative and courage. Combat leadership, at the company level, commonly receives little help from anyone.

The 5th Infantry Regiment was one of the first U.S. Army units to become racially integrated. In addition to detailed accounts of combat, I have described the relationships between South Korean, Puerto Rican, African American, and Caucasian soldiers. Included are discussions of the problems and successes of the newly adopted practice of racially integrating units as well as the effectiveness of an integrated unit in combat.

During World War I, soldiers suffered from "shell shock." In World War II and the Korean War, the term used was "battle fatigue." Soldiers released from active duty in 1953 did not receive professional counseling, nor were they otherwise made aware of what they might expect upon reentering civilian life. The Korean veteran had a very difficult time explaining to his family what had really happened to him, since he had so little understanding of his own problems. By 2006, military authorities recognized that each individual engaged in combat reacts in a different way and began to provide additional staffing of trained medical personnel to provide counseling for combat veterans.

Veterans returning from the Middle East in 2006 experienced a type of combat that was different from what is described in *A Morning in June* (although house-to-house fighting is similar to trench fighting). However, infantry combat is still infantry combat. The fear, the destruction of the human body, and the deeply embedded memories of horror are still the same. Veterans of today who have participated in combat have the same problems as veterans of yesteryear. Fortunately, today's veterans have counseling and help available.

A Morning in June opens when I reported for my first combat assignment with the 5th RCT. The time is October 1952, during the Korean War, and the place is an area called the "Punch Bowl," an ancient volcanic crater in eastern Korea. I describe my experiences and the challenges I faced until I finally rotated back to the United States.

Traveling by jeep from the bottom of the Punch Bowl to its northern rim, I reached my assignment as an infantry platoon leader for Able Company. I participated in infantry combat under intense artillery fire, was scared by a friendly tank, blown off my feet by enemy artillery, and shot at by an NKPA machine gun. While on the rim of the bowl, I lived in a bunker, walked the trenches, and ran ambush and combat patrols.

This book relates the many difficulties of living in trenches during the bitterly cold Korean winter of 1952–1953, including the complexities of being in combat for some six weeks without relief, showers, or clean clothes. In addition, the trenches of the UN troops, how they were constructed and defended, and how men lived and fought in them are discussed. Interlaced with tales of the fighting are noncombat segments of life during the Korean War. These include photographs that show the beauty of the Korean countryside in sharp contrast to the horror of combat. I also chronicle such classic warrior activities as seven days of rest and relaxation away from the shooting.

In the spring of 1953, the 5th RCT repositioned itself in Korea from the Punch Bowl to the Chorwon Valley. The scenario for the "Siege of Outpost Harry" (as identified by *VFW* magazine) was being set. I describe the events leading up to the Outpost Harry conflict from the mistakes and confusions of a military movement to initiation into the realities of personal, close combat. The main battle event, Able Company's defense of combat Outpost Harry on 12 and 13 June 1953, was critical to the United Nations' truce efforts. If Outpost Harry had been lost to the Chinese People's Volunteer Army, the Chinese would have had ground observation capability to support an attack toward Seoul, the capital of South Korea. When the Chinese did attack Outpost Harry, bitter hand-to-hand combat in the trenches ensued for hours. The bravery of the American soldiers defeated the Chinese that morning in June. From the initial orders, issued on a morning in June, to move forward and defend Outpost Harry until we were relieved on the afternoon of 13 June 1953, the action was intense, confused, constant, and unbelievable. Able Company and its attachments suffered seventeen killed in action and eighty-three wounded in action, representing 80 percent-plus of the defenders.

After reading *A Morning in June,* the reader may wonder how anyone ever recovers, mentally or physically, from the horrors of hand-to-hand trench combat. No glamour exists in such combat. When a warrior meets the enemy in a trench, only one of the two will live. There are no time-outs, no referees, and no honor codes—nothing but the barbaric destruction of the other person. The message of this book is that a person can be engaged in the deadliest form of combat and, with the help of God, survive the horror. However, returning home and trying to live a normal life, with the memories of trench combat constantly lurking in the background, is a challenge for which no one can prepare. *A Morning in June* is the true story of how I survived combat and overcame the unexpected challenges I faced upon my homecoming. It is my hope that my success may help others.

Acknowledgments

With little understanding of the effort required to write a book, I did what a lot of novice wannabe authors do: I leaped from the world of dreams into the unknown challenges of authorship. Writing a manuscript about Outpost Harry, I surmised, would be easily completed in two to three months. After two years of labor, however, I realized that writing is a difficult task. Nevertheless, with exceptional help from some wonderful people, the manuscript slowly evolved and became a book. Now I appreciate and respect all who have earned the title "Author."

Many people have assisted me with their encouragement and constructive criticism. Of special help has been Richard D. Goldblatt, the first to review a draft, write a letter of recommendation, and edit the manuscript. Samuel M. Kier, author of *Thirty-Six Points* (Fireside Fiction, 2005), graciously provided reports and logs from which I could accurately reconstruct unit movements and a timeline for the trench combat. Timothy R. Stoy, James Hafer Jr., and Dr. Lester Dubnick also encouraged me with letters of endorsement, for which I shall always be grateful.

Comrades-in-arms who shared valuable documents and support include Raymond C. Anderson, Robert H. Baker, Patrick W. Burke, Dan Carson, Robert E. Cole, Jerry Cunningham, Paul Curtis, Floyd Deiwert Jr., Leonard E. Godmaire, Paul Gregory, Cornelius Hindall, E. Douglas Jones, Ernest W. Kramer, John A. Lenz, Robert H. Orheim, John M. Ross, James G. Steffan, Claude L. Williams, Mark Woods, and many others who shared information while attending meetings of the Outpost Harry Survivors Association.

Special thanks to those who contributed irreplaceable photographs—some never before released. These include George Boucher; Freeman H. Bradford; Robert J. Brandon; James Drew; James Hafer Sr.; James F. Jarboe, for his 15 June 1953 night view of Outpost Harry with descending flares; and Chic Pellegrino. Each of these warriors provided unique battlefield photographs. Only with the help of Charles S. Scott was I able to include the Associated Press picture presenting the results of our defense of Outpost Harry.

No longer available to acknowledge my heartfelt thanks is Delbert F. Tolen, an outstanding warrior who served as my executive officer. Another missing soldier to whom I am grateful is 1SG Clyde Shinault, with whom I had the honor of serving during the battle for Outpost Harry. Without these two outstanding men, there is a very good chance that I wouldn't have survived the fight.

Many thanks to Korean War veterans for the conversations we have shared over the years, where images, understandings, and perceptions of the Korean War were confirmed or discarded. Many conflicts that I have had with myself regarding actions, times, and people have been resolved to the best of my ability.

I am especially grateful for Jerry Cunningham's leadership in organizing and perpetuating the Outpost Harry Survivors Association. Exchanging stories, validating facts, and creating lifelong comrade-in-arms fellowship has been a rewarding experience for which I will always be thankful.

And, most important, I am grateful for the support I received from my wife, Anne, without whose encouragement and patience I would have never completed this book.

List of Abbreviations

5th RCT, Fifth RCT	Fifth Regimental Combat Team
APC	armored personnel carrier
Arty	artillery
AW	automatic weapons
BAR	Browning automatic rifle
BN	battalion
Btry	artillery battery
CCF	Chinese Communist Forces (also known as the CPVA or the CPVF)
CO	company-size unit—also used as commanding officer
CP	command post
CPVA	Chinese People's Volunteer Army
CPVF	Chinese People's Volunteer Force
CT495388	coordinates for a location on the ground
DIV	division
FA	Field Artillery
FDC	fire direction center
FPF	fire protective fires
G-2	intelligence
G-4	quartermaster
HMG	heavy machine gun
ID	infantry division

INF	infantry
KIA	killed in action
M39	full-track armored personnel carrier
MG	machine gun
MIA	missing in action
MLR	main line of resistance
OP	observation post
OP Harry	Outpost Harry
PW	prisoner of war
RCT	regimental combat team
REGT	regiment
S-1	personnel officer
S-3	operations officer
SA	small arms—such as pistols, rifles, and machine guns
TOE	table of organization and equipment
VT	variable timed (a shell set to explode above the ground, usually 105mm)
WIA	wounded in action

A Morning in June

I

5th Regimental Combat Team

Korea with Incoming Artillery

On the crisp, cool morning of 10 October 1952, I, 2LT James William Evans, along with other U.S. Army replacement personnel, was finally getting off a Korean train after a two-day ride from Pusan, Korea. From the window, I noted that the train stopped at a small railroad station. Gathering all of my gear, including my .30-caliber carbine, I disembarked and joined the other one hundred or so replacements standing beside the train. Glancing about, I noticed that the railroad station's roof was gone—blown off—a true indication that the country was at war.

Before long, a sergeant started calling out names. After each name, the sergeant would direct that person to one of several two-and-a-half-ton trucks waiting a short distance from the railroad station. The trucks would transport the soldiers to their assigned units. When I heard my name called, I climbed onto the bed of the truck that was designated to go to my unit, the 5th Regimental Combat Team (5th RCT).

Our truck left the railroad station, and we bounced around in the "deuce and a half" for more than an hour, stopping at various locations. Riding in the back of a two-and-a-half-ton truck is a rough ride. The truck didn't seem to have any rear springs, because every dent in the road meant a bump of the wooden seat that would move the passengers up and back down with a hard landing.

At each stop the driver called out the name of the soldier assigned to the unit, and the soldier would gather his gear and hop off. We riders didn't exchange a lot of conversation. No one seemed excited or joyful to be in Korea;

in fact, we were a rather somber group. When the truck stopped and the driver called out my name, I gathered my equipment and disembarked at a location in the northeastern section of South Korea. As I looked around, I noticed several large tents erected and arranged in a dispersed manner. I was, so I quickly learned, at the headquarters of the 5th Infantry Regiment of the 5th RCT.

After checking in with the sergeant major, I dropped off my gear at the transit officer's quarters, which was really just a bunker in the side of a hill. Since noon was approaching, the sergeant major suggested I get some chow before reporting in. I found the mess hall, had lunch, and then walked back to headquarters, reporting as ordered. When reporting to a new command, infantry officer protocol directs the reporting officer to report to the unit's highest-ranking officer first and then work his way down to his assignment. Being a second lieutenant, I would have to work my way a long way down.

"Sir, Lieutenant Evans reporting as ordered, sir." I first reported to Lee L. Alfred, Colonel, Infantry, commanding the 5th Infantry Regiment and the 5th RCT.

The colonel quickly reviewed my orders. "Welcome, Lieutenant Evans, to the 5th Regimental Combat Team," Colonel Alfred said. "I notice you're wearing a Ranger shoulder tab. I thought all Rangers were to be assigned to Ranger companies." I explained that as I understood the situation, in 1951 the army had inactivated the Ranger companies in Korea, so replacement Rangers now reported to regular line units. We chatted for a few minutes before Colonel Alfred said he was glad to see me and we shook hands; I saluted and turned to walk to the door. He seemed like a reasonable person.

The colonel then turned me over to the regimental S-1, a designation for a regimental/battalion personnel officer. A major was currently holding the regimental S-1 slot. I saluted the major, who acknowledged the salute and suggested we go outside and look around. After we left Colonel Alfred's office and took a short walk out of the headquarters bunker, the S-1 explained to me that I was going to be a platoon leader in Able Company. Then he described where we were.

"We are standing in the bottom of an area called the Punch Bowl," he began. "The area is so named because if you look all the way around, you'll feel like you're in a very large bowl. Mountains are all around us, with the northern series of mountains being the ones where we are engaged with the North Korea People's Army, the NKPA," he said. "The units that we have fought have been the 45th, 48th, and 50th Regiments, 115th Division, of the III North Korean Corps."[1]

Pointing to the edge along the top of the northern series of mountains, the

1. View from inside the Punch Bowl. This photo shows the northern rim of the Punch Bowl as viewed from inside the valley crater. The highest mountain peak, shown under the center cloud, is Hill 1243. Able Company started at the top of this hill and went eastward toward the flat area called the "saddle." The Turkish battalion defended the left side of Hill 1243 continuing westward. Although difficult to determine in this picture, the rim begins its southwestward turn just to the left of Hill 1243. The highest hill left of Hill 1243 is Hill 1181. The cut for the road along the contour line of the mountain is clearly visible. Right of Hill 1243, while standing in the "saddle," several photographs were taken that appear later in this book. (Photo courtesy of LT COL George Boucher, 5th RCT, 1953.)

S-1 explained that the edge was the "rim." He said, "We call the edge a rim because bowls have rims, and since we're in a bowl, we have to have a rim." That made sense to me.

Continuing, he explained that no pattern existed as to which battalion would be on the rim or in reserve for showers, rest, and other military training. Battalions are normally rotated every month or so. Turning so that I could see his shoulder patch, the S-1 continued. "Fifth Regimental Combat Team, formed in Hawaii in 1950, is made up of several different units. The base unit for the 5th RCT is the 5th Infantry Regiment, which has as an organic component a tank company, a medical company, and a 4.2-inch mortar company. The 5th Infantry is one of the oldest regiments in the United States Army, formed in 1808. As you may already know, like all infantry regiments, the 5th Infantry Regiment has three infantry battalions identified as 1st, called Red; 2nd, called White; and the 3rd Battalion, called Blue. And each battalion has four infantry companies." The S-1 didn't tell me, because I knew, that the 1st Battalion [BN] had Able, Baker, and Charley companies, plus Dog—the heavy weapons company; 2nd BN had Easy, Fox, and George, plus How—the heavy weapons company; and 3rd BN had Item, King, and Love, plus Mike—the heavy weapons company.

"One additional element that's part of the 5th RCT is the 555th Field Artillery Battalion, which we sometimes call the 'Triple Nickel.' The last additional component is 72nd Engineer Company. As you can see," he said, pointing to his left shoulder, "the shoulder patch for the 5th RCT has five points and is shaped like a pentagon, with the interior in red and a border in white. The 5th RCT is presently attached to the 25th Infantry Division, which is part of the X Corps."[2]

After telling me all about the 5th RCT, the division, and the corps, the S-1 asked if I had any questions.

"No, sir," I responded. Besides, I thought, I most likely would never meet anyone with the X Corps or the 25th Infantry Division. I may never even meet anyone from the Triple Nickel unless it would be a forward observer.

Again pointing to the northern mountains, the S-1 explained, "The 1st Battalion, of which Able Company is a part, starts from the highest peak, on the left side of the northern rim, and goes down eastward to just about the center of the rim. With Able Company occupying the left flank of the 1st Battalion, Able Company starts from the highest peak and runs east. The Turkish Brigade starts on the other side of the highest peak and runs toward the west. The joining point is the peak. You may be assigned to the platoon having the responsibility of defending the area on the east of the peak down." I guessed that climbing up the mountain to the peak and back down was the worst platoon location in the Able Company area. Surely a new second lieutenant would get that assignment.

Continuing to point toward the northern rim, he said, "Now the 2nd Battalion of the 5th RCT attaches to the right flank of the 1st Battalion and continues to the east."

The major explained that the bowl was about seven to eight miles across and that to travel from the bottom of the bowl to the rim by jeep took four to five hours.

"In case you're wondering, the NKPA soldiers are still very active on the other side of the northern rim. Get some rest, because you're leaving early in the morning."

I thanked the major for his help, saluted, and departed.

When I returned to the transit officer's quarters, I found my gear as I had

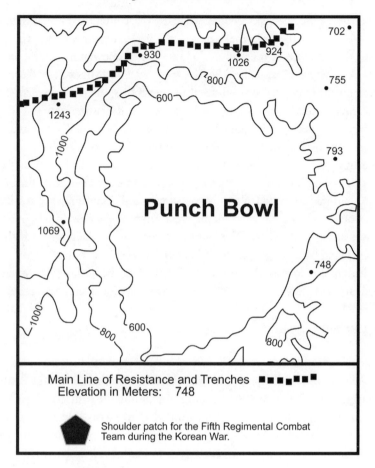

Map 2. Punch Bowl.

left it and started to settle in, hoping the chest cold that was threatening would go away. After looking around the quarters, I decided, as I first thought, that these quarters looked a lot like a bunker. I was learning that "bunker" was a generic term for any sleeping, mess, fighting, medical, or other type of facility. I had always visualized a "bunker" as a concrete structure like the ones the Germans used during World War II when the Rangers scaled the cliffs on D-Day. Not so in Korea. In Korea they used logs, tar paper, and sandbags as building materials. Sometimes, if available, the bunker builders would use twelve-by-twelve-inch square timbers that were twelve feet long instead of logs.

Here, soldiers had constructed a bunker using logs that were ten feet long and eight to ten inches thick. My bunker for the night had been cut out of the side of a hill. Bunkers were constructed using these procedures because four of the sides wouldn't require sandbagging—the floor, the left wall, the right wall, and the rear wall. All of the walls used logs stacked one on top of another. Logs on the roof were laid side by side. The front wall and the roof had sandbags stacked on the logs. This procedure of using sandbags had two benefits. First, small arms bullets would not normally penetrate the sand. Second, the sandbags would protect the bunker from the shrapnel generated from exploding artillery rounds. Frequently, the roof would have an additional layer of rocks. Theoretically, these rocks would trigger any incoming shells before they could penetrate the logs. With luck, the shell would then explode outside the bunker. If that shell had a longer fuse, the explosion would occur inside of the bunker and I would have a serious problem. The bunker I was now in was one room that was about five feet wide by eight feet deep, with a height of a little over six feet. There were three bunk beds installed along one of the eight-foot walls. By using smaller logs as side rails and pulling communication wire (a narrow-gauge wire covered with a plastic coating used to connect telephones) back and forth, thereby creating a web of wire, the bunks became racks on which to support a bedroll. By placing a sleeping bag on the web of wire, the bunks became a bed.

The lower bunk was about six inches off the floor; the center bunk, about two and a half feet off the floor; and the top bunk, about four and a half feet above the floor. The height of each bunk (including the width of the logs) was approximately eighteen inches high, which left room to slide into and out of the bunk. Earlier, when I was reporting as ordered and found my home for the night, I hadn't seen any other gear in the bunker. I supposed I was the only officer in transit. There were many stories about big rats in Korea running around the bunker floors looking for food. Not wanting to sleep too close to the rats, and not eager to climb and try to squeeze into the top bunk, I had put my gear in the center bunk before I reported to the colonel.

After my introductions at headquarters and killing some time wandering around regimental headquarters, I went back to the mess tent—the kitchen was partially in a bunker—and had a good evening meal. I guess it tasted so good because I was hungry and the food served was available. I was tired and still feeling as if I might be catching a cold.

While leaning against the bunker where I would be spending the night, and watching the sun drop behind the mountain rim, I started smoking a cigarette and thinking about the day's activities. In this first week of October, the Korean evening had been beautiful. This was such a restful and quiet place it was difficult to believe a war was going on. I hadn't heard a shot fired or an artillery shell land. And except for catching the damn cold, my first day in the bowl had been a good day. I had arrived safely, met the colonel without making any dumb mistakes, and the major S-1 seemed like a good person. The 5th RCT wasn't so bad after all—not the Rangers, but not bad.

I finished my cigarette and went inside my home for the night. In my small room was a candleholder made from an empty C-ration can (about the size of a soup can) cut four times. Each cut went from the top of the can halfway down toward the bottom. Then three of the four sides were bent out and down to form handles. The fourth side was bent inward to form a base on which the candle was placed. The candleholder was a good idea, because as the candle burned down, the stub would fall into the bottom of the can and go out. I lit a candle and placed the candleholder on a small table. The bunker contained no chairs or other furniture.

As I unrolled my sleeping bag, I remembered that it incorporated a new design. According to the supply sergeant who issued the sleeping bags to us, the bag had a "quick release" manufactured into the zipper. All you had to do was pull the zipper tab all the way up and the whole zipper would release, allowing the bag to completely open.

"Now, the reason why they added the new design," the supply sergeant had said, "is that a couple of years ago at the beginning of the Korean War, we didn't have any winter clothing to issue, and everybody was very cold. You'll learn that the temperature in Korea can drop to minus ten to twenty degrees in the winter. In trying to keep from freezing, soldiers would put on everything they had to wear, crawl into their sleeping bags, zip the zipper all the way up, and try to stay warm and get some sleep. The North Koreans would attack at night while the American soldiers were sleeping. The yelling and gunfire by the NKPA soldiers would awaken the GIs, and before they could get out of their sleeping bags, the enemy would bayonet them." Suddenly we all thought the quick release zipper was a good idea.

Wearily, I took off my clothes, which didn't mean much, since it simply meant removing my boots, socks, and field jacket. I had taken off my flak vest and helmet as soon as I entered the bunker after dinner. Since a chill was in the air and seemed to be getting colder, and with no heater in the bunker, I decided I would sleep in the rest of my clothes. The bunker where I slept had a woolen blanket hung over the small entry door to keep the candlelight from shining out. I didn't understand why the blanket was necessary, since I didn't think any North Korean soldiers were near this position for miles. I carefully slid into my sleeping bag and pulled the zipper up. The sleeping bag was warm, and even the wire bed felt good. I quickly went to sleep. Maybe even snored.

KERWHOOM
    KERWHOOM
      KERWAM

What was that? Without thinking, I quickly rose up, and my head hit the log railing on the bunk above. The candle had gone out and I was in total darkness. I could taste dirt from the dust rolling in through the opening. The ground was shaking. I was afraid the bunker would collapse.

KERR—WHHAM
    KERWHOOM
WHAMMEM

Bright flashes—then total darkness. *Incoming artillery! The noise must be incoming artillery!* I heard someone screaming in great pain. I tried to rise, but I hit my head on the bunker railing again. I couldn't get up. *The quick release! The quick release!* I remembered the quick release. I grabbed the zipper tab and pulled upward. My head was in the way. I ducked down in the sleeping bag to get the zipper over my head. The quick release still wouldn't release the zipper. The quick release wouldn't work. The zipper was up. I couldn't get out. I strained as much as I could to rip open the sleeping bag, but I couldn't break the zipper open.

KERWHOOM KERWHOOM
WHAMM

More bright flashes. The concussions from the shells hit me. The smell of burned powder came in with the dust. More dust. I knew the bunker would collapse. I was coughing, trying to get the dust out. I couldn't get the release to work. And I still heard the man screaming. I had to get myself under control. I rose up. *Damn!* I kept forgetting that I couldn't raise myself without hitting that damn log on the bunk above me. *Can't see—*

WHAMM!
KERWHOOM

—*anything. Total darkness.* The North Koreans were firing three rounds at a time. *Concussions closer. Have to get out of here.* I could feel the dirt from the bunker falling on me. The damn thing was really going to collapse.

I finally quit coughing for a few seconds. *Think fast. Will this thing open if I slowly unzip the sleeping bag the normal way?* Would the zipper work? *Have to try.* My hands were shaking, but I slowly got the zipper grip. *The goddamn thing has to work.* I pulled the zipper tab toward my feet, and the zipper released. My mummy wrap let me go! I was FREE!

KERWHOOM

Not quite so loud now. Must be shifting fire. Only one round that time. Maybe the barrage was about over.

In total darkness, I slid out of the bunk after hitting my head on the log again. I stumbled over my boots and sprawled on the floor. I was in total darkness with my head hurting from hitting the damn bunk log. I started to feel my way out but didn't know which way to go. The shelling seemed to be over, but I wasn't concerned if the shelling was still going on or not. I had to get out of that bunker or it might be my grave. I could hear people yelling and running toward what I figured was the soldier who was still in pain. I moved toward the noise, too. The yelling and screaming guided me to the front opening of the bunker. The blanket was still in place. I burst through the blanket and was finally outside. Thank God. Now I was coughing like crazy, but I didn't care. I was out!

The wounded soldier's screams had changed to a series of loud moans. Someone must have given him some morphine. The way he was screaming, I was certain he had taken a very bad hit. I didn't want to go over and see him. I would just be in the way. Besides, I had had enough excitement for one day.

Slowly, I looked around to see all of the damage caused by the North Koreans' shelling. The campsite looked the same to me as it had before when I went to bed. In fact, I couldn't see any craters where the shells had landed. As I began to regain my senses, I saw beautiful stars in the night sky and noticed the smell of burned powder from the North Korean shells lingering in the evening along with the drifting haze. The incoming artillery seemed to be over. I took several deep sighs of relief.

My feet were cold. Very cold. I had forgotten to put my boots on. I hadn't even thought about boots. I had no field jacket, either. My whole body was cold and I was shaking. The weather must have been close to freezing. I yanked down the blanket that covered the bunker opening. I had no flashlight, and I didn't want to go back into the bunker in total darkness, but a little natural illumination from the stars lit a path for me, so I quickly moved back inside and retrieved my socks, boots, and field jacket. Outside again I sat on the ground, put my socks and boots on, and wondered what I was doing in a place called Korea, surprised and scared. Still shaken from the experience, I lit up a cigarette and sat outside for a long while.

I had thought I was a goner, a dead man—captured in a straitjacket and buried alive. I was positive the bunker was going to collapse. What an experience! The noise from the incoming artillery had been terrible. One thing was for sure: I would never sleep in a bunker again without a working flashlight. And I would never sleep in a sleeping bag without testing the quick release zipper. I thought about never again sleeping without my boots but gave up the idea. They were too big. I would just have to be sure they were nearby. What an education!

Well, I had completed both my welcoming to the 5th Regimental Combat Team and an introductory course in infantry combat in the same day.

Need to get some rest. Tomorrow is going to be a long day.

I crawled back into the sleeping bag and decided to keep my boots on. But I would not zip up the zipper.

How in the world did I ever end up here?

2

Lieutenant Evans

Preparations for Infantry Combat

Born in 1929 in Fulton, Kentucky, to Sebra and Roberta Evans, I enjoyed a happy childhood. I had one brother (Jack) and three sisters (Julia Rose, Martha Ann, and Nancy). The Illinois Central Railroad employed my father, and my mother was a schoolteacher. Fulton was located in the southwestern corner of Kentucky on the Tennessee border. Like every other poor country boy, I attended a rural grammar school, rode my red wagon, fell off, and skinned my nose. In 1938 my father transferred with the railroad and we moved to Belleville, Illinois. In 1940 the family moved to New Orleans, Louisiana, where my father supervised the railroad freight movement to the port city in preparation for World War II.

Our home was in a nice neighborhood in New Orleans near Tulane University, the home of the Sugar Bowl stadium. In 1942, as the soldiers gathered in New Orleans for transportation to parts unknown, housing facilities for the soldiers were very limited. One solution to the lack of housing was to place cots on the football stadium ramps in the Sugar Bowl. The army placed hundreds of cots side by side there to bed the troops. To protect the civilians living nearby, the military police (MP) established positions on every corner in the neighborhood. At the age of twelve, having learned by radio of the fighting in Europe, I was interested in the soldiers and what they were doing. Whenever I could get permission from my mother, I would walk the few blocks to the stadium to watch the soldiers' activity. As I watched taxicab after taxicab pull up, I couldn't understand why the soldiers couldn't get out of the cabs by themselves. Instead they required an MP on each side to pull them out and into the stadium. Someone told me the soldiers had been drinking in the French Quarter.

The year 1944 featured another move for our family—this time to Memphis, Tennessee, where I entered Central High School. For my summer vacation between the eleventh and twelfth grades, I decided to follow the excitement of Mark Twain and secure a job on a Mississippi River tugboat. Traveling by rail to New Orleans, I joined the Federal Barge Lines as a deckhand and worked on a tugboat from New Orleans to St. Louis, Missouri, and back south to Memphis. It was a great learning experience. Since I was the only deckhand who could read and write, I became the union representative and, as such, would read the union mail to the crew.

In my job on the tugboat I learned about a system of using knots tied on a rope to determine the depth of the water. A deckhand standing on the side of a barge positions himself so that he can toss a weight tied to the end of a rope ahead of the barge. As the barge moves over the spot where the rope enters the water, the deckhand notes how many knots, or marks, are visible on the rope and calls out the number to the captain who is running the pusher tug. The first mark on the rope is referred to as "Mark Twin" (yelled as "Mark Twain"), meaning the water is twelve feet deep, or sufficiently deep to navigate. The second mark is "Mark Three" (yelled as "Mark Thigh-ree"), meaning the water is eighteen feet deep. No mark is referred to as "Deep Water," meaning the river bottom is over twenty-four feet deep. Even in poor or windy weather, the three depth-measurement calls are easily distinguishable by the boat captain.

After graduating with the class of 1947, I decided not to go to college. In January 1948, however, I changed my mind and enrolled at Memphis State College, because I became convinced that having money was a lot better than not having money. I also found a much-needed night job as an overhead electrical linesman with the Memphis Light, Gas, and Water Division. The hours—4:00 PM to 12:00 AM—required by the linesman job severely affected my study and dating time. Therefore, I limited my study time. In 1948 I joined the Navy Surface Reserve, because I needed the money and I thought the uniform would attract girls.

When the North Korean People's Army attacked South Korea in the summer of 1950, our Navy Surface Reserve chief took us to the Millington Naval Air Station, located just outside of Memphis. We were being considered for transfer to the Naval Air Reserve, so he wanted us to see the facility and our assigned aircraft. Since the NKPA didn't have a navy, the need to activate the surface reserve was unlikely. The NKPA did have an air force, however, so a need to activate our Naval Air Reserve was very likely. The chief said, "Evans, you're going to be a radio operator on that torpedo bomber."

Not realizing I was making a life-changing decision, I climbed into the airplane through the side door. The plane's interior was small. I had to slide sideways along the wall to get past a radio to reach the little seat used by the radio operator. Slowly and carefully, I looked around and found only one small window. The window was about eight inches square and positioned on the rear wall near the floor. Looking through the small window, all I could see was the tarmac. I noticed another seat just above my right shoulder. This, I guessed, was where the machine gunner would sit. The airplane reminded me of the World War II movies in which the torpedo bombers would drop their torpedoes toward the Japanese aircraft carriers and then fly right into the Pacific Ocean.

I realized that if the plane caught on fire, I could never get out, because I would be wearing a parachute and would be unable to slide past the radio on my way to the exit door. I wasn't very happy with my assignment, and from the mumbling and talking I did to my shipmate, it was apparent that I didn't want the job.

Finally, I had been in the airplane long enough. When I climbed out and back onto the tarmac, the chief said, "Evans, you didn't sound very happy in that aircraft."

"Yes, Chief, you're right," I said.

He grunted, "You can always get out of the navy."

"I can? How?" I responded.

"Join the army, and the navy will discharge you," said the chief.

Within a week I was at the U.S. Army Recruiting Station. I didn't mind going to war; I didn't mind going into the army. However, I very much wanted training so that I would have a chance to survive.

I was still an employee at the Memphis Light, Gas, and Water Division. Two of my coworkers, James Watts and William Allen, decided to enlist in the army with me. We all wanted to become paratroopers, since being a paratrooper meant a soldier would fly somewhere rather than walk as the infantry did. I made sure the recruiting sergeant listed me as volunteering for airborne duty. He kept writing "Infantry" on the volunteer form, and I kept making him change the form to "Airborne." The recruiter looked at me as if I didn't know what I was doing. He was right, of course. I soon learned that the army did have a division known as the Airborne Infantry. With my right hand raised high, I took the oath to defend the Constitution of the United States. I became a Regular Army recruit volunteer from the state of Tennessee. At twenty years old, recruit James William Evans, RA-14321088, was now subject to all rules and regulations of the military as well as orders from just about everybody else in the U.S. Army.[1]

In September 1950 I reported to Fort Jackson, South Carolina, for basic infantry training. We spent our first week there cleaning up the barracks and the yard of our company area. The section of Fort Jackson where our quarters were located had been vacant since World War II. The barracks were in bad repair, the furnace didn't work for hot water, the interior was dirty, and the yard was overgrown. With nothing else to do, we started to improve our environment.

The army schedules a period for new recruits to take a series of tests to determine their intelligence level. Upon completion of these tests, the soldier's skill classification is determined. These aptitude tests determine what, if any, type of specialized training the soldier should receive. Each morning, right after breakfast, we loaded onto trucks to go to a testing center where we were given a series of aptitude tests. Because I knew so little about the army, I didn't realize the importance of these tests. On Friday, when we completed the last test of the series, I heard my named called along with the names of a few other soldiers. The army then offered the selected few a chance to take another test, identified as the OCT. I didn't know what the OCT test was all about, but I agreed to stay for it; otherwise, I would have had to go back with the rest of our group and start cutting grass. Sometime later I was surprised to learn that I had passed with a very high score. Individuals who did well on the OCT (Officer Candidate Test) would academically qualify for Officer Candidate School.

After the week of tests, I reported to an infantry training company for seven weeks of basic infantry. The training company consisted mostly of draftees from Philadelphia, Pennsylvania, and its surrounding area. Several members of the training company were former German soldiers, some of whom had served with Rommel in the North African campaign. Some had fought on the Russian front while serving in the German army. All had volunteered to be in the U.S. Army. Apparently, if an ex–German soldier completed three years of satisfactory service with the U.S. army, he could receive his U.S. citizenship under the Hodge Act. The German immigrants were excellent soldiers and taught us how to kill effectively.

William Allen, one of my coworkers who enlisted with me, had been in the U.S. Marine Corps. He was exempt from having to retake basic training and immediately left for the 82nd Airborne. James Watts, another coworker, completed the infantry training with me and entered airborne training with the 11th Airborne at Fort Campbell, Kentucky. Neither of the two went to Korea.

After seven weeks of learning all the skills of an infantryman—marching, shooting, making up a bed "correctly," cleaning the barracks, scrubbing pots and pans, and numerous other tasks—I started the second seven-week training phase. However, we were now in advanced infantry training, which was a lot like the basic training, just more of it. I proudly moved from being a recruit to being a private in the U.S. Army.

I completed my advanced infantry training in January 1951. Many of the members of my training company left immediately for the Far East Command, which was most likely an assignment to Korea. However, I took advantage of an offer to attend a leadership course instead, because upon completion of the course, I would receive a private first class (PFC) stripe. At the time, I didn't realize how lucky I was, but I later learned that while I had stayed in the States many of my training company classmates died in the early days of the Korean War.

After completing leadership school, which was four weeks of learning to be a squad leader, I transferred to a holding company, a place where the army puts you when they can't think of what else to do with you. I was in limbo until my next set of orders came through. Now was the time for the army to fulfill my enlistment agreement and send me to an airborne unit. My next assignment was supposed to be the 82nd Airborne Division at Fort Bragg, North Carolina. However, my career path didn't quite work out that way. Those of us in the holding company did all types of brainless work, including policing the barrack area (picking up small bits of trash), serving as kitchen police (which meant getting up at 0300 and working in the mess hall all day), and standing guard (walking around warehouses being a fireguard). If I were lucky, I would slip off to the post library to read.

One beautiful Sunday in South Carolina, while still in the holding company, I was on kitchen police (KP) duty. Being the pots-and-pans person was a good job, because those pots were so dirty from the coal-burning stoves I had the option to take them outside to get them clean. On a day when the weather would permit, working outside, even cleaning filthy, greasy aluminum pots, was an enjoyable relief from working in a hot, steamy kitchen. Besides, the move outside got me away from the mess sergeant. On this particular Sunday, a little after lunch, while scrubbing away, I glanced across the street. The scene changed my life. A second lieutenant was strolling down the sidewalk with a beautiful girl on each arm. He was all dressed up in his winter Ike jacket (a short dress uniform jacket) with gold bars on his shoulders, a starched khaki shirt, and a black tie. And here I was, filthy with grease and coal smoke all over me. I was in the wrong place. The next day, I applied for Officer Candidate School (OCS). I didn't know much about being an officer, but it certainly had to be better than scrubbing pots and pans. I'm not sure I was right.

I reported to the Infantry Officer Candidate Course at Fort Benning, Georgia, and began some six months of intensive training. OCS taught me a lot of leadership skills as well as military skills, such as field exercises, scouting, patrolling, and attack maneuvers. Each level of training in the army seemed to put more and more stress on an individual to determine if he would be able to respond under pressure. OCS was very selective in deciding which candidates completed the course. Our class had a dropout rate of about 40 percent. Candidates resigned (or were dismissed) because they didn't want to put forth the effort, couldn't demonstrate a command presence—anything and everything. Strangely, I rarely knew when someone wouldn't be staying.

At OCS, while standing in a morning formation, someone would be called out to report to the orderly room. The callout could also happen while someone was in class. These callouts could be for any cause: an emergency at the candidate's home, a visitor, or for just about any other reason. However, if the candidate called out left OCS, we wouldn't know until we returned to our barracks. One of the first indications something had happened was that the count of beds in a row would be down by one. A clothes locker and footlocker would also be gone. Every trace of the dismissed candidate would have vanished. If one of us asked a tactical officer (training officer) what had happened to the candidate, where he had gone or why, the cadre wouldn't reply. What happened to our classmate was none of our business. Perhaps the person had never existed. Perhaps keeping us from knowing about our classmates was part of the training program. We needed to learn how to react to suddenly losing fellow officers in combat. When OCS started the count was fourteen beds in the row where my bunk was located; at graduation, however, the bed count in my row was down to four. The barrack was nearly empty.

Fort Benning was very hot in the summer of 1951. None of the candidates' quarters were air-conditioned, and the tightly woven fatigue clothing we wore didn't let a lot of air in. According to our uniform standard, candidates couldn't roll up their fatigue shirtsleeves nor pull their shirts out of their pants to let some air in. In addition, during field exercises we wore steel helmets and web belts. The coveralls we wore were also hot, because our belts kept the air from circulating. Officer candidates went to the field in ninety-five-degree, high-humidity weather dressed as if we were going to a dance: neat, clean, and all buttoned up.

Candidates were required to be proficient in firing every infantry weapon. One particular firing event always comes to mind when I think about Fort Benning in the summer. Sometime in July or August our class started to train on the 60 and 81mm mortars. Firing an 81mm mortar requires the same basic procedure as firing a 60mm mortar. A soldier drops a mortar shell into a steel tube wherein the shell falls and strikes a firing pin at the bottom of the tube. When the shell hits the firing pin, the powder burns, and the shell exits the tube on the way to the target. A few sighting differences existed between the 60mm and the 81mm mortar. However, both use a tube, which sits on an appropriately sized steel base plate. The base plate absorbs the recoil from the round being fired and prevents the tube from sinking into the ground. Because of its weight, the heavy 81mm mortar must be separated into three parts for carrying: the base plate, the tube, and the front bipod, on which the tube rests.[2]

One steamy Georgia day, we each carried one of the three parts of our 81mm mortars to a field for simulated firing. The grass in the field was about three feet high. As we spread out and positioned our base plate, we were getting hotter and hotter. After we put the tube on the mortar base plate and added the front legs, we lay down in the field so that the "enemy" wouldn't see us.

Never will I forget lying in the field directly under the glaring sun, no breezes blowing, and all wrapped up in fatigues. We were perspiring profusely. Our steel helmets transferred the heat directly into the tops of our heads. When the class was finally over, we all drank plenty of water. Somehow we had avoided heat stroke. We should have died. I never decided whether the training exercise was a good or bad learning experience. I did learn, however, that a soldier's safety is more important than rules of clothing.

I completed Officer Candidate School in a little over six months. Upon graduation on 22 October 1951, I was commissioned as a Second Lieutenant, Infantry, O-2028570, United States Army. After commissioning, instead of going to the 82nd Airborne as I had expected, I was transferred to Fort Jackson and assigned to an infantry training company for several months to convert raw recruits into soldiers. It was a very enjoyable job, and it was good to see how new recruits could change into real soldiers. While stationed at Fort Jackson, I completed the requirements for and earned the Expert Infantryman Badge (EIB).

Qualifying for the EIB was a strenuous and difficult task. A twenty-mile

2. Officer candidate James Evans (standing, right) relaxing with other soon-to-be officers. (Photo courtesy of the author.)

forced march was one of the requirements. Having just completed OCS, I was in excellent physical condition and was sure I could complete the challenge. Some 250 soldiers of varying rank and physical condition started the twenty-mile march. Three of us eager, young lieutenants led the applicants by running downhill and walking uphill. The testers had checkpoints en route, and the three of us were the first at every checkpoint. Completing the course in record time, the other two lieutenants and I climbed into an automobile for transportation back to our barracks. Upon arrival at the barracks, I opened the door to get out but couldn't move my legs. They simply wouldn't function. Moreover, my shins started to hurt. Someone told me it was shin splints. I believe we overdid our march. "Doctor Ego" had grabbed us, and now it was time for suffering. Somehow we got out of the car and stumbled into the barracks. It was a good lesson on what *not* to do.

Because of an experience at Fort Benning, I had not forgotten my desire to become an Army Ranger. While at OCS, we candidates shared a dayroom with members of the Ranger companies.[3] I was impressed with the discipline and respect the Rangers had for one another. I decided to apply for the Ranger training course at Fort Benning. However, my Ranger application ran into a snag: the comptroller at Fort Jackson didn't want to pay for my Ranger training. Since I wouldn't be returning to Fort Jackson, they wouldn't be able to take advantage of their investment in my training. The comptroller's decision didn't sit well with me, so, since I had accrued leave, I decided to use some of that time for a short vacation. I was now an officer of the United States Army and didn't like illogical arguments.

From Fort Jackson, I drove to 3rd Army Headquarters in Atlanta, Georgia, and met with the colonel responsible for all 3rd Army training. After explaining the situation that I had encountered with the Fort Jackson comptroller, the colonel instructed me to go home and not worry. When I reached Memphis for a short family visit, orders for me to go to Fort Benning for the Ranger school were awaiting me.

Ranger training was a great learning experience, as it seemed to bring all of my other infantry training into perspective. I have no doubt the training provided me with the knowledge of myself necessary to be able to lead men into combat. But the program was also tough. When I started the program, I thought I was in good physical condition and weighed 174 pounds. When I finished, I was down to 168, the lowest I could ever remember weighing. The concept behind Ranger training was to put the maximum stress, both physically and mentally, on participants, using various techniques. The physical pressure came from tactical problems such as twenty-four-hour patrols that required walking and running for many miles intermixed with other difficult activities. The mental part was subtle. For example, the stress would start at breakfast when the students were served half-cooked eggs, nearly raw bacon, and burned toast. I really hated the green, half-raw eggs. The psychological food warfare made sure every student started the day with a bad attitude. And that was only one of many little tricks used to tweak students' frustration.

However, we had some fun times, too. While at Elgin Air Force Base, located near Pensacola, Florida, our training cadre explained, "Since you men are members of the first officer Ranger class, you can help us with our collection of snakes. The camp commander decided it was important to have a collection of snakes of various types to show subsequent classes. We want all types of poisonous snakes. As you participate in a patrol or other training exercises, capture any snakes discovered and return them to the camp headquarters." On a clear night, another student and I were walking down a sandy trail during a patrolling exercise. The moon illuminated the path, providing an easy walk for us. Suddenly we noticed a colorful snake lying in the middle of the trail. It had black and yellow bands and was approximately three feet long with a girth that looked like some ten inches. Sensing a successful snake capture, we crept up to the snake. We looked at each other and shrugged our shoulders, indicating that neither of us knew whether the snake was poisonous. We hoped it was. As we got closer, the snake started to move. Then as it moved faster, it headed to a hole in the ground. We raced to catch the snake but only caught its tail. Then the two of us started to pull the snake out of the hole, but we couldn't do it. I don't know about other snakes, but this snake could easily slide into a hole, and its skin would flare and create a resistance when being pulled out of the hole. Finally, after a struggle and with great effort, we pulled the snake out and placed it in a sock—a tight fit. I tied the sock to my belt, and we continued on our nightly patrol.

The camp cadre had built a rectangle pen to hold the captured snakes. The structure was about four cinder blocks high with an interior that was about six feet by eight feet. Returning from our patrol at about 0630, we eagerly told the instructor about our capture. The cadre instructed me to drop the snake into the pen with the many other poisonous snakes our class had secured. Just as I started to put the sock in the pen, the instructor yelled, "Stop! Don't let that thing out! It's a Kingsnake. It will kill all of our poisonous snakes."

We had captured a nonpoisonous Eastern Kingsnake, which is immune to the venom from snakes such as rattlesnakes. In addition to its diet of frogs and birds, the Kingsnake kills and eats poisonous snakes. I yanked the snake-filled sock up and handed it to the instructor. He made a separate pen for the "good snake." I always wondered about what a wonderful fight and how exciting it would be to watch one good snake take on all of the bad guys.

I recall that the dropout rate of our Ranger class was nearly 60 percent; only seventy students graduated out of a class of about two hundred. Our class was the first officer class of the new Ranger Training Command. In 1952 it was protocol for officers and enlisted men to train separately. I understood that three classes of enlisted men had completed the Ranger course before our class. I have no knowledge of the fourth class. Those graduates became the cadre for the school. The Ranger training classes today instruct enlisted and officers together. The training curriculum is virtually the same today as it was for class number five.

Since I hadn't completed airborne training, I was to remain at Fort Benning for the three-week airborne school upon completing the Ranger course. However, the army decided I couldn't complete the three-week airborne class, have the authorized thirty days' leave en route, and meet my overseas reporting date. If I entered the airborne class, I would have only twenty-five days' leave rather than the required thirty days. Thus, my orders were to report for Camp Stoneman, Pittsburg, California, for transportation to the Far East Command

(Korea) as ordered. After a visit home, I rushed to California to arrive on time, but after arriving at Camp Stoneman, I had to wait nearly three weeks for transportation to Korea, meaning I could have finished the airborne course and still gotten to Korea on time. However, I did get to go into downtown San Francisco several times.

Finally, we replacements gathering at Camp Stoneman were on our way to the Far East so that some of us could participate in the Korean War. We would be flying to Japan via Hawaii and Wake Island and then traveling by ship to Korea. The government had contracted with a civilian company to provide transportation by air. We were loaded onto a DC-6 aircraft. The aircraft seated three soldiers on each side of the center aisle, leaving barely enough room to walk down the aisle. The plane was a four-engine propeller-driven aircraft and was loaded to the maximum. We were told by the flight attendants that the takeoff path took most of the runway at Travis Air Force Base in order for the plane to get airborne. The plane slowly climbed up and flew to Hawaii without incident. Everyone was as nice as one could expect, knowing we were going to war and were jammed in on top of one another. The first leg of our flight took about twelve hours, during which we covered some 2,390 miles of the Pacific Ocean. Upon landing in Hawaii, we off-loaded and then wandered around the hanger. After the plane was refueled and serviced, we departed. My visit to Hawaii was short.

The next leg was to Wake Island, another two thousand miles, where we were to refuel before continuing to Japan. However, just after the pilot had announced over the intercom that we had passed the point of no return (meaning the distance to our destination was less than that of returning to our starting point in case of trouble), I felt a shudder. I didn't notice any change in the way the aircraft was flying, but I happened to glance out the window and noticed that the propeller on the outboard starboard engine wasn't turning. But the pilot announced that everything was okay and said we were not to worry. After another hour or so (still about five hundred miles from Wake Island), I felt another bump and the plane seemed to slow down. Having just seen one propeller not turning, I suspected another one may not be turning. I was right. The inboard engine on the port side had stopped, yet we were still in the air. The pilot again announced that everything was under control and that we were not to worry.

However, when I looked out of the window and saw what looked like a B-17 bomber with a big orange pontoon underneath the body, I did start to worry. The flight attendant explained that the rescue airplane was just a precaution in case we had to ditch. All of us onboard had had to go through the ditching procedures. We all looked at one another nervously as we put on our life vests and settled down in our seats. We hadn't had much room before, and wearing the life vests added to our misery. I was getting very worried now.

The plane kept on going but seemed to be slowly losing altitude. With frequent glances at the B-17 following us while we tried to determine if we were gradually going down, the time passed very slowly. If we ditched, the B-17 was to drop the big orange lifeboat down to us. The rescue plan was reassuring—that is, unless the B-17 dropped the boat *on* us when we were floating around. I had a difficult time trying to determine if we were slowly going up or down with no point of reference except miles and miles of water. The pilot came on the intercom and explained that since we had burned a lot of gasoline, the weight of the airplane had lessened. With a tone of confidence in his voice, he told us that the two remaining engines were sufficient to carry us to Wake. None of us believed him. Somehow, though, we safely completed the trip to Wake, and as we disembarked, many of us kissed the ground.

We stood around for about twelve hours while the plane underwent major repairs. Then reluctantly we boarded the aircraft. Now the engines ran smoothly, and in approximately twelve hours we were in Japan. As the aircraft flew to Tokyo, we passed over Hiroshima, where the first atomic bomb had exploded seven years earlier. Still no buildings were standing. Only a few steel girders were sticking up. Some roads were free of rubble, but I could see no people or traffic on the few open roads.

At the Army Reception Center in Tokyo, the medics reviewed our shot records. The army relieved us of all of our civilian travel bags, claiming they would safely store them for us while we were in Korea. None of us believed them, but we gave up our luggage as ordered. I gave them my B-4 bag, which had my clean, starched khakis inside. When I reached the front of the shot line, there was a problem. For some reason, my records didn't contain the necessary medical validation that I had already received my required shots. The medical team was very nice and let me go through the line so that I could receive another complete series. They were hitting me in both arms at the same time. I was disappointed and disgusted, because on the plane trip across the Pacific, we all had been talking about what a great time we would have in Tokyo. But when I got the shots, I knew my night of sightseeing and partying in Tokyo was gone. Every time I received the triple typhoid booster shot, I would get sick like a dog. Within four hours I started having chills, then cold sweats, and other unpleasant symptoms for about eight to ten hours. Unfortunately, I spent my first night in Japan in bed. I'm sure being sick saved me a lot of money, but I'm also sure that it cost me a lot of fun.

I recovered as usual in a day or two and was then transferred, along with a contingent of other officers, to an old Japanese fighter training base near Gifu, Japan. During our two weeks at the Gifu site, we attended an officer's CBR (chemical, biological, and radiological warfare) course to learn all about how quickly we can die. The school was a nice break, and in a beautiful valley that had been a hidden runway for Japanese fighter planes (Zeros), there was an officers club. A Japanese doorman stood guard there, wearing a Japanese sword on his belt. It was a curved sword with a long handle, which was suitable for two hands. When we entered or left the club, he would demonstrate how fast he could move the sword. He was very good. We worried that perhaps he hadn't heard that the Japanese had lost the war and that he wasn't supposed to wipe us out. No one in our group ever argued with him.

The curriculum at the school provided for an examination upon completing the required two weeks of CBR warfare. The exam was to be held on a Saturday, our last day of school. After the exam we were to load onto a train that would take us to Sasebo, Japan. From Sasebo we would travel by boat to Korea. On our last Friday night at the school, another officer and I had completed packing for our train trip and decided to have a drink at the club. The officers club was very nice, but instead of currency, the club used a booklet with ten-cent chits. One drink cost one chit, regardless of what was ordered. As the other officers were leaving the club, they would throw their chit books to us with any remaining chits, since the chits would no longer be valid.

The problem on this Friday night was that we had gotten to the club so late that it was beginning to close. So, being intelligent young officers, we decided to cash in all of the chits on the table for a fifth of bourbon to go. We wandered back to our barracks, sat on the sidewalk, and sipped on the fifth while discussing our future in Korea. After going to bed that night, I awoke several times through the night not feeling very well. When morning came, someone awakened me and I got up and dressed and got my gear ready to go. I still felt sick, so I skipped breakfast and laid down again. Then I got up and went to class for the exams.

There were four exams, each allowing one hour for students to complete. The exams required the student to fill in circles marking his answers. As soon as you finished your test, you would turn in your test sheet and leave the classroom. You could go outside, smoke, rest, take a break, and wait until the next test was scheduled. I didn't believe that if I failed the test I wouldn't have to go to Korea, or that if I passed the tests I would get a pass back home. I would be going to Korea regardless of my test results. I marked the circles as quickly as I could, turned in my paper, and went outside. It was a beautiful day, so I took a break by lying on the grass between exams. Someone always woke me up and got me back into the classroom for the next test. After everyone was finished with the tests, we were loaded onto the train bound for Sasebo. Some weeks later I received a certificate showing that I had passed the CBR course.

As we traveled along, I started to feel a lot better and enjoyed the ride. The trains in Japan were clean, comfortable, and speedy—I believe they were electric trains. And Japan in early October was beautiful. I was amazed at how the people of the country utilized their land. Every square yard that I could see either had a structure on it or was farming some type of food. In the late afternoon the land looked peaceful and quiet.

Once we got to the dock at Sasebo, we found a small ship waiting to take us to Pusan, Korea. I did learn one thing about traveling on a ship: If you get to the highest point on the ship and keep your eyes on the horizon, the roll isn't too bad. Don't look at the waves, and don't think about food. Also, be careful what you do the night before you get on the ship.

Our first view of Korea was from the top deck of the small transport ship. The scents of Japan were just fading away when we picked up the odor from Korea. After we landed in Pusan, we received additional equipment before we headed north. At the depot, issuing uniforms and equipment, was a sergeant I remembered from Fort Jackson. I remembered him as being tough. He certainly looked the part. Square jaw, muscular build, and dark complexion—tough. I was very surprised to see him on such mundane duty. Certainly, he should have been leading the fight somewhere in Korea. Later I realized that perhaps he was smarter than I was. There would be no bullets in the clothing depot. However, seeing him there was a disappointment. My image of what a real combat soldier looked like had suffered a blow.

Unlike the Japanese train we had been on, the South Korean passenger train we boarded for our trip north was very uncomfortable. The roof of the station was gone. The Korean trains were always jam-packed, because they ran so infrequently. The train had wooden seats that were too small for most Americans. Most of the windows were broken out. A coal-burning steam engine pulled the railroad cars. Of course, black coal smoke blew through the broken windows and filled the cars, so we enjoyed a cold, smoky, and dirty passenger car. With no place to lie down and sleep during the ride, we had to sleep upright in our wooden seats or stretch out on the floor. And the train stopped frequently to take on coal and water. During one of our stops at a station, I observed passengers disembarking from a nearby train. Even with all of the discomfort of the Korean passenger train, the native people who were on the train were laughing and talking as people do everywhere. The resiliency of the Koreans and their ability to get on with their lives was admirable.

When we finally disembarked, trucks carried us to our various units to replace the troops who were already there. Since the Ranger companies had disbanded, the replacement Army Rangers were assigned to various line units to boost their esprit de corps. I had no idea whether we Rangers would help the moral of line units, but I was ready to try.

3
Punch Bowl Rim
North Korea People's Army

The next thing I knew, someone was yelling at me to get up. My driver was ready to go to the rim. Still tired from the night before, I packed my gear, went to the mess hall, ate breakfast, and got into a jeep for my trip to the top of the Punch Bowl. I wondered if the mess hall meals were free now, since I was in a combat zone. No one had asked me to pay for my meal the day before, which was unusual. Officers were required to pay for their meals in noncombat zones and usually paid cash for each meal. In some locations officers just signed a mess hall form so that the mess hall would get credit for serving a meal to a visitor or officer. Someone told me the army had decided to start deducting the meal charges from our pay, even in a combat zone. I thought that was dumb. Did they plan on the mess sergeant tracking down officers in combat so that the officers could sign for their meals? The rumor also stated that married officers in a combat zone wouldn't have to pay for their meals. Whether we received our pay in cash (scrip) or allotment money was sent home, I don't recall ever receiving a report of my payroll deductions. In a short time, however, I had much greater worries than whether I was paying for my meals.

Just two of us—a young, black PFC who was the jeep driver, and me, along with my duffel bag, carbine, helmet, and other gear—were in the jeep. The driver was friendly; we were in no rush, so we had time for some conversation. He liked to talk, but his talking did little to make me feel comfortable about what I was about to get into. Three times, he told me, he had suffered attacks on the road to the rim. Each time, he said, he had to drive like a lunatic to get away from the attackers, but at least he had managed to kill several North Koreans while he was escaping. I was impressed with the PFC and his bravery but later learned that the tales he told were merely figments of his imagination. He was just having fun educating a new, dumb second lieutenant.

To put the trip to the rim in perspective, the single-lane dirt road we traveled on was nerve-wracking. The elevation change from the bottom of the Punch Bowl (450 meters) to its highest peak (1,243 meters) was about 2,500 feet. There were no barriers installed along the side of the road leading up the mountain. This was a road with 120-degree turns, or switchbacks, back and forth up the mountain. A jeep could easily navigate the road. However, the two-and-a-half-ton trucks couldn't make such turns without backing up. The driver would turn as hard as he could, which would be some 40 degrees, and pull forward until his front bumper hit the side of the mountain. Then he would back up to the edge of the road and attempt another maximum turn. The second turn would put him at about 80 degrees toward his target of 120 degrees. The driver would then repeat the backing up maneuver and turn as hard as he could again. Usually the truck would then be in position to start the climb up to the next 120-degree curve.

Going back down the mountain, the same procedure was used except the driver would pull to the edge of the road, stop, back up and hit the mountain, turn the wheels, go to the edge again, and so forth. Going to the edge was the part that worried me. I rode in the right front seat. When the driver stopped at the edge as we went down the mountain, I was looking straight down the mountainside, knowing there were no barriers to keep us from careening over the edge.

Like all the other equipment I had seen since arriving in Korea, the two-and-a-half-ton trucks were from about World War II with stick shifts and bad brakes. The exciting times in the trucks were when the engine would cough and stall out during a turn on the mountain road. The bad brakes would start to slip while the driver tried to restart the engine, and the heavy truck would slowly start to roll toward the edge of the road. Then the engine would finally catch and start running again. I would be ready to jump, but after the engine restarted I would settle back until the next curve. My educator, the jeep driver, kept pointing out spots where trucks had fallen off the road and slid down the mountainside. I didn't believe any of those stories, but they certainly sounded real. (Later recalling the road and my other experiences with the two-and-a-half-ton trucks, I knew that the wrecks the driver described certainly *could* have happened.) Every time I went up and down this road, I looked for the wrecked trucks, but I never saw one.

After several hours of going back and forth to get up the steep mountain-

Copyright © James Evans 2006

3. The rim of the Punch Bowl as viewed from a rest area at the bottom of the bowl. This view of the rim from this location is toward the north-northwest. The highest point on the right end of the rim is Hill 1243. On the right side of the peak is the location of Able Company. On the left side of Hill 1243 the trench line goes westward and is not visible in this photo, since the rim turns southward at this point. Continuing south on the rim from Hill 1243, the highest point is Hill 1181. (Photo courtesy of the author.)

side, our jeep reached a flat area, the Mobile Army Surgical Hospital (MASH) helicopter-landing site. The helicopter would air-transport the seriously wounded to the hospital located in the bottom of the bowl.

Continuing along the road, we came to a bunker on the left (the mountain-side). The driver explained that the bunker was the battalion aid station, which I was supposed to visit. As we walked into the bunker, a black major came to greet us. The major had an emblem on his left shirt collar identifying him as a medical officer. The driver and I saluted. I briefly explained that I was on my way to Able Company, 5th RCT, and that we had stopped because I was on an orientation trip. The major introduced himself as a medical doctor for the 5th RCT Medical Company and welcomed me.

"Yes," the doctor said. "This bunker is my aid station, and I'm always ready to help."

As I looked around the room, I noticed that everything I thought should be in an aid station was in place. At least all of the equipment looked good to me.

Nevertheless, I didn't really want to end up in here after this visit, because returning would mean that I, or someone I was with, had been badly hurt.

As I continued to look around the bunker, I noticed a soldier lying on a stretcher on a small table. I didn't recognize the wounded soldier's uniform. Another soldier was standing beside the stretcher and talking to the man who was lying there. The standing soldier also wore a uniform I'd never seen. And I had no idea what they were talking about, since I had never heard the language they were speaking. The unusual thing about the soldier on the stretcher was that his right foot was gone. Blown off. The flesh on his right leg bone was also gone—blown off—for about another six inches toward his knee, which left the exposed bone. The exposed bone ended about ten inches below his knee. I couldn't help looking at the wound.

"These are very tough soldiers," the doctor said. "They are Turkish. Look at the man on the stretcher. I haven't given him anything for pain yet. I don't think anyone else has, either."

It was a strange sight—the first time I had ever seen a leg with no flesh and a leg without a foot. My jeep driver and I both stared wide-eyed at what was left of the Turkish soldier's leg. I don't think my driver had ever seen anything like this leg, either. I didn't know anything about injuries, but seeing the bone sticking out of his leg didn't help increase my comfort level. The major doctor said the wounded soldier could either be very tough or in shock. I like to think he was tough. He sure looked like he was.

I glanced around the station again and then thanked the doctor for his time. We didn't want to be in his way, so it was time for us to leave and let him take care of the Turkish soldier. The driver and I saluted and left the bunker. As we hopped into the jeep, we looked at each other, wondering if the other one was going to be sick, and we both shook our heads as if to say, "Not me." We headed for Able Company.

I never questioned why a Turkish soldier was in an American aid station. Perhaps the aid station was preparing the soldier for his trip by helicopter to the MASH facility at the bottom of the bowl. I hope he survived.

My grasp of combat was growing daily. Only two days and I had already learned a great deal: incoming artillery is loud, it can hurt people, and the job can be very dangerous.

When we left the medical bunker, we entered a stretch of the dirt road that my driver identified as "Skyline Drive." Skyline Drive ran eastward along the south side of the mountain and followed the contour for a couple of miles. As the northeastern section of the bowl turned southward, the road also gradually turned to the south, descending into the bottom of the bowl. This meant that in case the enemy blocked one way, the engineers had constructed a second way to travel to the top of the rim and return to the bottom of the bowl.

After driving approximately one-half mile farther, we stopped near a bunker constructed just above Skyline Drive. The bunker housed the headquarters for the 1st Battalion, 5th RCT. I entered and reported to LTC James Richardson, 1st Battalion commander. I was welcomed to the 1st Battalion, and after a short conversation Colonel Richardson sent me on my way.

The jeep driver knew where he was going and drove us toward Able Company. As we slowly proceeded along Skyline Drive, he pointed out the command post (CP) for Able Company. The bunker that housed the CP was located quite far up the side of the mountain. Finally arriving at a drop-off point, I retrieved my gear, thanked the driver, and started up the steep climb.

Looking up at the company command post from the road, I was concerned about being able to complete the climb. The command post *was* a long way up and reaching the bunker *was* a hard climb. All of my gear, including my duffel bag, flak vest, helmet, carbine, and sleeping bag, was on my back or shoulders, because I had to use my hands to hold the rope placed beside the dirt steps that had been dug out of the side of the mountain (then fitted with sandbags to prevent erosion) to get up the hill. The climb up the mountain was like climbing the stairs of a twenty-story building. But these stairs were muddy, icy, and uneven.

My cold was progressively reducing my strength, and I felt terrible. I was sure the dust from the incoming artillery the previous night combined with the dust on the dirty train ride had produced the germ or virus that was causing the fever I was beginning to feel. Of course, these factors were only my guess as to the cause. The alcohol at the CBR school could have been a contributing factor, too. I finally reached a bunker located about halfway up the mountain to the command post bunker. I could go no farther. I staggered into the bunker and asked someone to get the word to the company commander that I had made it to Able Company but was feeling very ill.

A medic came to see me. After he examined me, the medic told me I was sick. I already knew that. What I wanted was some medicine. The medic told me all of his supplies were for treating wounded soldiers. Other than bandages, morphine, and such supplies he only had the military version of aspirin. He didn't even have Vicks, the standby for treating all colds. The medic said he would check back on me later, then gave me some military aspirin and left. After taking several aspirin, I crawled into my sleeping bag and started sweating. Three days later I was slowly recovering. I was continuing to learn a lot about the war: no shower to wash in, no chicken soup to help me get well. So far the war had not been a lot of fun.

A steep climb faced everyone trying to reach Able Company from Skyline Drive. Skyline Drive provided a contour road on the side of the mountain for transporting our supplies. All food, ammunition, water, and bunker logs were transported by hand from the road up to our position. Wounded soldiers were carried down the steep slope by hand. We had to be careful not to drop them, because they would have a long way to fall. This was a tough place to live. Just climbing up to the bunker could completely exhaust a person.

The 1st Platoon, which was my new command, occupied a position even higher than the Able Company command post. To get to the highest point occupied by the platoon was a climb equal to that from Skyline Drive to the command post. The west end of the 1st Platoon's area of responsibility was at the peak. The peak was 1,243 meters in elevation—nearly 4,079 feet—so following the military tradition of referring to hilltops by their elevation, it was referred to as "Hill 1243" (without the comma). From Hill 1243 there was a wonderful view of the Punch Bowl when looking south.

I was welcomed by 1LT Murray D. Smith, Company Commander, Able Company, 5th RCT, who told me to call him "Smitty." He, too, was a Fort Benning Officer Candidate School graduate, and I was assigned as platoon leader of the 1st Platoon. Smitty showed me on a map where the North Koreans were positioned, and we discussed some of the things I should expect while on the mountain. Smitty seemed like a good person and was dedicated to his military career.

Still half sick, I made my way to my platoon and tried to get oriented. I met with my platoon sergeant and squad leaders. All of them greeted me, seemed very professional, and didn't laugh at the new, sick second lieutenant. My platoon sergeant and a number of other platoon sergeants were veterans of World War II. The 3rd Platoon had a sergeant who had fought in the Netherlands as a machine-gun platoon sergeant. Being older didn't necessarily make these men good sergeants, but they were experienced. I listened, I learned, and I respected their knowledge.

One of my squad leaders was an African American sergeant. I mention race here, as I did with the African American doctor and African American jeep driver, because the integration of African American soldiers with Caucasian soldiers had just started in the army, and the 5th RCT was one of the first to implement the program. I learned that the plan for integration was to have 10 percent of a unit be composed of African Americans. Furthermore, I learned why.

When President Truman signed Executive Order 9881 on 26 July 1948, the military resisted implementing integration at many levels. The order stated, "It is hereby declared to be the policy of the President that there shall be equality of treatment and opportunity for all persons in the armed services without regard to race, color, religion, or national origin. This policy shall be put into effect as rapidly as possible, having due regard to the time required to effectuate any necessary changes without impairing efficiency or morale."[1] The army had operated under the "separate but equal" philosophy for some time and wasn't eager to change. However, the air force and the navy, both of which had been previously closed to African Americans, decided to integrate a year before Executive Order 9881 was made.

In 1945 the only remaining all–African American unit was the 24th Regiment, assigned for training and other duties near Gifu, Japan. However, all of its senior officers were white. African American officers believed that white officers tolerated weakness in black troops that they wouldn't tolerate among whites simply because the white officers were doubtful the African American soldier could do any better. According to one white intelligence officer, there was "a climate of cover-up, benign neglect, acceptance of inadequate performance."[2] Unfortunately, the 24th had received little training for cold weather or night combat. The 24th Infantry Regiment remained racially segregated, and the effect of the segregation system incessantly ate into the bond that held the unit together. These segregation problems were often hidden at Gifu, which had become an artificial island for blacks—"our own little world," as some of the men described it.[3]

In June 1950, before the invasion of South Korea by the NKPA, the 8th Army, under the command of GEN Douglas MacArthur, was still not desegregated. Since the 25th Division, stationed in Hawaii, and the 24th Infantry Regiment (assigned to the 25th Division), stationed in Japan, were close to Korea, they were among the first units sent to stop the NKPA invasion. The 24th went into battle much as the other regiments in the 8th Army did—poorly trained, badly equipped, and short on experience. The unit carried baggage that none of the others possessed, including all the problems of trust and lack of self-confidence that the system of segregation had imposed. Disturbing trends emerged within the 24th as it entered into combat, and no one took immediate action. When the soldiers' straggling increased to epidemic proportions, the leadership did little more than return the men to their units. Some units became so accustomed to withdrawals that their men abandoned their positions at the mere sound of gunfire.

On 31 August 1950 the NKPA forced the 24th Infantry to withdraw. Official records show that mass hysteria seized the regiment and they ran before the NKPA fired a single shot. The 24th coined the term "bug out," and they became known as the "Running 24th." Although the experiences of all-white units were similar in many respects to those of the 24th Infantry Regiment—all having heroes and cowards, successes and failures, good times and painful memories—the 24th was stigmatized for its deficiencies while its accomplishments faded away. After many disgraceful encounters with the enemy, it became the only regiment recommended for dissolution.

General MacArthur was relieved of his command after a dispute with President Truman. General Matthew B. Ridgway assumed command of the 8th Army, and on 26 July 1951, a full year after the invasion by North Korea, he ordered complete desegregation of the army in Korea. In addition, General Ridgway ordered the 24th Infantry Regiment disbanded and the personnel distributed to other units in Korea. It was the last all-black regiment in the United States Army.[4]

Interestingly, in August 1950, while segregation remained in most army units, the training command at Fort Jackson decided to implement integration of troops immediately. Because of the many African Americans drafted along with Caucasians, Fort Jackson didn't have the facilities to provide segregated training and cadre. Therefore, in August 1950 Fort Jackson became a model for an integrated training command.

In Korea, after the order from General Ridgway, "Negro" soldiers were listed separately on the company's official morning report as in the following example:

Negro Enlisted	27
Other Than Negro Enlisted	186
Total Enlisted	213[5]

An initial view of the morning report would indicate that the Negro soldier was identified separately to enhance segregation when, in fact, exactly the opposite was the objective. Reporting the Negros separately was done because General Ridgway wanted to be sure that no one would create an all-Negro company thereby violating his desegregation order. Any pro-segregation action by a unit commander would be cause for a court-martial.

African Americans were in my training company at Fort Jackson when I arrived there in September 1950. They also shared combat with me in my first combat command as a platoon leader and later joined with me in combat while I was a company commander. I had a good opportunity to observe the quality of the integrated African American soldiers. Since the majority of soldiers in the Korean War were draftees, I also had the opportunity to evaluate Caucasian, Asian, and Hispanic soldiers. Throughout my military experience, I found that the African American soldier was both as good and as bad as any other soldier regardless of race. Some African American soldiers were very dedicated. As with other races, some of them really did and some really did not want to be in the army. Like soldiers in other races, some were well educated and some were not. Overall, the level of performance by trained black soldiers was no different from trained soldiers of all other races. The 5th RCT, to my knowledge, never had a discipline problem with any black soldier. As far as I knew, African American soldiers never disobeyed an order and were as brave in combat as any other soldier. I never knew of a single court-martial or loss of enlisted stripe by an African American soldier.

Although a separate category on the morning report wasn't required, about 10 percent of my platoon consisted of KATUSA soldiers. (KATUSA is the abbreviation for Korean Augmentation to United States Army, which refers to soldiers from the Republic of Korea who were assigned to the U.S. Army.)

Fortunately for me, the platoon sergeant for the 1st Platoon was well qualified and knew what he was doing. In the army, it is a tradition that noncommissioned officers train new lieutenants and hope those lieutenants will live long enough to become good officers. Otherwise the sergeant will have wasted a lot of time and effort.

The elevation of the mountain where the 1st Platoon was defending was high enough that the ice and snow on the north side of the rim never melted. The trench on the forward (northern) slope facing the North Koreans had ice, so the only way to go up or down the steep slope was to hang on to a rope. It was difficult to check our fighting position when we had carbines, helmets, flak vests, pistols, and all, and had to pull ourselves up the trench.

Still sick from the last throes of my cold, I struggled to get up and down the trench. I had on the usual gear and also carried my .30-caliber M2 carbine with two thirty-round banana clips. I taped these clips side to side so that I had effectively sixty rounds in the carbine.[6] Of course, I wore the steel helmet along with two fragmentation grenades hanging on my flak vest. With the weight of my gear, I was tired before I started.

World War I was the last war in which trenches had been used extensively, and the trenches had been structured differently than those used in Korea. The trenches that British soldiers occupied in Belgium during the Great War were ten or more feet wide and about ten feet deep. The soldiers had to stand on ladders or build up the side walls to see over the tops of the trenches. Many

World War I trenches had wooden walls to prevent the dirt from collapsing into the trench. The primary location for French trenches was in a low area. As expected, the trenches would fill up with a foot or two of water that caused "trench foot" or rotting and infections of the feet. The soldiers would build a floor in the bottom of the trench that would be higher than the water. Another major difference between the French trenches and the Korean trenches was that we didn't have to attack from our trenches (except when we had to counterattack), only defend. In World War I the soldiers from both armies would have to climb out the front of their trenches into a battle zone without cover and attack. Such a maneuver cost hundreds of thousands of lives.[7]

"Checking the line" was a term we used to describe the inspections that I would do every day and frequently again at night. In addition to other duties, checking the line entailed examining the trench walls to make sure that they weren't collapsing and that the trench was clear. The trench walls in Korea sloped from the top of the trench toward the center at the bottom. If the walls were not sloped correctly, incoming artillery hitting close to a trench or even a heavy rain could cause the walls to collapse. We didn't use wooden supports for the trench walls as were used in World War I. The Korean War trenches in which I served had floors of dirt or rock. Wooden floors in the Korean trenches were not necessary, because most trenches in mountainous areas drained well.

As a rule, Korean trenches didn't have drainage problems. However, during the rainy season—June through August—some sections of the trench collected water, making those sections muddy and slippery. Usually we dug the Korean trenches to at least six feet deep. Most were three feet wide at the bottom. It was important for the trenches to be wide enough to facilitate carrying a wounded soldier on a stretcher if needed. Since the sides sloped outward (away from the center of the trench), the height at which one would carry a stretcher would be wider than the two- to three-foot width at the bottom.

The most desirable way to construct a trench was to make it as narrow as functionally possible, because a wide trench would increase the opportunity for incoming artillery to explode inside rather than outside of the trench— front or rear. A narrow trench was safer. Walls often crumbled from the concussions of artillery shells, from the rain, and from the normal wear and tear of soldiers moving through the trenches. Keeping a trench clean was a very important and continuous job.

The army used various types of trenches during the Korean War. A "fighting trench" was normally located on a slope facing the enemy (forward slope). Along a fighting trench would be bunkers with apertures for firing weapons placed at strategic positions to defend the friendly area. Large rocks often prevented us from digging trenches as deep as necessary. The depth for these sections of a fighting trench was sometimes just a few feet; a soldier would have to move fast when he met one of those rocky spots.

A "communication trench" connected the fighting, or "forward," trench to the rear, or sleeping/eating, area thus providing cover and protection for soldiers moving to and from a fighting position to a sleeping or eating position. The terrain determined the trench's configuration. Movement using the communication trench prevented the enemy from observing any personnel changes, such as unit transitions.[8]

Trenches don't run straight by design, because if a trench were in a straight line, shrapnel from a shell exploding in the trench could travel for some distance and cause additional injuries. An infiltrator with a rifle could control the trench. The zigzag path of a "defiladed" trench prevents the exposure of troops to enemy fire as described above. The defensive position, the mission, the location, and the terrain determine the direction in which the trench is constructed. Soldiers traditionally take the easiest route through the dirt and rocks when digging a trench, which is another reason why trenches are not in a straight line.

During our "checking the line" activity, I inspected each firing position to make sure nothing had gotten in the "field of fire" that would prevent a clear path for shooting a weapon. A clear field was particularly important for machine guns, since they were heavy and more difficult to redirect. I also inspected weapons and ammunition on position, including hand grenades (fragmentation and white phosphorus) and flares. Squad leaders would secure any additional items as needed to improve the defensive position.

The soldiers I worked with were outstanding and rarely required any corrective action. Able Company continually required trench and bunker maintenance, so we couldn't perform physical training as a unit. However, when the men were in the trenches positioned away from the enemy, they were able to gather in small groups to exercise. We made an effort to keep everyone busy and productive. Morale was excellent. My checking the line really wasn't a difficult chore and became a routine job to keep me busy during the boring days. As may be expected, all of us wanted to finish the war and return home safely. We emphasized to the men that remaining alert, maintaining their equipment, and taking care of their personal health would greatly increase the probability of their returning home.

A 5th RCT medium tank from our tank company parked in my platoon sector just below the crest of the rim (ridge). During the daylight hours the tank would pull back below the ridgeline out of sight of the North Koreans. The pullback was a good plan, because if the North Koreans saw the tank on top of the ridge during the daytime, they would try to destroy it. Trying to destroy the tank would bring in an awful lot of artillery, which would hit in my platoon sector—not a good plan.

The 5th RCT Tank Company had received the newer medium-size tanks, the M46 Pattons, each armed with a 90mm cannon. This 90mm cannon used a muzzle break to allow the gases that are created when firing a round to escape early, thereby reducing the gun recoil. When deployed on a mountain ridge as was done during Korea, the mission of the M46 was to be surprise tactic to kill North Koreans. Since it was impossible for North Korea's tanks to attack the rim of the Punch Bowl by coming up the mountainside, the tankers really didn't have a lot to do. The only access to our position by tanks was the single-lane Skyline Drive, and it was highly unlikely that the North Koreans would use that road for an attack. Most nights the tankers would pull into a shooting position just above the rim and wait until they thought they had a target before firing. The location of the tanks' shooting position placed their main guns some fifteen to twenty feet above the top of our trenches.

Part of the tankers' mission was that when they couldn't zero in on a real target, they would fire in the general direction of a potential target, hoping to catch the enemy in the open by surprise. Firing in such a manner was called "H & I" or "harrassment and interdiction" fire. The concept behind the H & I methodology was to shoot randomly at known or suspected targets, thereby keeping the enemy worrying about where we would shoot next. One of many objectives of H & I firing would be to catch the North Koreans on a patrol coming down a finger (also known as a ridge) leading into the valley in front of our position. I don't know if the tankers ever hit anyone or anything except the side of a mountain. They fired frequently, and when they fired the 90mm cannon, the smoke and noise were impressive.

In addition, on the rim of the Punch Bowl there was a station for a half-track (full tracks like a tank on the back and two tires in the front). Mounted on the back of the vehicle were four .50-caliber machine guns, referred to as a "quad fifty." The half-track would move to a position off the line during the day and pull back up on the line at night. The quad fifty was a great weapon. The .50-caliber bullets were loaded in belts so that every fifth shell was a tracer. In between the tracers were a standard ball shell, an explosive shell, another ball, and another explosive shell. All four guns would fire at the same time. When the quad fifty walked up and down a finger searching for suspected North Koreans, anyone on the targeted finger was in great danger.

Normally the platoon sergeant would accompany me while I checked the line in case any corrections were needed. Corrections were rare, however, since the platoon had been on position for several weeks. Sometimes I would check the platoon alone. Late one evening, a couple of weeks after I had recovered from my cold, I was checking out the fighting position just to be sure everyone was awake. As described earlier, the 1st Platoon, Able Company, started near the very top of the highest point on the northern rim of the Punch Bowl and went downward (eastward) toward the center of the rim. At 1,243 meters, the peak was some 4,040 feet high. As noted before, the western side of the peak was the responsibility of the Turkish army. Holding on to the rope, I slowly worked my way down the ice-covered trench and—*WHAM*—just as I passed under the 90mm tube on the tank, it fired a round. It scared the hell out of me!

I released the rope and slid down the trench as if I were on a luge. My carbine went one way, my helmet another, me another. I must have dropped down the trench fifty feet. The trench had several small turns, but a big turn finally stopped me. Several soldiers saw me going down and tried to stop me, but I was moving too fast. I think I set a new Olympic record. I got up, checked for broken bones, and realized I had suffered little or no damage.

As I gathered up my gear, I explained to the soldiers on site that I was okay. Slowly I realized that they were trying to hide their smiles. When I started thinking about my bouncing between the walls of the trench, I started to smile, too. Then I started laughing. Then we all had a good laugh. The soldiers described what I looked like sliding down the trench. I wish I had a movie of the feat.

The tank firing incident was the tank crew's way of welcoming me to Korea. I started to go up and raise hell but decided I wouldn't give them the pleasure of knowing how scared I was. I never mentioned my bouncing down the trench to anyone, but I'm sure most people in the company knew about my experience before long. Stories like what happened to me travel fast in the army. My ears rang for a week. I was much more careful the next time I checked the line. I was always aware that some damn tanker might catch me off guard again and send me quickly down the trench.

In October 1952 the bunkers were very cold, even with a heater. Since the bunkers were very small, anyone opening the door would immediately let all of the heat escape. The Korean winter was so cold that we had learned to get in and out of the rest, or restroom, facilities quickly. The longer a person is exposed to the cold, the greater the chance of something bad happening. At zero degrees

4. Second Lieutenant Evans, in a cozy UN forces bunker, studying a map to determine his company's location. Notice the flak vest, the low ceiling, and the clothing worn inside a bunker. (Photo courtesy of the author.)

Fahrenheit, it doesn't take long for body parts to begin to freeze. At fifteen to twenty degree below zero, it takes even less time. Our rest facilities were not heated. One slip on your way to use the facilities could mean you would completely miss that visit. Instead, if you didn't hit a tree, you took a slide and fell a long way to the bottom of the bowl.

Our rest facility was outdoors and had no heat, air-conditioning, or running water. And it didn't have a front door, allowing the air to circulate. Depositing a chemical in the facility kept infections down and improved the odor to the point where we could breathe, but the chemical created an aroma nearly as bad as the odor it replaced. We had to remember not to breathe too deeply!

Rest facilities available to the soldier usually faced uphill, because creating the necessary pit was much easier when using sandbags. Using sandbags saved work, as we wouldn't have to dig a hole in the rocks. However, the bad news was that because the entry faced uphill, any incoming shells hitting above the structure would cause all loose rocks and logs to roll into the facility while it was being used. How exciting! If the shell was long and passed over the facility, whoever was inside would hear a great booming but would probably not be hurt. In either case, soldiers had to learn to have better body control so that they wouldn't have to use the facilities during incoming artillery.

No fires were allowed in the bunkers. A fire in the fighting bunkers at night would attract the attention of the North Koreans, and they would take a shot or two hoping to kill someone. We didn't allow any type of fire or light in the bunkers facing the North Koreans at night, including smoking. Others had a different idea, however. The Turkish soldiers stationed next to us on the rim proved the "no light" theory false. They built fires each night to stay warm and cook their food. Of course, those fires were visible to everyone for miles. We could see a few of the fires from our position and wondered how the Turkish soldiers got away with their campfires. But after several weeks of the campfires, the North Koreans must have decided enough was enough and opened up on them. One night a very heavy artillery barrage hit the Turks. We thought the North Koreans were making a ground attack, but no North Korean soldiers appeared when the artillery barrage lifted. However, the Turkish fires went out immediately and all was quiet and dark on the Turkish position. The next night there were no fires for the Turks.

The following morning, a rumor started that the Turks had moved out independently and attacked the North Koreans. Of course, moving out and attacking was a terrible thing to do. No one was to attack and occupy terrain in front of the proposed peace line without an order. Most likely, the independent and unauthorized attack by the Turks had everyone shaken from the headquarters of the 8th Army all the way to Washington, D.C. The magical, though not yet agreed upon, Panmunjom line of contact (to become known as the demilitarized line) was changed. There was now a bulge in our line.[9]

Most of us in the 1st Platoon moved to where we could see the Turks. We went to our left front and looked down and across the valley to watch the combat. A small hill was on the North Korean side of the valley, and we could clearly see the Turkish soldiers. They were running from one spot to another but firing very little. We hadn't heard any shooting the night before, when the Turks attacked. We surmised (never confirmed to my knowledge) that the Turks had taken their knives and slit the North Koreans' throats before the enemy soldiers knew what was happening. Even in daylight very little shooting by either side was happening.

Jeeps started to arrive loaded with senior officers. Everyone was excited at seeing a general officer hopping out of his jeep up here in the freezing combat zone. If the North Koreans had been astute, they would have known that U.S. generals would be on the rim to correct the line. The North Koreans would have unloaded many rounds of artillery on us. For some reason, however, the North Koreans didn't fire a single shot at our positions on the rim. Looking toward the west on Skyline Drive, we could see jeeps converging on the Turkish position. After thirty to forty-five minutes, the fighting appeared to have stopped, but we couldn't see any Turkish soldiers returning to our side of the valley. Another hour or so passed before we noted any movement by the Turks who had been engaged to break off and return to our side. Observing and following the Turkish soldiers who were returning to our lines was difficult. Nevertheless, we believed all of the Turkish soldiers did return to their pre-attack positions later in the day.

Night fires were burning again the next evening for the Turks, and we still couldn't smoke in our bunkers facing the North Koreans. We rotated off the hill shortly after all of the excitement. I don't know whether the Turks kept burning their fires, but for their sake, I hope they did.

Most days on the line consisted of a few rounds of incoming artillery from our enemy, the North Korean Communists. I guess the NKPA were as bored as we were and took a few shots for fun. Attacking our position would be extremely difficult; however, the North Koreans were continually probing our positions, looking for Americans they could take as prisoners. We took a few 105mm shots at them to let them know we were still awake. Most shots from the North Koreans missed, but occasionally one would kill an American soldier. I never figured out what they were shooting at—target practice, I guess. We blew up a lot of ground with our 105mm shots and maybe even killed an enemy from time to time.

A week or so after my "Olympic luge tryout," the days were still cool, but they were also sunny. I had been there for a few weeks—it was now late October—and the chill was getting colder every day. It was a good feeling to get a little warmth and sunshine. I was wandering around the platoon's position chatting with some of the soldiers and just making sure everything was okay. Earlier that morning we had received several incoming artillery rounds but no assault. Incoming artillery rounds were common, so there was no need to rush. The platoon sergeant, or at least the squad leader, would be with me when I checked the line. However, today, for some forgotten reason, I wasn't checking the line, just wandering around in a section of the trench by myself. Everything looked normal, so I decided to take a smoke break and get a little sun at the same time.

Finding a flat spot where the sunshine was hitting the side of the trench, I leaned with my back to the North Koreans (the sun was from the southern sky). I had to stand up, since the sun wasn't reaching the trench floor. I lit up a cigarette, took my helmet off to get some sun on my face, and relaxed. It really felt good.

Whack! Whack! Whack!

What was that? I wondered. *Sounded like rifle fire. Could be machine-gun fire.* The shooting was nothing for me to worry about, since I was in a deep trench. However, I quickly put on my helmet.

Whack! Whack! Whack!

Same noise. Strange. Someone must be shooting. I moved around a little, looked up and down our trench, but saw no one firing. I wondered what was going on.

Whack! Whack! Whack!

Then I heard in the distance—*Whoom! Whoom! Whoom!* The sounds reminded me of when I used to pull targets on the rifle range.[10] *The bullets must be going right over my head. Could someone be shooting at ME?*

A chill went down my spine as I carefully peeked over a mound on the trench wall to determine if I could see the person who was trying to hurt me.

Whack! Whack! Whack!
Whoom!Whoom!Whoom!

I could see dirt popping up a few yards just to the right of my position. Somehow the sniper must have seen me, even though I thought I was well hidden in the trench. Nevertheless, I had a very strong feeling that I was his target, so I decided to leave that section and move on down the trench. I held on to the rope and slowly slid down the trench, keeping low, alerting everyone as I descended the trench that an enemy sniper was out there looking for someone. He fired a few more times but didn't seem to track me.

I dropped my cigarette in my rush to move down the trench, so I found another sunny spot, stopped to rest, and have a smoke. I had a few puffs of my cigarette and started contemplating what had just occurred when

Whack! Whack! Whack!
Whoom!Whoom!Whoom!

The sniper must have seen my cigarette smoke. He was good. Even more, he was serious. Now, for the first time, I knew someone was trying to kill me. We received at least one incoming artillery round every day, but artillery rounds are impersonal. When someone fires a machine gun at you—now, that is a very personal experience. Very disturbing!

If I could have gotten a message to our 555th forward observers, I'm sure we could have given the sniper a thank-you return with a 105mm shell. However, we had no radio or telephone close by. I asked several soldiers if they could spot the gun, but no one could. We didn't return fire. I very slowly moved on down the trench and continued to alert everyone to the sniper's presence. He fired a few more times and then gave up. All misses. No one hurt.

Somebody had really wanted to kill me. It was a strange sensation, a very strange realization. A chill ran through me, and I shuddered. Near the bottom of the platoon sector, I found another quiet, sunny spot in the trench and lit up a cigarette. No shots. I was safe. A trench provided a sense of protection. I guess it was because I was close to Mother Earth.

In late October 1952 the 40th Infantry Division, which assumed responsibility for the defense on Line Minnesota, replaced the 25th Infantry Division. The 5th RCT then became part of the 40th Division.

On 2 November 1952, Able Company was relieved on the Punch Bowl and replaced by the 40th Division Reconnaissance Company. Able Company then moved to division reserve, where we would get clean clothes and a little rest.[11]

4
Shower Relief
MASH for Treatment

By 1 November 1952, only four weeks had passed since I had joined Able Company on the line, and I was surprised at how much I had learned. Moreover, I had earned one badge. An infantryman could earn the Combat Infantryman Badge (CIB) in three ways. The soldier had to have an infantryman's Military Occupational Specialty (MOS) number to qualify. Then he had to either

- be assigned to a company that received enemy fire for fifteen or more days in a given month
- be wounded and receive the Purple Heart
- be killed in action.

I was happy not to qualify for the last two; however, I had qualified under the first requirement. I was very proud to join the elite group of men who had earned the CIB.

The day before we were to be relieved and leave the rim, an incoming North Korean artillery shell knocked me off the side of the mountain, and I fell several feet before stopping. I recovered and checked all of my important parts to see if they were still working. Everything checked out okay, and I found no fresh blood. I felt a sharp pain on the left side of my back and some soreness on my left side. Since there was no blood, I didn't think my injury was serious. I was very lucky.

Our rotation off the rim started on 2 November. The 40th Division Reconnaissance Company relieved us, and we proceeded to the 40th Division Reserve for delousing, showers, clean clothes, and some rest.[1] However, the army's philosophy was that a busy soldier is a happy soldier. Whenever we rotated for a shower break, getting ready to return to the rim would normally require a week to ten days. First, we would get clean and enjoy wearing fresh fatigues. Then, to keep our climbing ability in shape, we would start doing physical training (PT) on the first morning and then every morning thereafter while we were in the reserve camp.

As part of our program in reserve, the armorer would inspect all of our weapons to be sure they were functioning properly. They would also check to make sure no one had filed the sear on the M1 Garand rifle and M1 Carbine to make these weapons fully automatic. The reason the guns were checked wasn't in order to stop soldiers from shooting faster and killing more NKPA soldiers but to make sure they weren't burning up the gun barrels, thereby making the guns inoperable. To hold an automatic weapon on target when being fired in the fully automatic mode was very difficult. In the case of the M1 rifle, which operated with only an eight-round clip, the soldier would spend more time reloading than shooting.

The first morning in the division reserve camp in the bottom of the Punch Bowl, we fell out in formation and started our PT routine. First we did some warm-up exercises—jumping jacks. Throwing my arms up in the air quickly reminded me of my sore left side. Our next exercise was pushups. I dropped down on my hands and started to lower my upper body. Suddenly I felt a sharp pain in my left side. I just about lost my breath, my side hurt so much. I yelled and got up. A medic came over to see what was wrong. He pulled the back of my T-shirt up and noticed a bruised area about the size of a baseball. Because the bruise was toward my back, I couldn't see much of it, but I could certainly feel the pain when the medic poked me in the ribs. He wasn't sure what was wrong but told me I should immediately go to the MASH. Since we were in the bottom of the bowl, the hospital was just a few miles away. Wearing my helmet and carrying my flak vest, I got into a jeep. The driver took me to the 8063 MASH.

X-rays revealed I had three fractured ribs. A doctor told me I was very lucky not to have punctured my lungs with one of my ribs while I was doing exercises. As he taped up my side, we discussed how the ribs could have gotten broken. When I told the doctor about my incident with the incoming round while I was on the mountainside, he said he believed that the concussion alone from the shell could have broken the ribs but that it was more likely a piece of shrapnel or rock had hit my flak vest where the vest covered my left rib cage.

The large bruise on my back indicated that whatever had hit my body was so large that a mark might still be on my vest. We examined the section in question on the vest and found a slight scar. The doctor and I surmised that the shrapnel or rock must have been ready to drop to the ground from lack of energy when the object hit me. Otherwise, my whole chest would have been blown out. For the next two weeks, I wasn't supposed to remove the tape. And I couldn't participate in PT, especially pushups, for at least three weeks. By then the fractured ribs should have healed, the side should no longer be sore, and the bruise should be gone. No pushups sounded good to me.

Then the doctor asked me if I would like to visit other Able Company wounded, and I said, "Yes, sir, I would very much like to see them." He also asked if I would like to visit their officers club. Again I said yes. To see the doctor, get x-rayed, taped, and have lunch took all of the morning. It was early afternoon before I could go to visit the wards. A seriously wounded soldier was in one of the first wards we came to. When I saw the solider, he was sleeping and didn't look too bad. A doctor led me to a lighted screen on the wall and put up several x-rays that had just been taken of the wounded soldier. The soldier's body was covered with black spots. The doctor explained that the black spots were steel fragments of shrapnel. He continued to explain that at this stage the physicians were afraid to remove some of the fragments, because removing them might cause greater damage to the man's body. The hospital didn't have the equipment to attempt the operation, so arrangements to transport the man to a larger hospital had started. Each black spot was a piece of steel; some looked like tiny dots and others were the size of the eraser on a pencil. The doctor explained that the shrapnel was inside the soldier. Now I understood why they had to transport him to another facility. The MASH unit was just trying to stabilize him for the trip to a hospital in Japan. I never spoke with the sedated soldier. However, I did say a prayer for him.

I continued to track down and visit as many Able Company soldiers as I could find. Later in the afternoon, I went to the MASH officers club and found a couple of other officers from the 5th RCT. A raised table served as the club's bar, and several types of alcoholic drinks were available. As with other army officers clubs, in order to get a drink, one had to purchase a two-dollar coupon booklet. The book contained forty chits valued at five cents per chit. Each drink cost one chit. Having been on the line for a month without anything alcoholic to drink, only one or two drinks were all we needed before the three of us were ready to leave. As usual, we were happy to get away from the hospital. In our case, we *had* to leave, because we were drunk—"smashed at the MASH." The MASH had a good program even if they wouldn't allow us to cash out the remaining chits. Fortunately, our driver didn't drink, we didn't fall out of the jeep, and it was just a short distance to our quarters.

I can't say enough good things about the medical care we received from the U.S. Army medics, nurses, and doctors. From the time a medic started to help the wounded on the battlefield until the soldier completed his stay at the hospital, everyone had just one goal in mind: save that soldier—and to be careful with him while saving him. I will always hold the military medical personnel in the highest regard.

I returned to Able Company and wasn't required to participate in PT for a while. However, the army never rests. When we were in reserve for our shower cleanup and a little rest, we would start military training again. Our training entailed reviewing the infantry tactics for the attack. At first I thought such training made little sense, since the 5th RCT hadn't attacked anywhere in Korea in a year or so. We had always been in a defensive position, such as trenches and listening posts. Nevertheless, we started to practice "attacking on a village," moving in a "dispersed formation," squad maneuvering, and assault, among other actions.

In our discussions about our training, the only reason we could come up with for not being trained in defensive tactics was that apparently no one in the army had ever written a field manual for trench warfare. In 1952 the only field manuals I knew of had been about attacking, fire, and maneuver. If a field manual on defensive tactics for a rifle company existed, it wasn't available, and one cannot train soldiers without the proper field manual. I would have preferred classes on how to prepare a line of fire, proper construction of a fighting bunker, and the best way to store ammunition in trenches. We also should have received training on how to protect our weapons when we were in the trenches, how to string barbed wire, how and where to place defensive mines and napalm, and other tricks of the trade that are necessary in trench warfare. What I learned about all of these activities and many other subjects was from hands-on training. Learning on the job, as we did, while fighting a war in the trenches was a very dangerous and deadly way to learn.

Nevertheless, the army goes into detail and does an excellent job of training. Actually, I realized it was important for us to review and rehearse maneuvers in an attack. In the event a position was lost to the enemy and we would have to retake it, these rehearsals would have been well worth the effort. The only thing we didn't have to do while we were in a reserve position was to march in formation. And the reason for that was because the level ground needed for a parade field was difficult to find.

The weather grew progressively colder, so the army issued us winter equip-

5. Parkas with fox fur around the hoods, winter 1952–1953. (Photo courtesy of James A. Drew, 5th RCT, standing on right.)

ment, including new winter-insulated boots that we called "Mickey Mouse" boots. They worked very well unless you stepped in a pool of melting snow or ice and the pool was deeper than the mid-calf top of your boot. With a boot full of water, your foot would quickly freeze in very cold weather. To save your foot, you had to take the boot off and pour the water out, since the boots had no leak holes. If you were on a patrol and couldn't stop to get the water out, you had a problem. Walking around with your foot in a chunk of ice wasn't a good experience. The secret was "don't step in pools of water deeper than your boot." The new boots worked very well for ambush patrols where you had to sit in the snow for several hours waiting on a North Korean soldier.[2]

In World War I the trenches were often filled with water six to ten inches deep. A World War I soldier would use rubber boots or hip waders whenever he could find them. However, the boots or waders didn't last long, since shrapnel, barbed wire, broken weapons, and other such sharp instruments were lying in the bottom of the trench ready to punch a hole in the boots or waders and thus making them useless. Fortunately, our Mickey Mouse boots were made of tough material, and I was never aware of anyone puncturing a boot.[3]

The army decided to improve our chances of living in the extreme cold. In addition to our new boots, each soldier received a parka with a hood. The hoods had fox fur around the face opening. The fox fur covered an embedded wire. Using the embedded wire, we were able to shape the fur into various forms. Only fox fur was used for covering the embedded wire, since ice doesn't adhere to the fur. If the fur used on a hood iced up, it was fake and a contractor was delivering illegal hoods. Amazingly, correctly formed fox fur around the hood would allow me to look directly into the freezing Siberian winds without hurting my eyes. We didn't have goggles, so if we hadn't been able to mold the fur, we would have been unable to look at the North Koreans. The U.S. Army took much better care of its soldiers than the North Korean army did of its soldiers, who wore heavy, quilted uniforms—two pieces, with top and bottom. If the quilted uniforms became wet, the soldier would freeze to death. They also used a reversible khaki/white covering for patrols in the snow.

The official report of our activity while in reserve was that the 1st Battalion engaged in intensive training. We were now clean, rested, and trained. Weary of the training exercises but with excellent morale, we were ready to get back to the excitement on the rim of the Punch Bowl.

5
Christmas 1952
Winter Combat on the Mountain

On 16 December 1952 we returned to defensive positions on the rim of the Punch Bowl, relieving the 40th Division Reconnaissance Company, the same unit that had relieved Able Company on 2 November.[1] Winter war in an inhospitable environment, such as we were in at 3,500-plus feet, involved several unusual factors. First, we had to stay alive, which meant we couldn't freeze. The Punch Bowl's temperature during the winter months ranged from thirty degrees below zero (forty-four below on the top of Hill 1243) to twenty-five degrees above zero, with most temperatures being between ten below and twenty above. The windchill factor was unknown, since we had never heard of such a thing in 1952. However, we knew the weather was cold. Second, to stay alive we had to be alert, and the freezing conditions we faced made it very difficult to stay alert, especially during the nighttime.

In all of our activities we had to deal with a great amount of snow and ice. Making the situation even worse was that the fighting bunkers faced north, since that was where the North Koreans were located. With the bunkers' gun apertures open toward the North Koreans, the cold northern winds from Siberia blew right through the apertures into the fighting bunkers. The army had issued each of us a Russian-style fur hat, which was nice and warm, and the hats had earflaps to keep our ears from freezing. But if the North Koreans attempted penetration on a freezing-cold night and our ears were covered with the flaps, we would be unable to hear the enemy soldiers coming up the hill.

Another problem with staying alert was that in the cold night weather a soldier would wear as much clothing as possible. Becoming warm and comfortable, he couldn't stay awake very long. A practical rule was that a soldier should have to stay awake for only a couple of hours before relief. A two-hour rotation with another soldier would provide each of them a break from the weather, and each could get a little rest. If the fighting bunker was too far from a communication trench, which the soldier would use to reach a rest bunker, the soldier wouldn't have much rest time for the two-hour rotation procedure. One solution would be for both the alert soldier and the resting soldier to stay inside the fighting bunker. Because we couldn't have fires in the fighting bunker, the resting soldier wouldn't be able to fall asleep, because he would be too cold.

In these cases, another solution was to cut a resting place out of the side of a trench wall close to the fighting bunker. The cut would be about two to three feet into the side of the trench, about three feet high, five to six feet long, and about two feet above the trench floor. A blanket, a poncho, or a piece of tent taken from somewhere would cover the open side. Even with the resting place opening covered with a blanket, the weather was so cold that the soldiers would take a number 10 can (a large can for bulk supplies), punch holes in it, and use it as a stove to burn charcoal to warm the resting place. Of course, we didn't realize then that burning charcoal in a confined area wasn't healthy. Had we known of the dangers of breathing charcoal fumes in a confined area, everyone still would have considered breathing charcoal fumes a heck of a lot less risky than freezing to death. The charcoal burners didn't smell very good, but they did generate some heat. After a while we all smelled like burned charcoal. Nevertheless, the rotation to the charcoal-burning, blanket-covered resting place did provide a warm break.

Remember, we were all wearing several layers of clothing plus our flak vests and parkas. The weather was too cold to take off all of our clothes. I usually wore a T-shirt, long woolen underwear, a wool sweater, a fatigue shirt, a field jacket liner, and a field jacket. When I went outside the bunker, I added a flak vest, a parka, helmet with liner, pistol belt with holster, canteen, ammunition, and a few grenades. In addition, I wore heavy wool pants, field pants, insulated boots, and thick mittens. Under my helmet I wore a fur cap with earflaps. Even with all of the clothing, however, we were still cold. Some days the weather on the mountains was so cold the .30-caliber carbines couldn't be carried on patrols, because the carbines froze up faster than the BARs (Browning automatic rifles) or M1 rifles.

We couldn't put the charcoal burners in our fighting position for the same reason we didn't allow smoking or any other type of light in the fighting positions: a light of any kind in the bunker would draw fire from the North Koreans. We could use charcoal-burning number 10 cans in the cutouts, though, because the blanket-covered cutouts were in the side of the trench and not visible to the enemy. A more important reason for not allowing the burners in the fighting position was that staring at the light of a charcoal fire in a can or lighting a cigarette could diminish a soldier's night vision, and perhaps the soldier on guard would miss an infiltrator.

Able Company, 5th RCT, spent Christmas 1952 on the rim of the Punch Bowl. We were quiet and melancholy, wondering what in the world we were doing in Korea. Christmas Eve was a clear night, and of course the bad joke was watching out for Santa. Especially for the Christian soldiers, it was a very lonesome evening. We all dreamed of being home, prayed for deliverance, and suppressed the emotions soldiers always have when they are away from their loved ones on Christmas Eve. At least on Christmas Day we had a good, hot meal.

On 12 January 1953, COL Harvey H. Fisher assumed command of the 5th RCT.[2] On 15 January a patrol from Able Company engaged a North Korean squad and killed one enemy soldier.[3] Contact with enemy probing patrols was normal.

An exciting winter warfare adventure was patrolling in the deep snow. The land in front of our fighting bunkers (our front trench line) was considered no-man's-land, and anyone in that position would be assumed an enemy and therefore subject to being shot.

The North Koreans were always trying to sneak into our trenches and create havoc. To try to stop them before they got too close we ran two types of patrols. One of these was an ambush patrol, which was usually a six- to eight-man operation. The objective of the ambush patrols, which were generally run every night, was to go somewhere in the valley separating the U.S. forces from the North Korean forces. At some point the patrol would set up a small defense perimeter and wait for the North Koreans to visit. Most times the patrol members would sit in the snow without talking, smoking, drinking, or thinking for four to five hours. Each soldier had to keep his fingers and toes moving and his body functions under control. When the ambush ended, the soldier would get up (if he wasn't frozen) and climb back up to the trenches. I would guess that in only one out of every five ambush patrols would the patrol even think they heard an enemy soldier. And only one out of ten patrols would actually see the enemy. Ambush patrols were so boring that sometimes the patrol leader would call in an artillery concentration to keep everyone awake and interested.[4]

The other type of patrol was a "contact patrol," which was a moving patrol looking for indications that the NKPA soldiers were moving into positions for an attack. Even though the contact patrols were more interesting than the AM-bush patrols, the contact patrols experience little contact. However, when contact *was* made with the North Koreans, a firefight would result. The NKPA also ran ambush and contact patrols. And they often tried to penetrate our defensives in hopes of capturing one of our soldiers.

We were extremely fortunate to have the 555th Field Artillery Battalion supporting us. When preparing for contact patrol, we would work with the 555th forward observer to decide, based on the patrol's path, where the artillery would prearrange their concentrations. Several points along the patrol path were marked as locations where the patrol would likely need artillery support. Concentrations were given simple numbers and names, such as, "1," "2," or "3." The patrol leader would then call in "Fire C 1" (or the code for day), and the 555th would drop a round at the proper map coordinates. The wonderful thing was that when we left the safety of our trenches, the Triple Nickel would track our movements, which meant if we needed artillery, all we had to do was call in the concentration number. The gunners would change their settings as we moved to a different concentration number. Whenever needed, the 555th guns would immediately respond with "on the way," meaning that a round had been fired and was in flight. Then the message "splash-wait" came within seconds. "Splash-wait" meant that the round was about to impact, so the soldiers requesting the artillery would have a chance to duck. The round would land exactly in the right place. The 555th was a truly outstanding bunch of warriors.

As a platoon leader of Able Company, I had the responsibility, as did the other platoon leaders, of taking a newly assigned officer or a new senior enlisted man out for his first ambush patrol. I didn't mind taking them out and helping them get set up for the night. After they were in position, I was free to return to the trenches. I made sure that everyone in the ambush patrol was in position and that the radio was working and had an extra battery. I could then head to the warmth and relative safety of a bunker.

The soldiers making up the patrols were a mixed group. We tried to make sure each patrol included one of the most recent replacements and one of the more seasoned soldiers. To complete a patrol, the leader would then select from his platoon four to six men, one of whom had been on patrols before. As a rule, Able Company deployed one or more patrols every night. The majority were under the supervision of noncommissioned officers, since a lot more noncoms were available than commissioned officers.

Once the ambush patrol is in position, whoever set up the patrol is free to return to the trenches and warmth. Moving back up the mountain was a much longer and lonesome walk than returning to the trench with the patrol. With the patrol there would be a sense of safety in numbers; by oneself there was the fear of being alone. Imagine this: Beautiful stars fill the sky, the moon is shining brightly, and the snow is sparkling. Your patrol is in position and settled. You are ready to leave the patrol with the patrol leader and start your solo trek back up the snow-covered mountain finger. Wearing over-whites helps you blend into the snow. The climb back up the mountain is an elevation change of some two hundred feet, equal to a twenty-story building.

There is no cover anywhere on the return trip—no trees, no bushes, no ravines—nothing on the finger except a lot of white snow on a steep hill. You are climbing back up to the trench using the ridge of a finger, because the snow is too deep to walk in the ravines on each side of the finger. You know the North Koreans can see you struggle through the snow as you climb, and you wonder what the bullet will feel like. You are defenseless.

At this point you do as every soldier does—you pray. Perhaps you recite the 23rd Psalm: *Yea, though I walk through the valley of the shadow of death, I will fear no evil, for thou art with me, thy rod and thy staff they comfort me.* God answers your prayers, and you become calm.

No bullets, no artillery, nothing happens. After a very worrisome twenty-minute climb, you are breathless and your muscles are aching. Then a second great concern leaps into your head. The time is about midnight now. What if a half-awake machine gunner on duty sees a figure moving up the hill toward him? Will he be aware that it is you out there? Does he know the password? In a half whisper, you start calling out the password. Finally, someone responds and you hear him pass the word to the others on the line. *Thank you, God. You are still with me.*

After finally reaching the barbed wire in front of the trench, you're not exactly sure if the opening to go through the wire is to your left or your right. And since you left the patrol in the valley, there's no one to ask. You know that finding the opening is very important. Antipersonnel mines and planted napalm are buried somewhere nearby. Tin cans with rocks hang on the barbed wire to alert the men in the trench if someone is in the wire. Usually, the noise would be from a North Korean trying to slip into the trench.

Prepare to duck, because if you miss the correct path, you'll make a lot of noise. When the mine goes off or the machine gun opens fire, everyone will awaken and they won't be happy with the chaos you have created.[5]

You look very carefully for the footprints that were left in the snow when the patrol exited the trenches on their way down to the valley. You think you see the footprints. As you look closer, they seem to be pointing downhill. *Thank you, Lord, for not allowing snow or rain to destroy our footprints.* You now follow the footprints and finally see a break in the wire.

You're not there yet, though. Once you enter the spot where the barbed wire is broken, the path to safety zigzags up to the trench. Tonight the moon has been a great help in lighting your way. You take a few steps, look carefully, and continue. Very alert and aware, you search for the turns, hope you make the correct movements, and keep looking up at the trench.

With a big sigh of relief, you see the outline of a bunker. Mother Trench looms, and finally you see where it dips to provide an easy entrance to safety. You are overjoyed to be back. You have done a lot of soul searching, praying, and guessing during the climb back to the trenches. You have just lived through an unforgettable experience.

Patrolling was one of the main courses taught during the Ranger course. I was a lot luckier than most soldiers, because I had the best teachers the army offered. Unfortunately, at Fort Benning they forgot to tell me about the lonely and dangerous climb back home.

Contact patrols usually took less time than ambush patrols, because the mission required covering a certain amount of ground. Normally the patrol, using the necessary caution, would move to predefined points on the ground while looking for enemy tracks, equipment, or other artifacts. The patrol leader would be debriefed. I never knew of a patrol failing to cover the required ground as ordered.

When Able Company returned to a defensive position on the rim of the Punch Bowl on 16 December, we were in the "saddle" of the northern sector, which was approximately halfway between Hill 1243 and Hill 1026. During these winter months, I learned a great deal about winter warfare.

One clear day, I was standing near the company command post on the rim, and a roar passed just over my head. I ducked immediately, thinking of new artillery shells the North Koreans must have. I looked up and realized what I had heard wasn't a new shell but a jet aircraft flying very close to the rim of the bowl. I couldn't tell if the jet was an American fighter or a North Korean plane. Immediately I heard another roar, started to turn, and saw two more jet fighters roaring by. It appeared that the two jets in the rear were chasing the first one and appeared to be American F-86 Air Force jet fighters. Then all three quickly disappeared into the distance.

About five minutes later, someone yelled that a parachute was coming down. We all rushed outside to see what was going on. Yes, a parachute was floating downward. If the parachute was on the back of an American, he was in for some trouble, because it appeared to be coming down in North Korean territory. As we closely watched the parachutist's descent, we recalculated and decided he might reach American lines if he continued to drift eastward.

Our main line of resistance (MLR) ran just about due east along the rim of the Punch Bowl. On the eastern edge of the bowl, the MLR and associated trenches turned to the northeast. Since the parachutist was drifting just about due east, too, if he continued on the same path, he would land in friendly territory. He continued on the track, and we thought we could see him land on what should have been friendly territory. We never did know if he landed safely. If he did, he was very lucky. (Of course, if the parachutist was North Korean, he may not have been so lucky.)

U.S. Air Force and Navy jets flew whenever the weather was good. The jets would make bombing runs against North Korean positions generally to our northeast. We would stand outside and try to guess whether the air force (silver) or navy (blue) jets would go lower on their bombing runs. It appeared to me the air force would stop their dive at one thousand feet above the target while the navy (or marines) would go down to about five hundred feet. In either case, the dropped bombs would shake our mountain. I didn't see anyone directing the bombing, nor did I know what the bombing was trying to destroy.

I was used to seeing 105mm and 155mm howitzer shells landing, but those explosions were very small compared to the bombs the planes dropped. It would be a difficult task for anyone to withstand the shock of those bombs. I'm sure the North Koreans felt the same way.

We were also all jealous of both navy and air force pilots. Of course, I didn't blame them for not wanting to stay in a bunker with us. After their brief contact with war, the navy and marine pilots returned to a clean environment on an aircraft carrier for a nice, warm bed. Even better, the air force pilot returned to a nice, warm officers club at an air force base with girls (in Japan, anyway). We, on the other hand, had to go back into our sandbagged, dirt-filled bunker, communication-wire beds, and, at no additional cost, large rats.

When infantry units took their turn on the rim of the Punch Bowl, there was a rule that we would have one hot meal each day whenever possible. The hot food was prepared in a mess bunker and then loaded into marmite-insulated containers. Each container was about the size of a five-gallon gasoline can. The insulation worked well except on very cold days. On those days, the cooks would place a padded cover on each container. The containers were hand-carried from the road up to our sleeping and fighting bunkers. Each platoon received their allocated containers, and small groups of soldiers would line up to receive their food. Usually the food would be located at one place and the squads would rotate through the chow line. After the meal, if we were lucky, we could rinse our mess kits in a pot of boiling water.

For the other meals, we would munch on our C rations (these may have been K rations—I never did learn which was which). The rations were generally fairly tasty. Sometimes we would place an opened can of food on an oil heater or a number 10 can charcoal stove to warm the food and make it palatable. Most of the time, though, we just spooned the rations out of their original container and ate them cold. Then we would stick the spoon in the dirt, rinse the mess gear and spoon with water, and wipe them off, which seemed to be sufficient to kill any germs.

A selection of several foods such as hot baked beans or beef patties were on the menu. Condensed milk made a box of cereal taste very good if you didn't cut the milk with water. In each box of individual rations, one of the cans would contain a package of cigarettes, matches, toilet paper, and a small bar of candy. The best rations I ever had were the "assault rations." These were packaged in a sardine-type can to reduce the size and weight a soldier would have to carry for long distances. The assault rations were well prepared, concentrated, and had something added for a high level of energy.

If too much ice had accumulated on the road or on the trail up the hill to our position, we would miss a hot meal. However, most days the mess sergeant would make a real effort to prepare a hot meal and get it to us.

One night in mid-January 1953, at about 2300 hours, a machine gun opened up on our right flank. The gunner fired two or three short bursts and then all was quiet—except for the horrible sound of a man screaming. I went outside to find out what was happening. A couple of flares illuminated the night sky but revealed nothing. Our telephones were working, so I called the company command post for Baker Company, the unit on our right flank.

"Baker, this is Able 1.[6] What was the shooting?"

"Able 1, sir, a machine gun fired. Hit our listening post."

"North Korean?"

"No, sir. We think the shooting was just an accident, sir."

"Can you get him?"

"Sir, not sure. He may have fallen in the wire."

"Thanks, out."

His message was very upsetting. We had suffered enough deaths at the hands of the North Koreans without shooting our own people. Unfortunately, a machine gunner didn't know or forgot about Baker Company having a listening post about fifty yards in front of their barbed wire. When the gunner saw movement, he shot, and the soldier he hit was in bad shape. I could tell from the way he was screaming.

Apparently the wounded soldier had fallen into barbed wire that was in an area of a known minefield. Mines, napalm, and other devices had been placed in and among the barbed wire to create a barrier to stop the North Koreans in an attack. For anyone to crawl to the soldier and bring him back in the dark of night would be extremely dangerous—nearly impossible—as anyone making such an attempt would very likely trip a mine or other device and kill them both.

For hours the wounded man let the world know he was hurt. No other sound could be heard during the night except for his screaming. Someone had to make a decision, and whoever he was ended up making a very difficult decision: The soldier was to remain where he was until daylight. Then perhaps recovery would be possible without risking several additional lives.

It was a most terrible night. The poor soldier was crying and begging for anything to relieve his pain, for someone to get him, for someone to help. Then he would scream in pain for a while. Then he'd start begging. But helping the badly wounded soldier was beyond our ability. Sending anyone out to him would have been suicidal.

The soldier's crying became weaker and weaker. He died just before daylight. I'm very glad I didn't have to make the decision to leave the fellow to die. However, I'm sure I would have made the same decision.

Everyone in the whole battalion heard the cries for help. Most of the North Koreans on the other side of the valley probably heard his cries. Everyone—American and NKPA soldiers—who heard his screams imagined himself in the man's place, thought of his home and loved ones, and realized that war was one hell of a way to live.

You may recall that I had had some problems with a tank firing its 90mm cannon just when I walked under the tube. The M46 tank has a nuzzle brake on the 90mm tube that causes a flashback and reduces recoil when fired.

In early January 1953 a tank went into a firing position along the rim as they usually do for H & I activity. The next morning, after completing all of his firing missions, the driver started backing the tank from the firing position to the parking position for the day. Somehow he backed completely across Skyline Drive and went over the side toward the bottom of the bowl. Realizing what he had done, he threw the gears to the forward position and jammed on the gas. The motor raced and the tank's tracks started spinning as they tried to get traction. With dirt flying, the tank slowly slid backward down the side of the mountain above the Punch Bowl. It slid toward another finger near the bottom of the mountain that ran across its side and formed a V. As it continued to slide down the mountain, its motor was running full blast. The back of the tank jammed into the V and the tank stopped sliding.

It appeared to be about four hundred yards down the side of the mountain and was wedged in tightly. Several of us debated as to how anyone would be able to get the tank out of the wedge. Apparently it would be impossible to pull it out. I learned that the tankers took out the sight, radio, and other removable parts and then exploded a thermite grenade in the cannon's tube, melting it and making the gun inoperable.

When we left the Punch Bowl, the tank was wedged in the mountain crease. If a salvage crew was unable to cut it up, it's very likely the tank is still wedged in the crease today.

When General Eisenhower was campaigning to become president of the United States in 1952, he pledged to have all soldiers in Korea who had accumulated thirty-six points or more to be immediately rotated out of Korea. In the 5th RCT, numerous soldiers had earned more than that number of points, and some had accumulated more than forty-five points. I had several men with "over points" in my platoon. The Able Company first sergeant had nearly sixty points—or so he told me.

The point system was based on the time a soldier had served overseas. The normal overseas tour of duty was three years. In a noncombat zone, each month military personnel could accumulate one point. Soldiers closer to combat zones would accumulate two or three points per month. In a unit that was receiving enemy fire for fifteen days or more in a month, soldiers would accumulate four points per month. The greatest number of points that should have been earned by a soldier who served all of his tour in a four-point combat zone was thirty-six, the equivalent of nine months. If a soldier was killed or seriously wounded after completing his service of thirty-six points, it was considered a disgrace to the U.S. Army and to the commander in chief for allowing the soldier to stay too long in combat. Apparently, President Truman didn't know or didn't care about the soldiers and allowed many to overstay their required time. As a result, the many wounds and deaths to soldiers with more than sufficient points to rotate home were reprehensible. In the fall of 1952 the secretary of the army intervened to restore the thirty-six-point criteria after the Far East Command raised it to thirty-nine points. However, the point level was immaterial if replacements didn't arrive to fulfill the obligations of the army.

Sometime after we went back on the line on 16 December 1952, Able Company, 5th RCT, received some twenty-five Puerto Rican soldiers as replacements. At first I was glad to get the extra soldiers. If all of the men with "over points" were pulled from the regiment by President Eisenhower, as he had promised when elected, we believed that replacements would not be reporting to the regiment for several months. From experience, we had always been short of the soldier requirement of our TOE (Table of Organization and Equipment). When the Puerto Rican replacements reported, they explained that they had been with the 65th Infantry Regiment, 3rd Infantry Division, and had recently fought a battle for a hill called Jackson Heights, located some 140 miles west of the Punch Bowl.

As I mentioned earlier, integration of infantry units had started in Korea when General Ridgway took command. In compliance with orders from General Ridgway, we tried to keep a ratio of at least 10 percent African American soldiers and the balance a combination of white and KATUSA. With the addition of the Puerto Ricans, however, the ratios were changed. We now tried to keep a ratio of 10 percent Puerto Ricans, 10 percent African Americans, and 80 percent whites (including KATUSA).

When I learned that the new men spoke little, if any, English I wasn't too sure how the situation was going to work out. Able Company divided the Puerto Rican soldiers among various platoons and then assigned them to squads. These assignments placed one or two former 65th Infantry Regiment soldiers in each squad. The plan was to have at least one English-speaking Puerto Rican soldier in each platoon to assist the platoon sergeant in communicating with the newcomers. It was a good plan—except only one English-speaking Puerto Rican soldier was available for the entire company. The language challenge was especially difficult for the squad leaders, who had to teach these replacements how we did business. They had to supervise these soldiers without knowing how to speak Spanish and with the new soldiers understanding little or no English. I wasn't sure how the squad leaders could effectively train the Puerto Ricans, and since I didn't speak or write Spanish, I couldn't help.

When the 65th Puerto Ricans arrived at the 5th RCT, I was still the platoon leader of the 1st Platoon and received our seven replacements. We had started to wear our parkas now that the weather was colder. We also used our newly issued fur caps with the fur pull-down flaps for the ears. With the ear-flaps tied under the chin, the caps were very warm. One of the most important rules I had for my platoon was that *no one* could wear the flaps down over his ears while standing guard duty unless the weather was extremely cold. When appropriate, I would approve wearing the flaps down and advise the platoon sergeant. As I wrote earlier, the flaps, when worn down, were so warm they cre-ated an environment where the soldier became sleepy. More important, when the flaps were down over a soldier's ears, it substantially reduced his ability to hear.

One night, a week after the Puerto Ricans arrived, I started to make a quick check of the line. All was quiet, so I decided not to bother the platoon sergeant and let him rest. This was going to be a very quick walk-through check. As I proceeded down the line, everything seemed to be okay and the guards were alert. However, I did find one of the Puerto Rican replacements standing guard with his earflaps down. The time was about 2300, and the weather was cold but not frigid. A light Siberian wind was blowing through the apertures into the fighting bunkers. This soldier had his flaps pulled down and tied. I immedi-ately ordered him to untie the flaps and tuck them under his helmet. He acted as if he didn't understand me, but he finally untied the earflaps and tucked them up and under his helmet. I made a mental note to discuss what had hap-pened with the platoon sergeant.

The next day I had a long chat with my platoon sergeant, and he called the squad leaders together to discuss the "flaps down" situation. I was sure everyone had a refresher course regarding the earflaps. Several nights later, however, I was once again checking the line and came across the same Puerto Rican standing guard. He was leaning against the wall on the right side of the bunker, dozing, and didn't hear me when I walked into the fighting bunker. Dozing or sleeping was even worse than having earflaps down. And this soldier was not only dozing but also had his earflaps down and tied.

"WAKE UP!" I yelled as I shook his shoulder.

He slowly came to life, and I could feel my anger rising.

"Stand up and take your helmet off," I ordered.

He acted as if he didn't understand, so I made sign language of sorts and he got up. More sign language and he took off his helmet.

Anger was slowly overtaking me. I knew that the solider had received in-structions about the danger to the platoon and to the company of wearing his earflaps down and sleeping on guard duty. He also knew he was to stand when an officer was present. Not being able to think of another appropriate move, I grabbed the fur cap with the flaps off his head and threw it as far as I could over the front of the trench. It landed in the barbed wire, trip mines, and other defense devices placed in front of each fighting position.

"If you want your flaps down so bad that you would risk the lives of the rest of the company, then climb over the top and go get your cap," I said.

I don't think he understood many of the words, but he did understand that he didn't have a cap. Sleeping on guard duty was a serious offense, and he could have been court-martialed. Without a witness (he was alone in the bunker, as his partner was on his two-hour rest) the soldier could have claimed he wasn't asleep, just dozing, and the court-martial would be one person's word against another's. He was lucky I didn't file charges. And I don't know if he ever got his hat back. I turned the problem over to his platoon sergeant.

Unfortunately, the 65th Infantry Puerto Ricans developed quite a bad reputation while staying with us. They grudgingly followed orders, and they refused to do their part of the work. They claimed they didn't understand the English language. If the task was to clean the trenches, pull the barbed wire, bring the heating oil and water up from the road, or whatever else, they put forth only 40 percent effort, if not less.[7] The following are excerpts from a recent report regarding the 65th and Jackson Heights (original footnotes have been removed).

The Battle of Jackson Heights (October 1952)

During October, Chinese forces launched yet another series of strong local offensive operations aimed at seizing key terrain in Eighth Army's western and central sectors. These included an attack against Jackson Heights in the 3rd Infantry Division sector, which pushed the 65th Infantry Regiment to the breaking point.

Colonel [Chester B.] DeGavre assumed command of the regiment on 11 October, while the 65th was in IX Corps reserve near Changmol, North Korea. . . . A shortage of ammunition, however, firing restrictions, division inspections, and over-supervision by both division and regiment greatly degraded the value of the training, leaving the 65th less than prepared for the trials that lay ahead. Complicating matters, DeGavre issued an ill-advised order for all personnel of the regiment to shave their mustaches "until such a time as they gave proof of their manhood." Interpreted as a demeaning gesture by the troops, the measure generated open insubordination in two of the regiment's three battalions, further undermining morale and unit cohesion.

On 22 October the regiment moved from Changmol to Topi-dong, two miles north of Chorwon....

The outpost at Jackson Heights was located on the eastern edge of the Chorwon Valley, approximately eight miles northeast of Chorwon and six miles southwest of Pyonggang, North Korea. It comprised the southern portion of a large hill complex known as Iron Horse Mountain (Hill 388). The peak of Iron Horse Mountain, located 750 meters to the north of Jackson Heights, and a second hill known as Camel Back Mountain (Hill 488), located 2,800 meters to the northeast, dominated the position. Located more than a mile in front of the main defensive line, the position at Jackson Heights consisted of solid rock. All of its bunkers, as a result, were in unsatisfactory condition. Complicating matters, the position lacked barbed wire and mines because of supply shortages and heavy enemy pressure dogged every attempt to make even marginal improvements in its defenses. Company G had charge of the outpost. Facing it were elements of the 3rd Battalion, 87th Regiment, 29th Division, 15th CCF [Chinese Communist Forces] Army, well supported by artillery.

Enemy action against the outpost followed closely on the heels of the 65th's arrival.... By 1245 [on 27 October, the company had suffered thirty-six wounded], and its commander, Captain George D. Jackson, was radioing higher headquarters for assistance in evacuating the company's wounded from the position. By 1700 all but seven members of the company's Mortar Platoon were casualties and only two mortars were still in action. At 1800 Jackson Heights received another heavy shelling, this time followed by a reinforced company-size attack consisting of an estimated 250 men and supported by fire from nearby enemy positions. Company G repelled the attack but at the cost of 14 more friendly casualties....

Tensions increased as night fell. Between 2035 and 2100 the Chinese unleashed an immense artillery and mortar barrage on Jackson Heights. Charging from two directions but mainly from the southeast, two companies of Chinese infantry attacked at 2100. Company G responded with small arms fire and its remaining mortar rounds, but its ammunition dump was hit a second time, causing confusion among its men. Casualties mounted. Jackson called for final defensive artillery fires at 2120. They inflicted heavy losses on the enemy, allowing Company G to begin withdrawing at 2130. By 2240 the unit's first elements were safely behind the 65th's main defensive line. The company had suffered 87 battle casualties.

On 28 October, Colonel DeGavre ordered his 2nd Battalion under Lieutenant Colonel Carlos Betances-Ramirez to retake Jackson Heights....

Betances-Ramirez planned to use only one of his companies for the attack, Company F. He received permission to borrow a second, Company A, from the 1st Battalion. Once Jackson Heights had returned to American hands, he intended to use Company F to remain on position to defend the outpost while Company A returned to its parent unit. . . . . Confusion immediately arose within the two units over which would stay to defend the heights and which would depart.

The attack began at 0645 on 28 October. By 0955 Company F was on the objective and was reporting it secured. By 1115 both companies were on the hill, having taken 17 casualties while inflicting 22 casualties on the enemy. . . . In the confusion that followed, the men of the two companies became intermingled, destroying the cohesion of the outpost's defense and presenting the Chinese with a lucrative target. As enemy artillery and mortar rounds slammed into it, inflicting numerous casualties, the defending troops began to move off the position. With the situation deteriorating, the Company A Commander, 1st Lieutenant John D. Porterfield, called a meeting of his officers to decide what to do next. The group had hardly convened, however, before a Chinese 76-mm round fired from Camel Back scored a direct hit on it, killing Porterfield, his artillery forward observer, and one of his platoon leaders, along with an officer from Company F. The death of these leaders had an immediate impact on the men, who began to abandon the position in even larger numbers.

Since communications with the two companies had gone down during the attack, Colonel Betances-Ramirez only learned of the situation at 1500. He ordered Company F to remain on Jackson Heights and Company A to return to the main defensive line. There matters stood until 1705, when the 2nd Battalion command post received a message from Captain [Willis D.] Cronkhite on Jackson Heights stating that the fighting strength remaining on the position was down to ten men and requesting permission to withdraw.

At 1715, a lieutenant from Company H reported that some 80 men from Companies A and F had congregated in the vicinity of Hill 270 and were refusing to go back to Jackson Heights. Betances-Ramirez ordered these men, including 1st Lieutenant Juan Guzman, a Puerto Rican National Guard officer and the Company A Executive Officer, to go back up the hill to rejoin Captain Cronkhite. Regarding the order as suicide, most of the men again refused. At approximately 1730, Cronkhite ordered the remaining men on Jackson Heights to withdraw. . . . .

Early in the morning of 29 October, Company C, commanded by 1st

Lieutenant Robert E. Stevens, departed the 1st Battalion area for Jackson Heights. The unit reported the objective secured at 0720, but shortly thereafter its men began abandoning the position. By 1050, 58 of them had assembled near the battalion command post. The number grew over the hours that followed, even though 80 agreed to return to the hill. In the end, the 1st Battalion's Commander, Major Albert C. Davies, had little choice but to order Stevens and those of his men who remained to return to the main defensive line. The equivalent of "a company less its officers and a few men," wrote Colonel DeGavre afterward, "withdrew from Jackson Heights without an enemy round being fired or a live enemy being sighted . . . [since] there were . . . however, bodies of both friendly and enemy dead on the position . . . [the] unauthorized withdrawal is believed to have been solely from fear of what might happen to them." On 29 October, the 3rd Division relieved the 65th of its sector along Line Missouri. The next day the regiment, less its 3rd Battalion, which remained on the line under the 15th Infantry Regiment, reverted to IX Corps reserve at Sachong-ni, North Korea.

The 65th had suffered a total of 259 casualties for the month, including 14 officers. Of these, 121, including 97 battle casualties and 24 non-battle casualties, occurred while the regiment was stationed on Line Missouri. The reputation of the regiment and the Puerto Rican soldier, which had suffered a heavy blow after the battle of Outpost Kelly, was shattered irreparably. A total of 123 Puerto Rican personnel, including one officer and 122 enlisted men, were in the division stockade pending court-martial for refusing to attack the enemy as ordered and misbehavior before the enemy. The regiment's only Puerto Rican battalion commander, Colonel Betances-Ramirez, had been relieved of his command. To make matters worse, on 3 November, 39 more enlisted men of the 3rd Battalion's Company L refused to continue with a patrol while attached to the 15th Infantry Regiment in the vicinity of Jackson Heights. They were also placed under arrest. The following day, the 3rd Division's commander pulled the 3rd Battalion out of the line at the request of the 15th Regiment's commander.[8]

How could members of a United States infantry regiment be as disorganized and poorly trained as the 65th Puerto Ricans assigned to us? The 65th was a colonial regiment in the U.S. Army (regulars). The Puerto Ricans claimed they didn't have Puerto Rican officers, since many Puerto Rican officers and senior enlisted men had rotated back to the United States. Even though the white officers were partly responsible, blaming white officers for their own poor performance was no excuse.[9]

We had some very good Puerto Rican soldiers in the 5th RCT, but they were not 65th Infantry Puerto Rican soldiers. In one sense, I felt sorry for the 65th Infantry soldiers assigned to Able Company. They were not trained and they certainly were not ready for combat. The 65th soldiers were required to do things they didn't know how to do and, unfortunately, for some reason didn't seem to want to learn. They needed some extensive, hard-nosed military training, which we couldn't give them while we were engaged in combat.

Everyone who is physically acceptable to the army is capable of learning the basic functions of a soldier. Until the 65th men learned, we needed to make sure the Puerto Ricans didn't occupy a responsible combat position. No one, regardless of race or gender, should be in a combat unit who can't or won't perform the duties of an infantryman. Trench-warfare combat units operate differently than maneuvering combat units. Because of the restrained combat zone, it is particularly important in trench warfare for everyone to perform his duty. Not being responsible may have been what the Puerto Rican troops wanted. If so, such an attitude would be shameful to anyone wearing the uniform.

I felt a sense of frustration in not knowing what to do to salvage these soldiers. They were as exposed to combat as I was, yet they were ill prepared. Perhaps they should have been rotated back to the United States for more training, but such a move would have been grossly unfair to the soldiers who were still in combat. It was a tough question. Regardless of why, the result was that we didn't have time to fool with them.[10] Ultimately, a reconstituted 65th Infantry Regiment fought bravely in June 1953 with one company being awarded the Distinguished Unit Citation, Distinguished Service Cross, numerous Silver Stars, and other awards.

African American soldiers filled another 10 percent of our company. With several different races in our unit, Able Company was fully integrated. As proof that integration of black soldiers into white units was successful, when I arrived in Korea, I found that, as a rule, the black soldiers performed as well as the white soldiers. We were all alike. Those of us who were trained fought well.

Once they faced similar combat experiences, the African American, Hispanic (other than the 65th Puerto Ricans I knew), Korean, and Caucasian soldiers all performed equally well. Until the African American or Caucasian soldier participated in combat, some of the South Korean soldiers had an advantage, since several of them had been fighting for months. South Korean soldiers who had been augmented to the U.S. Army (KATUSA) made up approximately 10 percent of the company and performed their duties extremely well. KATUSA soldiers sent to the U.S. infantry units in 1950 transferred back to the Republic of Korea (ROK, pronounced "rock") army units in 1951. In 1952 GEN James A. Van Fleet arranged with the Korean government to transfer KATUSAs to the 8th Army to supplement the U.S. Army's efforts to provide sufficient replacements. Most of the KATUSA soldiers I knew learned English, were excellent on patrols, and understood the importance of their duties. Those with previous combat experience were extremely valuable, and we appreciated their willingness to share their knowledge with us.

I had only one problem with KATUSA soldiers: with their homes so nearby, when they would take leave, many of them would return to their homes, and some of them would bring back a bottle of Korean whiskey of some type. We had strict orders in our company that no one was to consume or possess any whiskey while engaged with the enemy. While in a reserve position, soldiers could drink alcohol with caution. The "nothing on line" rule included officers as well as enlisted men, and the KATUSA soldiers were well aware of the rule. These men were the only ones in the company who had access to alcohol. We inspected the soldiers upon their return, and if we found alcohol, we were required to break the bottle of whiskey. I often wondered why we couldn't have saved the whiskey until we went into reserve—the company could have had a great party. But I never got an answer. Unfortunately, I never did get a drink of Korean whiskey. The Korean soldiers told me that their Korean whiskey (soju or rice vodka) was very good. From what I have learned, the 5th RCT was one of the few units that didn't allow whiskey while we were committed to defending the rim. Nevertheless, I would much rather be sober and alive than drunk and dead.

The conclusion from my experiences with South Korean soldiers was that they were very good soldiers, and it was an honor for me to have served with them. The South Koreans assigned to our unit were brave and outstanding soldiers. I would serve with them again anytime.

Not once did I ever witness discrimination between any of the races. We all knew what we had to do, and everyone tried to do his job. The enlisted soldiers realized that their lives depended upon their squad and platoon leaders. A mutual respect developed, because the leaders realized the lives of the men serving under them were their responsibility. We all respected the good qualities in one another and put up with the bad ones.

The white solders represented a cross-section of the United States with no selected region predominant. A large percentage of these replacements were draftees who upon completing their fourteen weeks of basic training were sent to Korea. A few replacements transferred from the army in Germany and ended up in Korea to complete their enlistment. I didn't make a judgment as to which soldier group performed better than the other did. Moreover, I never reviewed any soldier's 201 file (military personnel record), performance report, or other such documents. Either these records were not available or no one told me where they were located.

One of the disadvantages of individual replacement versus unit replacement is that with individual replacement the leadership—at whatever level—doesn't have an opportunity to know the individual. The advantage of the individual replacement system is that I accepted each soldier on his merits at the time, not based on incidents that had happened before. Each replacement had to prove himself as a soldier.

I served with a superb group of men. To my knowledge, while I was with Able Company, 5th RCT, we never had a single charge for a court-martial and rarely any disputes that required company-level action. I couldn't be more proud and honored than to have served with all of these warriors.

By mid-January 1953 I had earned enough time to qualify for R & R (rest and recuperation) in Japan. Upon my return I learned that I had missed an engagement on 24 January in which Able Company engaged three enemy squads cutting wire in front of the MLR. The company had detonated a napalm mine and defended the position with small arms, automatic weapons, and hand grenades. The 555th Field Artillery placed artillery on the enemy as requested. The enemy returned automatic weapon fire but was repulsed as our fire inflicted an estimated fifteen enemy wounded.

On 3 February 1953 the 1st Battalion, 5th RCT, including Able Company, was relieved by the 19th Battalion Combat Team (Philippines) and received orders to the reserve position for delousing, showers, and clean clothes.[11] After six weeks of living in a bitter cold dirt bunker, a soldier, his clothes, and his possessions tend to become filthy. The grime in his hands and the dirt on his body will take more than one shower to remove. Able Company needed the relief, if only for a few weeks.

6
R & R

Seven Days Rest, Then Return to Korea

By mid-January 1953, I was eligible for R & R in Japan. My date to leave for R & R was the third week in January. Later I would learn that I had missed the combat that took place on 24 January between Able Company and three enemy squads.

I left as scheduled, and my five days in Japan, not counting travel time, gave me a much-needed break from the war. One of the first things I did upon arriving in Tokyo was to purchase a camera, since the one I had been using didn't work properly. I took some pictures, as did every soldier pretending he was a tourist. The R & R facility I qualified to visit was on Mount Fuji, the highest mountain in Japan.

Late in January, just before the 19th Combat Team (Philippines) relieved the 1st Battalion of the 5th RCT on 3 February, I returned from R & R to rejoin the 5th RCT. Much to my surprise, I learned I was no longer a member of Able Company but was now assigned to the Communication Platoon, 1st Battalion, 5th RCT. My new assignment was to be the 1st Battalion communication officer. Wondering why I had been transferred, I learned that the previous communication officer had recently rotated. I was the best-qualified replacement. S-1 (Personnel) had reviewed my personnel records and decided that since I had been a linesman I knew everything about telephones. I explained that I had been an electrical power linesman—handling 2,400- to 13,000-volt lines—not a telephone linesman. But the S-1 didn't care—my records revealed I was a linesman. Fortunately, I found the communication platoon sergeant to be very knowledgeable.

6. On Skyline Drive a Korean laborer approaches the MASH helicopter medical-evacuation landing spot. Note ambulances with Red Cross markers. (Photo courtesy of the author.)

The communication bunker was on the Skyline Drive running behind the MLR. The United States had a contract with the South Korean government to provide laborers, known as the Korean Service Corps (KSC), to help the troops build bunkers, carry timbers, work on the roads, and do other manual labor tasks.

Near the location where the accompanying photograph was taken (see figure 6), many Chinese People's Volunteer Army troops had died just a few months earlier in the battle for Heartbreak Ridge. When the Chinese occupied these hills, they had built one- or two-person firing positions. These firing positions were simple holes, approximately four feet in diameter, dug straight down. The tops of the holes were covered with straw to camouflage the positions. The Chinese soldiers stood upright to fire their weapons. When the Americans attacked and killed the enemy soldiers, the dead enemy bodies remained in their firing positions.

A number of stories circulated about large Korean rats—some ten to twelve inches long (not counting the tail)—feasting on the dead Chinese and digging tunnels between the Chinese one-man firing positions. In fact, one such tunnel ran along the back wall of our bunker. These rats would run along their tunnels day and night looking for food. Unfortunately, one of the rat tunnels ran alongside my bunk. We tried several different methods to close the tunnel, but the rats would dig around or through the closed hole. I decided to try another method. I placed food in the rats' tunnel and then stood in the doorway with a flashlight and .45-caliber pistol in hand, waiting. After a short while, I heard the pitter-patter of little running feet. I shot the rat when it stopped to take the food. The noise was loud in the bunker. I missed several of the big rodents but got a couple of them. It was kind of messy; nevertheless, the rats provided a little bit of excitement for bored soldiers.

Finally, I got some good news. A signal officer had checked into the battalion and taken over the position of the 1st Battalion communication officer, which meant I had lost my job. On 30 January the 40th Division released the 5th RCT to the 45th Infantry Division for operational control. On 3 February the 19th Combat Team (Philippines) relieved the 1st Battalion, thereby placing the battalion (including Able Company) in reserve.[1] When we reached our reserve position in the bottom of the Punch Bowl, I was selected (meaning "ordered") to command the Pioneer and Ammunition Platoon (P & A). Once again I was totally unqualified, which meant I was perfect for the job.

The P & A platoon was responsible for building bunkers, setting up tents for the battalion headquarters, and other construction activities. After a week of building bunkers, I requested reassignment to Able Company. I hadn't trained to be a combat officer for two years to end up spending my time building bunkers and latrines. Everyone thought I was crazy. No combat for the P & A platoon was expected unless the whole regiment was in great danger. I explained to the headquarters company commander that I was a combat soldier and wanted to go back and do the job I knew. The battalion commander sent me back as executive officer of Able Company. Since the 1st Battalion was in reserve, I was once again training with Able Company. I was happy to get back to my old company. I wasn't a staff officer. I was a combat line officer.

While we were in reserve, suspected guerrilla activity took place just outside of the Punch Bowl section on 22 February. Guerrillas attacked a two-and-a-half-ton truck, killing one soldier and wounding another with small arms fire. The attack occurred just as the truck crossed the road that ran through Line Kansas. Running across Korea was a main line of resistance known as Line Wyoming. About ten miles farther south, another defensive line of resistance had been constructed and named Line Kansas. At Line Kansas the trenches were completed, the gun emplacements constructed, and the barbed wire strung. Building Line Kansas was based on the premise that UN forces would be defeated in their defense of Line Wyoming. If the UN soldiers had to execute a retrograde maneuver (retreat), a fallback position, Line Kansas, would be prepared and waiting.[2]

Higher headquarters immediately decided that the attackers must have been North Koreans who infiltrated and were now living on Line Kansas. They also decided that the trenches had to be swept clear of any enemy soldiers. UN soldiers would start at various points along Line Kansas, investigate every bunker, and kill any enemy found. The 1st Battalion, 5th RCT, received an order to search an area on the line. One of the companies assigned to do the sweeping was Able Company. I led two platoons for the sweep.

We loaded onto two-and-a-half-ton trucks. A soldier from the 45th Infantry Division was our guide to the drop-off point along the Kansas line. When we reached what the guide said was the correct drop-off point, we disembarked. Our instructions were to go from the road up to the trenches and, once in the trenches, move to our left or toward the east.

The road we were standing on ran parallel to and north of the Line Kansas trenches. Another unit, about a mile to our left, was to move to their right after they reached the trenches. We would meet the left flank unit and trap any North Koreans in the trench between us. The trucks and our 45th Infantry Division guide left us.

The remnants of a light coating of snow were still on the ground. As we stood on the road, the distance to the trenches appeared to be between 200 and 250 yards. The terrain was fairly level for the first twenty-five yards and then began a steep incline up to the trenches.

I got everyone up and moving. We were to go single file up to the trench, with me leading. I started and had moved about one hundred yards before I felt the same sensation I had experienced earlier—a subconscious warning. I slowed down and looked around my feet. Suddenly I noticed something and froze. *What the hell is that? It can't be,* I thought. A small piece of metal was sticking out of the ground with three small steel prongs. These were the triggers for an antipersonnel land mine known as a Bouncing Betty. When the mine was tripped, a small propelling charge would launch the body of the mine three to four feet in the air, where the main charge would burst and spray shrapnel roughly waist high. Whoever tripped the trigger would lose at least one leg.

I looked up toward the trench line and noticed something odd about the trees we were nearing. When we got closer to the trees, I could see wires wrapped around them. Those wires would have to be trip wires—for napalm, mines, and anything else designed to kill someone. We were in a minefield!

I yelled, "We're in a minefield. Don't move. Listen to me." I had to decide how we could get out without anyone getting killed. We would have to get out the same way we got in.

"Turn around carefully. Stay in your own footprints," I said. Then quickly, "Wait a minute."

I carefully looked around where I was standing and couldn't see anymore three-pronged mines. Looking back to the road for another path out of the minefield, I noticed what appeared to be a path with less snow on the ground. It looked clearer and not much longer than the route I had taken to get us into this mess. We would try the new path. I decided if the men would step where I stepped, perhaps we would all be able to get back to the road.

"We're going back a different direction. Step in my footprints. Be careful and take your time," I said.

As I walked slowly out of the minefield, I carefully looked for other sets of three prongs. I stepped where my sixth sense—my instinct—directed. I saw about six or seven more sets of prongs. I would yell "Mine" and point out its position to the man behind me. The next soldier would then point out the location of the mine to the man following him, and so on.

We finally returned to the road with no one being hurt. By now I was one mad infantry first lieutenant. I would have shot the guide who had dropped us off and directed us to take the path we took had I known who he was. But I was even angrier with myself. I should have realized that one shouldn't approach a trench from the front. Of course, the mines were set and the trip wires pulled. Line Kansas was a fallback position and the trenches had to be prepared. I had made a terrible mistake but somehow didn't get anyone killed. *Thank you again, God.*

I decided I had no idea as to how we could enter the trench. Therefore, I deactivated the mission. I instructed everyone, "Take a break. Smoke if you have them."

The mess sergeant was late but did show up with the noon hot meal at about 1400 hours. As the senior officer, I always waited until all of the men went through the chow line before I got my rations. When I got to the food containers with my mess kit at the ready, I looked in and saw the bottom. There was not a drop—not a spoonful—none—nothing—*no food.* I was hungry, and I was still mad about my disgraceful minefield experience, and I knew we would have no food until we got back to camp later in the day. I had a frank and sincere discussion with the mess sergeant. If some soldiers other than me had been starving, I would have asked Lieutenant Smith to pull his stripes. I think my conversation with him had results. He never again, to my knowledge, failed to monitor the equal distribution of food at meals. Every soldier who was due a meal received at least one helping of food.

We waited for the trucks to take us back to the campsite. That was just as well, since none of the other searching units had found infiltrators. Able Company continued in a reserve position to train and have equipment repaired.

On 11 March a freak snowstorm hit our reserve area, leaving a deep accumulation of snow. Command Report for the regiment listed the snowfall depth as fifteen inches. The snow was a real shocker, being so late in the year. When it melted, the encampment turned into a mud bowl. A large section of the campsite was at a lower level and the melted snow runoff pooled there, creating a muddy mess.

The mud was so deep that a four-wheel-drive two-and-a-half-ton truck got stuck. The truck sank so deep that even with its own cable and power winch it couldn't pull itself out of the mud. We called for another two-and-a-half-ton truck to pull out the first one. However, while trying to pull out the first truck, the second truck sank into the mud, got stuck, and couldn't move. Finally a half-track appeared and with its tank-type tread on the rear was able to get some traction. With much cursing by the men involved, the half-track pulled both of the two-and-a-half-ton trucks out of the mud.

Our rest was over. We received orders to return once again to the rim of the Punch Bowl. We started the movement on 23 March 1953.[3]

7
Relocating to the Chorwon Valley
Finding the Doors of Hell

On 24 March 1953 the 1st Battalion, 5th RCT, having enjoyed showers and rest, returned to the rim of the Punch Bowl. We relieved the 19th Combat Team (Philippines) and assumed responsibility for the eastern portion of the rim.[1] The weather was becoming warmer, which we all welcomed.

The forward fighting trench line was east of and at a lower altitude than Hill 1243, which had been my first assignment when I joined the 5th RCT in October 1952. As the eastward view in figure 7 shows, the rim continues to drop lower going eastward before rising to the highest peak in the distance, Hill 1026. Company A's command post was to the left of where I was standing when I took this picture. In the distance was the Sea of Japan, which you could see on a clear day.

The 24 March deployment established Able Company in a position where the Republic of Korea Army (ROKA) was in contact with Able Company's right flank. The connection, which is not visible in figure 7, was about 150 yards of the trench lines farther east and around the curve from the position to which the red arrow is pointing. Our 3rd Platoon was defending our right flank, which placed the 3rd Platoon as the connecting platoon with the ROKA.

One evening in late March, the North Koreans sent a force of some two hundred soldiers to penetrate the line where the right flank of the 5th RCT joined the left flank of the ROKA. The North Koreans knew the weakest part of our defenses would be wherever units joined, because they knew that when joining forces spoke different languages, the defensive link was particularly

7. Facing east from the Able Company communications bunker on the rim of the Punch Bowl. Number 1 indicates the location of Skyline Drive, a road that runs along the rim. Skyline Drive was the main transportation road for supplies, medical evacuation, and other procedures requiring transportation. Number 2 points to the location of various bunkers on the rear slope that could be for eating, sleeping, or storage. Number 3 indicates a communication trench. Number 4 identifies a "forward" (fighting) trench line. (Photo courtesy of the author.)

poor. Our combined forces included men who people spoke English, Korean, and Spanish. The language barrier between units created difficulties in coordination, communication, and fields of fire support.

A fierce firefight developed between the North Korean and ROKA forces. The only thing we in Able Company could do was to contribute machine-gun support. Of course, the 555th Artillery Battalion started firing defensive fire to support the ROKA defenders. The North Koreans entered the ROKA trench, and we could hear the South Koreans putting up a good fight. After some thirty minutes of heavy small arms fire and grenades, the ROKA forces repelled the North Koreans and restored their trenches. Most of the enemy withdrew but then immediately returned to continue the fight. The North Koreans shifted their direction of attack to their right and attempted to enter our 3rd Platoon trenches at the point where the U.S. and ROKA forces joined. The battle was, as in all trench battles, at close quarters, with hand-to-hand fighting. Several North Koreans were wounded, and we could see them being recovered from in front of the 3rd Platoon by other North Korean soldiers. Rifle flares went up to assist in illuminating the scene. From the joining position,

8. Talking with my South Korean friend Pee Wee. This photo was taken from the same position as figure 7. The view here is toward the west. The peak (Hill 1243) in the distance (shown directly above my head) was where I had my first assignment as a combat officer. That was the same peak where I had my "Olympic luge experience." The side of the peak (Hill 1243) showing the snow faces the North Koreans. Down that snowy peak was the patrolling area for Able Company.

Pee Wee was a fine young man. The North Korean army killed his mother and father when he was about six, and I met him when he was seven or eight. Pee Wee had wandered around for months before he found us. He had just joined Able Company when I arrived in the Punch Bowl, and we treated him as if he were part of our family. He became our number one houseboy. Pee Wee had a great attitude, was respectful, and was a hard worker. When the 5th RCT moved to the Chorwon Valley, Pee Wee remained with a Korean family in the Punch Bowl. (Photo courtesy of the author.)

the trench curved toward the north and then back toward our position. The slight curve in the landscape made it difficult to see the fighting and provide supporting fire.

The illuminated scene revealed that two of the North Koreans, who did not appear wounded, were dragging a wounded American soldier from the trenches. The NKPA soldiers were moving in front of the 3rd Platoon's position. It was apparent that they were trying to take the man prisoner. They had dragged the American approximately one hundred yards down the slope in front of our wire. Sergeant Rewie, the 3rd Platoon sergeant, fired his M1 rifle three times at the fleeing enemy, killing both of the North Koreans.[2] Immediately, soldiers from our 3rd Platoon attempted to recover the wounded American. Unfortunately, he died before we could get him back.

The NKPA always tried to recover their dead just as we did. Knowing their mode of operation, we left the dead North Korean soldiers where they fell, hoping to catch the NKPA recovery team in an ambush. But we had no such luck. The next day we pulled the North Korean bodies in.

The morning after the attack, as executive officer, I received orders to visit the South Korean company commander and try to improve our coordination with the South Koreans. The problem was that we had received no information regarding a pending attack until the NKPA had entered the ROKA trenches.

On that cool, sunny day, we had late-in-the-year snow flurries early in the morning. My wardrobe that day consisted of a field jacket, the usual flak vest and helmet, and my carbine slung over my shoulder. As I walked down the trench, I chatted with those I saw and slowly made my way to where the Americans and South Koreans interfaced. Someone had strung barbed wire across the trench between our units. I suspected Sergeant Rewie had placed the wire there after the North Koreans penetrated the ROKA trenches and then entered our trenches. Very carefully, I ducked under the barbed wire and entered ROKA trench territory. As soon as I turned the first corner after entering the ROKA side, I froze. Lying on the ground in the middle of the trench was an NKPA soldier looking directly at me. Behind him I thought I saw a second NKPA soldier. I leaped back in the trench and just about fell into the barbed wire. My heart was racing, hands shaking, and knees knocking after such a surprise.

I flipped my carbine off my shoulder and took off the safety. *Prepare for a firefight.* But no bullets were flying from the North Korean. No grenades. What was wrong? I slowly peeked around the corner in the trench, carbine ready to fire, and noticed that neither of the NKPA soldiers had moved. The first soldier looked as if he had on overwhites. The light snow did a good job of camouflaging him. I continued to watch for a minute or so. The longer I looked, the more relaxed I became. Slowly I was calming down. I decided to move in closer. Both men were dead, stiff.

I stepped over the bodies and proceeded down the trench until I found a ROKA soldier. He took me to a ROKA officer and we discussed notification solutions, the idea being that we would call each other as soon as either of us observed the North Koreans and expected an attack. Fortunately, the ROKA officer spoke very good English. I told him about the barbed wire and my experiences with the dead North Koreans in his trench. He got a good laugh out of my fight with the two dead NKPA soldiers. Then he explained why ROKA soldiers left the dead North Koreans in their trenches for a while. He said it functioned as a morale booster. The dead soldiers were definitely a booster for me. I thought I had been careless and was a goner. I told myself that I must remember lesson number one: Never let your guard down in combat.

One evening, just after dark while we were still on the rim, 1LT Murray Smith received a call to report to battalion headquarters for a meeting. As executive officer, I would assume the responsibility for the company in his absence. An hour or so after Lieutenant Smith left, a soldier came into the command post and asked me to come outside for a minute. The particular location of our CP bunker was on the side of a hill, as were most bunkers on the rim. However, this bunker was different. It faced east toward the contour of the mountain. From the bunker entrance, a path turned sharply to the left and climbed up the side of the mountain for about ten feet. There our bunker path intersected in a T with another path, which led to the right or the left. The second path followed the contour of the mountain. A right turn onto the second path led to a third path leading down to the toilet facilities. A left turn onto the second path led to a larger path, which went down to Skyline Drive.

When I went outside with the soldier requesting my help, I found two other soldiers leaning against a row of sandbags bordering the larger path leading to the latrine path. They were looking intently into a deep gulley that fell sharply away.

"What's down in the ravine?" I asked.

"We don't know, sir. Sounded like someone walking," answered one of the soldiers.

I kneeled and listened. Then I took my helmet off and listened. Nothing. It was very dark in the ravine, which was full of leaves and brush. I kept listening. The wind was only a gentle breeze. Several minutes passed.

"Sir, we're sure we heard something in the ravine," one of the soldiers said.

"Well, I guess we could throw a grenade and see if we flush anyone out," I said. "But what if someone is in the latrine? The grenade will scare him to death."

The night was still very quiet. Just a few leaves rustling. Minutes passed. I was growing suspicious because I could hear no movement in the ravine. Perhaps the men were just pulling my leg. A rat, an owl, or any other small animal crawling through the brush could have made the noise they claimed to have heard. There were many small critters living in the area. Just to be sure, I decided to toss a grenade and see what would happen. Before I threw the grenade, I wanted battalion to know the North Koreans were not attacking but that it was me making the noise. I called battalion and told the telephone operator what was going on. I explained that we knew of no NKPA soldiers in the area but were suspicious. I hung up and threw the grenade. The fragmentation grenade exploded. No one was running, groaning, or yelling from being hurt. Just the same quiet, cool night. No one yelled from the latrine, which was good. I looked at the soldiers, shook my head, and sent them on their way.

In about ten minutes Lieutenant Smith came bursting through the door, wanting to know where the fight was. He was sweating from running all the way back from battalion. I explained the sequence of events, including my call to battalion, before I had dropped the grenade. He said the telephone operator had told the battalion commander that we were under attack. Smitty got on the phone and talked to battalion for a while. Miscommunication was not good in combat.

We were very fortunate to have as our artillery battalion the 555th positioned in the bottom of the Punch Bowl. The forward observer (FO) for Able Company from the 555th was constantly looking for new North Korean activity on the hills north of the Punch Bowl, and he enjoyed shooting. You could find any type of target, and he would log the exact position and then try to blow the new target away. He had two or three fire missions every day. These fire missions were either for targets of opportunity or for registering concentrations for later support of our patrols. The observation post was near our CP, and I visited our FO to learn something about fire missions.

On 9 April Able Company was relieved from the rim on the Punch Bowl and moved to the reserve position.[3] As always, we enjoyed a good shower and a chance to get some clean clothes. The weather was becoming springlike, a wonderful relief from the winter.

On or about 15 April 1LT Smith completed his tour of duty in Korea and rotated to the United States. My promotion to company commander of Able Company was without ceremony, without the transfer of the Able Company guidon (a military flag), and without a speech to the company. My promotion was simply made by LTC James Richardson, the battalion commander, calling me to his headquarters and informing me that I was the new company commander of Able Company. Of course, I was very proud and honored to be the commanding officer (CO). I don't recall ever receiving a copy of the promotion orders. The colonel and I had a very informal meeting ending in a handshake, which was my promotion party. Nevertheless, I did feel the responsibility of command and, like every other young combat commander, fleeting concern about whether I could do the job. Of course, at that time I couldn't imagine what the real magnitude of the job would turn out to be in a few weeks.

A few days later, while the 5th RCT occupied the reserve position, we felt some changes in the wind. For example, for the first time since I had been with the 5th RCT, we were to prepare for a command inspection, scheduled for 18 April. The inspection was to determine what shortages and worn-out equipment we might have after being on the line for such a long time.[4] Also, a rumor started about a possible move by the 5th RCT from the Punch Bowl area for the first time in a year. Perhaps we would be making a cross-country move to somewhere in western Korea. Since we constantly rotated up to and off of the rim, we were always ready to move. Relocation to a different part of Korea sounded like a good idea.

I presume we passed the command inspection, because we received movement orders. On 19 April we started the trek to the Chorwon Valley. Our new position was about 120 miles west of the Punch Bowl. We completed the trip in one day.

The 5th RCT was relieved from X Corps and assigned to the IX Corps, because our relocation movement crossed corps lines of responsibility. Additionally, the move resulted in the 5th RCT being relieved from the 45th Infantry Division and assigned to the 3rd Infantry Division for operational control.[5]

We arrived for a short stay at one of the prettier campsites. The encampment in a reserve position lasted only a few days. On the night of 24 April 1st Battalion, 5th RCT, moved to the main line of resistance on Line Missouri and relieved the Greek Expeditionary Battalion.[6] Our new enemy was the Chinese.

Line Missouri was in the Chorwon Valley. Able Company was to defend an area that was known as Happy Valley. This defensive position consisted of low ridges running northwest, rising in the valley in the west, and gradually lowering in the east. The Chinese People's Volunteer Army was entrenched in prepared positions on higher terrain approximately fifteen hundred meters to the front of the 5th RCT. This arrangement placed the Chinese in an advantageous position wherein they could observe battle positions, and it favored their defenses. From their dominant positions, the Chinese were constantly taking shots at whoever was defending the trench. The CPVA had their mortars so accurately zeroed in on stretches of trench that they could put a series of mortar shells directly into the trench. They would drop a mortar shell at one end of the trench and then drop six or eight shells down the line.

A basic rule of how to position troops was to secure the high ground when-

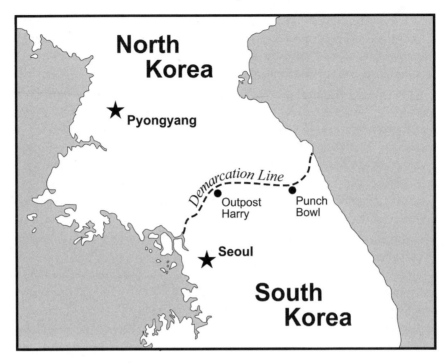

Map 3. It is approximately 120 miles from the Punch Bowl to Outpost Harry in the Chorwon Valley.

ever possible. Let the enemy have the low ground. We had no idea who had decided to place the UN trench down in the valley, but I'm sure he never had to spend any time in the trench to defend his position. What a dumb place to have to fight and die.

Able Company remained on the defensive position until the night of 15 May, when the 65th Infantry Regiment of the 3rd Infantry Division relieved the 5th RCT.[7] Because of the rumor of the Jackson Heights problems, we were all under the impression that the 65th Infantry Regiment no longer existed, but apparently the 3rd Division had retrained the regiment.

I understand that the defensive position had been named Happy Valley because whenever a unit got the hell out of the trenches in the valley, everyone was happy. We were all happy to get out of that valley and let some other poor soldier take our place. In addition to the sense of safety, the occupation of the reserve position from Happy Valley did provide us with a very nice set of sleeping bunkers someone had built.

On 18 May training started again for the 5th RCT consisting of military

9. The winding road that we traveled from the Punch Bowl to the Chorwon Valley. (Photo courtesy of the author.)

courtesy, field sanitation, supply economy, interior guard duty, assembly and disassembly of weapons, and scouting and patrolling.[8] Being far enough back from the MLR, these bunkers were in a relatively quiet location. We didn't receive frequent incoming artillery as we had experienced in reserve in the Punch Bowl. I had the opportunity to use my new camera.

June 1953 found the 1st Battalion of the 5th RCT continuing training. On 5 and 6 June the 5th RCT, minus the 2nd Battalion, moved to a forward position to assume the mission of a counterattack element for the 3rd U.S. Infantry Division.[9] The following are excerpts from the 15th Infantry Regiment, 3rd Infantry Division Command Report, June 1953. This is a very accurate description of the tactical situation and the combat impact on the battlefield.

During the period 16 May to 5 June 1953, the 15th Infantry Regiment, Third Infantry Division, had been relieved of its responsibility for the Outpost HARRY sector. After correlating and evaluating reports from various higher staff sections, the higher commanders were confident beyond any reasonable doubt that numerically superior Chinese forces were going to attack Out-

10. Chorwon Valley. The view is eastward. The Chorwon Valley is to the west, behind the photographer and the MLR is north (to the left) up Happy Valley. The numbers represent relative positions of Outpost Harry, Happy Valley, and the artillery observation post Howe: (1) The Chinese-occupied Hill 533; (2) Outpost Harry—the Chinese Star Hill is to the left, along the Outpost Harry ridge, but is not visible; (3) Happy Valley—the arrow indicates the direction where the trench running across Happy Valley was located, but the trench is not visible from this view; (4) Artillery observation post Howe, from which the night pictures of the fight on Outpost Harry were taken; (5) Location of Headquarters Company, 3rd Battalion, 15th Infantry Regiment; (6) The 15th Infantry Regimental Headquarters was located approximately five miles due south of the position of the photographer, which places the headquarters near the Han Tan River Pontoon Bridge that we crossed in moving to the Outpost Harry assembly area. (Photo courtesy of LT Freeman Bradford, P & A Platoon, 3rd Battalion, 15th Infantry Regiment.)

post HARRY. It was ordered that the 15th Infantry Regiment, a more experienced and battle tried unit, be made responsible for the Outpost HARRY sector no later than the 6th of June. To accomplish placing a more seasoned unit on Outpost Harry, the Third Battalion, 15th Infantry replaced the Second Battalion, 65th Infantry, Third Infantry Division. The 15th Infantry regiment prepared to meet the onslaught of the Chinese. . . .

Aerial reconnaissance from 1 June to 8 June showed much increased enemy activity. This activity included construction of new anti-aircraft artillery positions, self-propelled gun revetments, artillery positions, supply bunkers, personnel bunkers, a new bridge, and road improvements along the enemy main supply routes. An enemy offensive was obvious.

11. Weapons are clean and ready, illustrating the discipline of the men of the 5th RCT. (Photo courtesy of the author.)

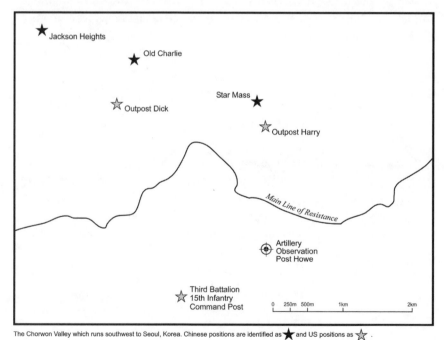

★ Jackson Heights

★ Old Charlie

Star Mass ★

☆ Outpost Dick

☆ Outpost Harry

Main Line of Resistance

⊕ Artillery
Observation
Post Howe

☆ Third Battalion
15th Infantry
Command Post

0   250m 500m   1km   2km

The Chorwon Valley which runs southwest to Seoul, Korea. Chinese positions are identified as ★ and US positions as ☆ .

Map 4. Positions of U.S. and Chinese forces in the Chorwon Valley.

During the same period prior to the attack of 10 June, reports were made of increased personnel sightings during daylight hours. During the period of darkness, an increasing number of vehicle lights were reported, generally in the rear areas moving south and southwest toward the enemy's main battle positions. Prior to the attack CPVA artillery battalions positioned to fire into the Third Infantry sector disclosed the enemy to be employing 102mm rockets for the first time in this area.

Also evident during this period was increased enemy counter battery fire on friendly artillery positions. Incoming artillery and mortar rounds reported in the regimental sector increased from an average of 275 per day to 670 per day, during the four to five days prior to the initial attack on the outpost. During the attacks on HARRY, a tremendous volume of rounds fell in the entire regimental sector, including service units and regimental headquarters.

The enemy disposition at this time were not pinpointed; however, it was well known that there were two unidentified battalions of the 22nd Regiment, 74th Division, in the left sector and two unidentified battalions of the 221st Regiment, 74th Division, in the right portion of the 15th regimental sector. The 221st Regiment, 74th Division was located in the sector immediately opposite Outpost HARRY. Reserves capable of intervention in the Outpost HARRY action were the two reserve battalions of regiments in contact with the 15th Infantry in the left sector, as well as three battalions of the 220th Regiment, unallocated, which were in the 74th Division reserve.

The concentrated enemy drive began, which was to last for a week, and was to cost the Chinese dearly for every engaged minute. At 1950 (7:50 PM) hours on the night of 10 June 1953, reports were made of the first CPVA sightings, and mortar and artillery fire engaged each sighting. At 2130 (9:30 PM) hours an ambush patrol west of OP DICK in the sector of the Greek Battalion reported Chinese numbering approximately 250 coming from JACKSON HEIGHTS (in front of OP TOM). Mortar and artillery began falling on the 15th MLR as well as outposts DICK and HARRY. After a short but intense firefight near Outpost DICK, including 2000 rounds of enemy artillery and mortar fire, the enemy withdrew. This was recognized as a possible enemy feint, and all units were alerted.[10]

8

Morning of 12 June

The Siege Starts

Somewhere in Korea's Chorwon Valley on 11 June 1953 a radio operator assigned to the S-2/S-3 Section, 15th Infantry Regiment, 3rd Infantry Division, monitored the traffic (incidents, messages, and orders) between Outpost Harry and the supporting units—artillery, supplies, medical, and others. The radio operator created a time log so that senior officers would be aware of the situation on Harry on a continuing basis. The log messages displayed here and in subsequent chapters are exactly as the radio operator wrote them from 31 May to 30 June 1953. To assist the reader, a radio icon ▶ along with the date and military time of the radio transmission indicates a logged message. Excerpts and notes from the original Headquarters, IX Corps Combat Operations Command Report are shown by the words "HQ IX Corps" followed by the date and military time.[1]

The log times reproduced here are as reported in the 15th Infantry Regiment declassified documents and reviewed at the National Archives. Because it has been more than fifty years since I was in the trenches, it was impossible for me to correlate the exact time of my actions with the times listed in the radio log. Nevertheless, the combat actions reported below actually happened and, as near as possible, are within the corresponding time frames of the radio log.

▶ *11 June 0440—5th RCT mortar observer Robinson has been recovered by friendly troops. Had relayed reports of situation back to Orange by radio all during the action while CCF surrounded his bunker.[2]*

The morning of 11 June started like a lot of others for Able Company, 5th Infantry Regiment, 5th RCT, with 1LT James W. Evans commanding.

▶ *11 June 0630—Fifth RCT under operational control of 15th Inf.*

Able Company, 5th RCT, was still in a blocking position since being relieved from the Happy Valley front-line position on 15–16 May. As mentioned earlier, our blocking position was in a very nice location. Everyone was as relaxed as possible, considering we were still in Korea. South Korea in the summer had a beautiful sunrise and an odor unlike any I remember from the States. It wasn't too bad if you were some distance from the rice paddies. Summer mornings were generally cool—sixty degrees—but later in the day the heat would be extremely uncomfortable. The high humidity really made us feel the heat. With all of us from the States being far from home, another day began.

We started with morning formation and, of course, physical fitness training. Then we would start our daily routine: head-count report, sick call, breakfast, cleaning weapons, bathing, washing clothes, and a few silent moments of reflection or prayer. It was also important to identify any illnesses that may be circulating among the troops.

The water in certain parts of Korea contained some type of dangerous microscopic parasite. While in the Punch Bowl area, the shower-point personnel washed our clothes in a special chemical solution to destroy the parasite. We would get deloused and exchange our uniforms for clean ones that had been washed with the chemical. Although we didn't seem to have the same risk with the water in the Chorwon area, we continued to check for signs of infection and dysentery frequently. On this hot day in the Chorwon Valley, all seemed to be well. Everyone felt safe after the Happy Valley experience.

At mail call I received a package and letter from Mrs. Grass Soups (the Wyler's Company), and couldn't figure out why, since I hadn't written to the company. Contained in the package, I found six small plastic guns along with twelve plastic "helicopters." Each helicopter consisted of a stem about three inches long. Attached to the stem were four plastic blades with a circular strip attached to the tips of each blade. To use a launcher (a plastic gun) we would insert the stem of a helicopter into the gun, pull the trigger, and the spinning blades would lift the helicopter. The faster we pulled the trigger, the higher the helicopter would go. Eventually I realized what was going on. I was a new company commander, and one of the men had decided I needed some launcher guns and sent in a coupon to Mrs. Grass Soups, which must have been running a special offer for them. I'll bet the soup company got a kick out of a first lieutenant writing them from Korea. I passed the guns around, and we started launching the helicopters to see who could send them the highest. For a short while we were once again just some boys playing with a toy. We all had a good laugh over the joke somebody played on me, the "old man."

After breakfast, signing the morning report, discussing the company head count, and other important business, such as using the launcher guns, I took a walk through the Able Company area. My walk on 11 June was pleasant (more like a casual daily unit inspection). When I returned, however, a rumor was buzzing about the Able Company area. By mid-morning, word was spreading about some heavy fighting that had occurred the previous night. No one seemed to know where the battle was centered or who was involved. I hadn't heard any unusual artillery barrages or seen any flares, so I had no idea where the action had taken place. Sometimes rumors were just that—rumors.

I received a message to report to battalion headquarters to attend a briefing at 1100 hours. When I arrived at battalion, I noticed that all of the other 1st Battalion company commanders were present. The 1st Battalion operations officer (S-3), MAJ Robert MacLane, started the meeting by confirming that the rumors of a battle the previous night were not rumors but were factual.[3] Apparently, a company from the 15th Infantry Regiment, 3rd Infantry Division, had engaged the Chinese in a terrific effort to defend a combat outpost called Harry. The Chinese had overrun the 15th Infantry's rifle company several times, but after fierce hand-to-hand combat the company was able to defend the hill successfully. The report Major MacLane received was that the company had suffered 70 to 80 percent wounded or killed. The battalion S-3 had no more information about the fighting except that we were on alert to defend the hill. He then dismissed us, leaving us wondering if we would be involved.

When the 5th RCT had moved to the Chorwon Valley from the Punch Bowl area in the eastern section of Korea, the 3rd Infantry Division assumed operational control of the 5th RCT. The attaching of the 5th RCT to a division was common. The 25th Infantry Division, the 40th Infantry Division, and the 45th Infantry Division each had operational control of the 5th RCT at one time or another when the 5th RCT was operating in the Punch Bowl area.

The 5th RCT reported to a division-size unit for logistical support and received provisions though the general supply chain. Attaching the 5th RCT to a division saved the 8th Army quartermaster (G-4) from having to allocate and provide transportation from 8th Army stores to individual regiments. Being part of a division worked well, and we received most of the supplies we needed, except for our beer rations.[4]

Regardless of which division had responsibility for the 5th RCT, the 5th RCT normally retained individual unit control. We were always under command of only 5th RCT officers. Except for now. At 0630 on the morning of 11 June the 1st Battalion, 5th RCT, was placed under tactical control of the

15th Infantry Regiment of the 3rd Infantry Division. This unusual move was apparently a response to the Chinese threat.[5]

When we had gathered for the briefing at 1st Battalion headquarters, we didn't know that we would soon be taking operational orders from the commanding officer of the 15th Infantry Regiment, a COL Russell Akers.

At approximately 1500 on the 11th, I again reported to the 1st Battalion headquarters and was given further orders. I noticed that all the company commanders were there except for the Baker Company commander. The orders that had been suggested at the 1100 meeting were now official: Able Company was to be ready to assist the 15th Regiment, 3rd Division, if needed. The briefing revealed that Baker Company was already preparing to move toward a staging area somewhat closer to the main line of resistance. My orders were to start preparing for a move to a new position closer to the battle area so that we could back up Baker Company if necessary.

I returned to the Able Company area and met with the platoon leaders. I told them everything I knew about what was going on, which was not a lot except that a company from the 15th Infantry had been battered. Continuing, I reviewed what I had learned about the slaughter on Harry the night of 10–11 June, including the report that the battered company had suffered 70 to 80 percent of its men killed or wounded. I explained that a good possibility existed that Able Company would move to defend Harry.

The group started to ask questions. What was Outpost Harry? A nearby outpost that wasn't very large. Where was Harry? Not far from our reserve position—maybe five miles—maybe a little more. I explained that I didn't know if we were going to accomplish anything more than repositioning ourselves to a closer support area. However, if we were to get involved in the fight, we needed to get everyone ready.

I could feel the tension building as we all realized we were most likely heading into a truly dangerous situation. I told the platoon leaders to tell the troops everything we knew about the situation. There were no secrets here.

The soldiers were to consider this a serious operation and be sure they were prepared. If they needed to write a letter home or take other steps to clear their minds or bodies, this was the time to do it. We discussed the equipment we would need and the general procedures for a move. I discarded the normal procedure of making an early reconnaissance of the new location, because we were running out of time.

After the meeting, the officers returned to their platoons to get the men ready to move. In addition to the normal checks for equipment, each soldier had to be sure he had more than the minimum load of ammunition. I wasn't sure where we were going, but I wanted to be sure we could fight when we arrived. Late in the afternoon, while we were waiting for the order to move forward, a quiet and somber mood settled around Able Company.

Infiltration, a type of replacement movement, was not new to us. We had previous experience with moving into positions to replace units that had just experienced fierce fighting. Most of the officers and noncommissioned officers had had at least one company-size relief. How many times had we rotated off and on the Punch Bowl? Three or four? We had just had a relief to and from our defensive position in Happy Valley. And although we had experienced little difficulty during the Happy Valley relief, there were some periods of danger. Most transfers in the Punch Bowl were under artillery fire. It seemed the North Koreans always knew when a transfer was taking place and greeted us with some artillery. Even though we would be very quiet, the NKPA loudspeakers would announce our arrival.

Around 1600 I received a message to report to battalion, where Major Mac-Lane confirmed the morning orders and the 1500-hour meeting regarding a move. Able Company was to immediately move to a holding position. However, when I received the orders, I didn't receive a map showing the exact position of where we were to report. On the map I did have, Major MacLane made markings representing a trail turning off the main road to where he thought the forward position was located. However, the road from the trail to the backup position was not on my map. No one at battalion had the turn-off road marked on his map or knew exactly where the turn-off road was located. In fact, no one knew if such a road even existed. Nevertheless, according to arrangements made with the 3rd Infantry Division, a road guide from the 3rd would show me the turn-off road and guide me to the backup location.

Major MacLane advised, "Continue down the trail until you meet a 3rd Infantry Division soldier stationed as a road guide. He's posted and waiting for you somewhere along the road. I understand the trail you'll be taking is close to an artillery battery. When you get to your holding position, you'll get some new orders. Good luck."

I didn't know, and wasn't told, if we were to prepare for a normal relief of another unit. Nevertheless, I presumed our normal relief process would not be in effect if one company were disabled. In most cases when we relieved another unit, we would occupy the position for several days, if not weeks. No one had told me this movement would be any different. As usual, I gave the order for the personal gear (duffel bags and sleeping bags) to follow the company in a trailer pulled by a jeep.

The distance to the backup position was about seven miles, which was too far to march and be ready to support in time, so two-and-a-half-ton trucks were used for the movement. A rifle company was composed of three rifle platoons and one weapons platoon. Each platoon had four squads. Each squad had nine men plus a squad leader. The fourth squad of a rifle platoon was the weapons squad. Each platoon had forty men plus a platoon leader (an officer), platoon sergeant, and a radio operator. As I recall, there were approximately 220 men for each rifle company according to the TOE. However, we were always short, because we didn't receive replacements as quickly as we should have for the men rotating, wounded, and killed. Even so, to move the company took about fifteen to seventeen trucks. (A trucking company furnishes the two-and-a-half-ton trucks used to transport the company.)

On the evening of 11 June, at about 2000 hours, the trucks appeared, the company loaded onto the trucks, and we headed to war. One officer or senior enlisted man rode with the driver in the front seat, and the troops under their command rode in the back. Each soldier carried his personal weapon—rifles, automatic rifles, and pistols. Machine guns, 60mm mortar tubes with base plates, and 57mm recoilless rifles were on the truck's floor while their gunners kept a close watch on their weapons. Each soldier also carried a bayonet for his M1 rifle or carbine. Rifles, carbines, and Browning automatic rifles were generally not loaded while we were in transit in order to prevent accidents. However, tonight I ordered the weapons to be loaded with their safeties on ("lock and load" position), since I thought we might meet some Chinese on the road.

Able Company had successfully defended the northern rim of the Punch Bowl during a very cold winter. And we had always done very well in the training we received while in reserve. We had the equipment we needed to fight, and our morale was very high. Since we had received the influx of replacements in January to fill the ranks of those who had rotated out with thirty-six points or more, the turnover of personnel had been low. This stabilization of personnel gave the company a chance to develop camaraderie and a high level of esprit de corps. But the usual chatter was not heard on the trucks this night. The men were very quiet and somber. I believe we all somehow knew that we were moving into a very bad situation. The men's defense was their exceptional knowledge of how to fight, how to use their weapons, and their trust in God. My defense was the same, so I also prayed when the convoy got started. The evening of 11 June was filled with foreboding.

The engines started creating the low rumble that only two-and-a-half-ton trucks can make. I signaled to my jeep driver to start rolling and waved to the rest of the company to follow. Able Company, 5th Infantry Regiment, 5th RCT was ready to move into battle.

We had orders and we were going to follow them. The men got into the trucks with weapons loaded, and I led the convoy out. As we rolled out from the reserve area, I had no idea where we were going or what we were getting into. I was riding in a jeep with a driver and the company radio operator. As we left the encampment, the road dead-ended to another crossroad forming a T-shaped intersection. After checking the map, I decided we should turn left.

Any time vehicles moved in areas close to the enemy they were required to use blackout lights. Blackout lights were also known as "cat eyes," because only a narrow beam of light was able to shine through a cut in the material covering the headlamp. The narrow-beamed blackout lights pointed downward, illuminating the road immediately in front of the vehicle.

After turning left, we proceeded along the road for a short distance. I glanced back to see if all was well, if everyone was following. To my surprise, I saw only two trucks behind me. Only two trucks. What had happened to the rest of the company? I was surprised at first, and then my surprise turned into anger. They must have had a truck breakdown. These heavily used trucks had a reputation for having a lot of trouble. Most of our trucks had been here for a long time and had many miles on them. In addition, the needed parts were not available. Did one of the trucks break down? Did the driver not know where he was going? Couldn't he simply follow the truck in front of him? *I had been a company commander for only a couple of months, and I had already lost most of my company! And that without having fired a single shot.*

I ordered the driver to stop the jeep while I decided what we should do—whether we should keep going or turn around and try to find the rest of the company. After studying my map, I decided not to go back just yet. If they had gotten out of the reserve area, perhaps they had turned right instead of left at the intersection. If just one truck had broken down, the others would be joining us soon. The broken truck would just have to catch up.

The more I studied the map, the more I believed whether the trucks were turning right or left didn't make any difference, because the map indicated that the road we were on was a circle. If the rest of the company had taken a right turn instead of following me, they would eventually meet us, since we were on the same circle. The jeep and the two deuce-and-a-half-ton trucks waited for about five minutes in case the lost trucks had eventually turned onto the correct path and were following us. Finally, I said we should get going and move on to the bridge.

According to our map, the next turn we should make would be a left turn only a few hundred yards farther along the road. We would proceed on our current road until we came to the left-turn spot and wait on the rest of the

convoy. There was no need to go back, so we would proceed onward. Maybe I
hadn't lost Able Company after all. With a big sigh of relief, I told the driver
to keep going until we came to the next left turn in the road. We continued on
for about a mile (covering what I had thought was a few hundred yards) and
came to the intersection where I knew we had to turn. The rest of the company
would join us eventually. They would catch up from the rear or meet us head-
on by coming around the circle. Either way, we would go on to our new position as a complete rifle company.

We remained in our vehicles as we relaxed and waited for the rest of the
company to arrive. A few men got out to stretch their legs and take care of
other necessities. The usual small talk and smoking started, as the men began
to relax as only soldiers who know they are heading into battle can.

Suddenly a tremendous roar filled the air. Incoming artillery! Big-time
stuff!

"Everybody! Out! Out of the jeep! In the ditch! Off the trucks! Down!" I
shouted.

The first shells hit before we could reach the ditch, and they were big ones.
The explosions were louder than any I had ever heard. With the shells landing
short of our ditch by about fifty yards, the concussion rocked us as we dove
into the ditch and shrapnel went screaming overhead. We hit the bottom of the
ditch and ducked. Dirt kicked up by the shells landed on us, and the fumes of
burning powder rolled over us. Then there was silence.

It's funny how fear changes what you do. I would never have jumped into a
drainage ditch in the dark with no idea how deep it was or how many snakes
or other unknown items were in the ditch. However, at that moment I didn't
think about anything but getting down. The deeper the ditch, the better.
Large-caliber incoming artillery makes most people want to find a deep hole.
We were no exception.

One soldier in our group had particularly good ears. Even kneeling in the
ditch he could hear the incoming. Before I heard anything, he would cry out,
"Here comes another one!" About a second later my own ears could pick up the
roar. Then we were shaking and ducking again.

Every two or three minutes the incoming shells would land. The Chinese
fired their artillery in groups of three rounds, and the shells were of a very
large caliber—I would guess 155mm. (There was a rumor that the Chinese had
a new 152mm artillery piece in Korea. The shells could have been from the new
152mm gun.) Thank God that one time the shells landed a few yards short and
the next time they were over our heads, landing maybe fifty to seventy-five
yards behind us, instead of making a direct hit.

We could see the red glow of the shells as they roared overhead. There would be an explosion, and then came the red-hot piece of steel screaming overhead as if the piece of shrapnel were consciously looking for a human. Even though we knew the shrapnel was missing us, it was still frightening.

I had experienced a lot of incoming artillery fire while we on the Punch Bowl. It seemed like every day there we had received a few rounds of artillery. However, nothing on the bowl compared to the size or noise of the incoming while I was in the ditch. Someone had told me that large-caliber artillery sounds like a freight train when the train is coming at you. But on 11 June at about 2315, the noise was horrendously loud—louder than any freight train I had ever heard, and I had once worked for a railroad. The next time you're in a thunderstorm and a lightning bolt strikes very close, creating a loud boom, the sound you hear will most likely be less than 50 percent of the sound of a 105mm artillery shell exploding. I wouldn't even begin to try to compare the sound of thunder to a 155mm shell.

The explosions continued for fifteen or twenty minutes, but it seemed like two hours. Finally, I could see the blackout lights of trucks coming down the road toward us. I hoped it was the rest of the company. On the chance I was right and the trucks I saw were the rest of Able Company, I ordered, "Quick. Everyone. Back in the trucks. Let's get going to meet the company." Amazingly, all of the engines started. None of the trucks or the jeep had suffered any apparent damage except that some of the canvas tops had large holes. Somehow, from the thousands of pieces of red-hot shrapnel flying around, none of them hit a gas tank in our vehicles. Just as we started to move out, we heard another incoming freight train. The last group of two or three shells was long. Again we could see the red glow from shells as they roared right over our heads. But the long guns never hit us.

The oncoming trucks we met were indeed the remaining platoons of Able Company. After a brief discussion with one of the officers in the first truck, we turned left onto the road headed toward our 3rd Division road guide. The rest of the company followed us. As soon as we turned left, the road dropped sharply to a narrow bridge over a deep gorge. The bridge, about fifty yards long, seemed to decline to a bow in the middle. At night with only blackout lights, we should have made our way across the narrow bridge with great caution. But the driver went as fast as the jeep could go, with me urging him on. After what we had just experienced, I wanted to get away from the intersection as quickly as we could. Luckily, we didn't go over the railing. I couldn't see the bottom of the gorge, but I believed it was a long way down. According to the following radio log message, I now know we were going over a river.

▶ *11 June 2120—A Co, Fifth RCT reported to be under shellfire at pontoon*
bridge on road 3d. No casualties.

On the other side of the river gorge were perhaps fifteen large tents standing and arranged in no apparent order. I had no idea what they housed, but I guessed they were for some type of headquarters operation, or perhaps a MASH. The operations these tents contained were likely the target that the Chinese had been trying to hit when we were under fire. They were probably aiming for either those tents or the bridge we had just crossed. The shelling was closer to the bridge, but they were still missing by seventy-five to one hundred yards. The tents were behind a protecting hill; I don't think the shelling was ever very close to them. The Chinese didn't utilize aerial observation, so unless they had a spy on the ground, they must have been firing from map coordinates. If there was a spy spotting the artillery, he hadn't done a good job of adjusting. It never occurred to me that the bridge might have been the target and received some damage before we crossed. If the shelling had destroyed part of the bridge, a lot of the company would have ended up in the river, because it was so dark that we wouldn't have seen the break in time to stop. Ignorance was bliss.

We continued on the road and easily found the trail we should take. At last we were on the right trail (according to our map), with all of the trucks of Able Company moving toward our 3rd Division road guide, who would lead us to our destination. The road we moved onto was a single-lane dirt road through an area of trees. The relatively flat terrain meant we were in a valley. Moonlight was providing sufficient light for the road. The ride was not at all an unpleasant one after our experiences at the bridge—except for an ominous rumbling in the distance. At first I thought the rumble was thunder, but since the rumble was constant, it could be artillery. If it was indeed from an artillery barrage, the barrage was certainly tremendous.

Still a little shaken, we rode quietly. Now these continuous, deep sounds of explosions reawakened our concern. Since we all smoked cigarettes in those days, I'm sure we all lit up, smoked very fast, and then lit up again. As we continued down the dirt road, I wasn't thinking about anything except getting to where our orders directed us. Suddenly, approximately twenty-five yards to our right, an artillery battery started firing. It sounded like a 105mm battalion. The noise surprised me, but since I was sure the battery was one of ours, I wasn't too concerned.

We traveled slowly, stopping every now and then, looking for but not finding the 3rd Division's guide post. The road became narrow and narrower, and the tree cover became thinner and thinner until there was no tree cover at all.

12. Outpost Harry (left of center) time exposure with flares descending. (Photo courtesy of Jim Jarboe, 3rd Signal Company, 3rd Infantry Division.)

The road turned to the right. The jeep started to bounce as if we were on a cord road (a road made of tree trunks laid side by side in very soft areas).

We were in the open. Then I realized where we were.

"*STOP!*" I yelled.

Three or four deuce-and-a-half-ton trucks were in the open area with our jeep. We were indeed on a cord road, which started at the edge of the tree line, turned slightly right, and proceeded down the valley. I looked around and couldn't believe where we were. *Unbelievable!*

We were in a valley on the cord road, which meant anything off the road was rice paddy mud. The Chinese were on the hills on the other side of the valley about one thousand to fifteen hundred yards away. Searchlights, the type used to shoot down German bombers during World War II, were directed at a hill at the end on the valley. The side illumination from the searchlights was also lighting up our position in the valley, which meant the Chinese could easily see us. About a half mile away was a hill. Hundreds of large explosions were coming from the top of the hill—exploding artillery shells. The hill had been the source of the constant rumble we had been hearing. So many shells were hitting the top of the hill that individual explosions couldn't be determined. White parachute flares floated down from the sky, lighting up the hill. The red flashes from the artillery reminded me of firecrackers going off. And they kept going off, kept going off, and kept going off. The searchlight illuminated the hill like a stage-show klieg light. The whole sight was like a fantasy movie.

I had never seen such an artillery display—one shell after another going off. And the rumbling only grew louder. I thought to myself, *Those poor bastards are really catching hell. I'm sure glad it's not us.* Then, *What the hell are we doing out here, and how will I get everyone turned around?*

I immediately ordered the drivers to back the trucks up on the road. Fortunately, the old rice paddy bed was not so soft that drivers going off the cord road had much trouble getting back on. We ended up making a two-lane road out of a one-lane trail but finally got everyone turned around and going the right way. We started back up the road without hesitation. I think the speed of the turnaround was due to fear. We were sitting ducks in the valley. However, for some reason, the Chinese never took a shot at us. If they had, they would have caused us a lot of trouble.

While going slowly back up the road, looking for our road guide, I discussed the situation with my radio operator. I recalled someone mentioning that our turn-off road was near an artillery battalion's firing position. And during the briefing for this move, I had received instructions to look for the road guide to be sure I took the correct road. But as we slowly retraced our path, I began to lose faith and trust in the 15th Infantry Regiment, 3rd Infantry Division, as there was still no road guide. I decided to take a chance that the artillery battalion we had passed earlier was the one that indicated our turn-off road. We continued retracing our path, and finding the artillery battery was easy. They were firing one shell right after another. They must have been shooting at the hill we had just seen. Just before we drew parallel to the battery, I saw a narrow road turning off to the left. Deciding to do something rather than nothing, I ordered the driver to take the road. The narrow road carried us directly under the muzzles of the 105s. Being under the barrels of a battery of five 105mm howitzers while they were firing was an exciting place to be.

Finally, the one-lane winding dirt road running under the battery led us to the open area where we were supposed to be. We were finally at the forward holding position. The time was about 0300 on 12 June. We dismounted, unloaded all of our weapons and gear, and sent the trucks on their way. As always after any movement, each platoon leader did a head count and reported to me that everyone was present or accounted for or otherwise. We had traveled from our camp site, and I thought that I had lost most of the company. Then we were under intense artillery fire. Surviving that experience we then traveled too far into an open valley, placing us under Chinese eyes. Yet, thank God, none of the men of Able Company had been wounded or killed.

When the jeep with the trailer full of sleeping bags arrived, I realized we might be in for some real trouble. The battalion S-3, Major MacLane, was waiting for us to arrive. He told the jeep driver to unload all the sleeping bags and then fill the jeep trailer with ammo, grenades, and water. Apparently we would be fighting somewhere soon.

9
Outpost Harry
Destruction beyond Comprehension

After Able Company, 5th RCT, survived the exciting trip from the reserve position and finally arrived at the backing position, we dismounted, assembled, checked equipment, and unloaded guns. The time was now nearly 0350 on 12 June, and the men were tired and ready to settle down for a rest.

"Listen up," I said to the platoon leaders and the first sergeant. "There's no sleeping gear. Just tell the men to get some rest any way they can. Looks like today is going to be a tough day." As the men sprawled wherever they could find a place to lie down, I realized that I had been up for twenty-two hours, but there would be no rest for me.

At approximately 0400 1LT Delbert "Del" Tolen, Able Company executive officer, and I again met with the S-3, Major MacLane, and received his orders: "You are to prepare Able Company to be ready to relieve another company on Outpost Harry." I thought, *I don't recall having ever heard of Outpost Harry before yesterday and know nothing about Outpost Harry, its layout, or its location.* Major MacLane started the briefing by showing me a map where we were currently located and where the position of Outpost Harry was in relationship to our current position. Suddenly I realized that Outpost Harry was the hill I had seen a few hours earlier—the hill that was receiving such a tremendous number of rounds. A cold chill came over me. I was afraid I knew what Major MacLane's orders would be before he told me. And my fears were correct. The details of the orders were simple: Get Able Company ready for a horrific battle.

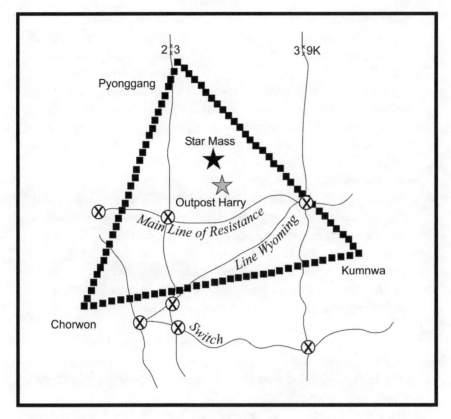

Map 5. The Iron Triangle in the Chorwan Valley. The markings 2^x_x3 indicate that the U.S. 2nd Infantry Division was responsible for the left of the line and the U.S. 3rd for the right. The 3^x_x9K indicates the U.S. 3rd and the Korea 9th Division areas of responsibility. Line Wyoming and Switch were prepared defensive positions in the event the main line of resistance fell.

The following descriptions of Outpost Harry are from the Outpost Harry Survivors Association and the 15th Infantry After Action Report for 29 June 1953:

Combat Outpost Harry was located in an area commonly referred to as the "Iron Triangle," which is an area bordered by three towns—Chorwon, Kumnwa, and Pyonggang—in Korea. This was an area approximately 60 miles northeast of Seoul, and the Chorwon Valley was the most direct route to the South Korean capital.[1]

Outpost Harry is situated some 400 meters northeast of the United Nations Forces friendly MLR, which runs diagonally northwest. The outpost elevation is approximately 420 meters. It is located on a small hill, which is 350 meters south, and part of a larger hill mass occupied by the Chinese People's Volunteer Army, referred to as Star Hill (also known as Star Mass), elevation 440 meters. The outpost commands a good view of the enemy terrain and its avenues of approach to the MLR position. Since the elevation of the outpost is greater than that of any friendly-held terrain within an area of 1500 meters, the position affords early warning of enemy approach to the main battle line.

The terrain within 500 meters is generally classified as non-trafficable to tracked vehicles and trafficable with difficulty to foot troops. The rugged nature of the terrain, with its numerous smaller ridges, offers some cover and concealment to advancing enemy troops. Intermittent streams on either side of the outpost flow south and connect at a point 1000 meters southeast of the outpost along the friendly MLR. The terrain in the immediate vicinity of these streams is trafficable to tracked vehicles during this period of the year.

The road approach to the outpost from the MLR runs north along an intermittent stream to the rear of the outpost, where the supply point is located. From here, movements to the position must be accomplished dismounted.

The position itself contains a communication trench which runs from the supply point forward some 300 meters to the forward observer bunker on the northernmost slope. Here this trench joins another trench which makes a complete circle around the forward portion of the outpost; this portion is usually referred to as the Loop. Approximately 75 meters to the rear of the loop, along a finger of the ridge running to the right side of the outpost, an additional trench extends for approximately 100 meters. This finger is mutually supporting with the loop position and helps to protect the probable avenues of enemy approach into the position.[2]

The trench line was approximately six feet deep, which was sufficient to enable a person "to walk around the perimeter unseen by the enemy."[3] Reinforced fighting bunkers, a command post, and a forward observation bunker constituted the fortifications. The trenches and bunkers could accommodate up to 150 infantrymen in bunkers. "The left side of the outpost [was] steep enough to afford a natural barrier to the attacking enemy forces."[4]

13. Outpost Harry (center) with exploding shell. (Photo courtesy of Jim Jarboe, 3rd Signal Company, 3rd Infantry Division.)

Since the Chinese did not have aerial observation, Outpost Harry was a strategic "military Hot Spot" and dearly desired by the Chinese. Its defense and preservation was viewed as critical because it blocked Chinese Communist Forces observation down the Chorwon Valley and shielded that portion of the MLR from enemy direct fire. If the UN forces lost the outpost, the U.S. 3rd Division and perhaps part of the 2nd Division would have had to withdraw approximately 5 to 10 kilometers to the next defensible line [Line Wyoming. At a minimum, a major attack would have occurred with a great loss of life.] . . . Furthermore, a CCF victory at Outpost Harry would have whet the Chinese appetite for more war and dishearten the American public to a point where it might accept an armistice term less favorable than eventually was the case.[5]

The CPVA was building for a major offensive. The enemy units identified were the 221st Regiment and 222nd Regiment of the CPVA's 74th Division. The 15th Infantry Regiment, 3rd Infantry Division, relieved the division's 65th Infantry Regiment for responsibility of the Outpost Harry sector. The 3rd Infantry Division replaced many of the original 65th Infantry Regiment Puerto Rican soldiers with recently arrived replacements and selected officers transferred from other units.

As Major MacLane continued his briefing, he explained what was happening and why Able Company had moved to a backing position. "The Chinese really want to take Outpost Harry. Our estimation is that a CCF regiment attacked the night before. That would be the night of 10–11 June. We're not yet sure, but we believe another CCF regiment is attacking at this time," he said.

"Sir, would you tell me a little more about Outpost Harry?" I asked.

The major agreed and started providing background information about the location we would be defending. "Outpost Harry," he said, "is a few hundred yards in front of the MLR. Three hills are located in the Chorwon Valley that would be excellent sites for a listening or combat outpost. In typical American fashion, 'Tom,' 'Dick,' and 'Harry' were the names selected for the three hills. Outpost Harry is the largest of the three," the major explained.

He continued, "At 2245 10 June, the Chinese attacked Outpost Harry with a regimental-size force with King Company of the 15th Infantry defending. The initial attacks to take Outpost Harry started the night before last, the night of 10–11 June. King Company of the 15th Infantry Regiment was defending Outpost Harry at the time when the Chinese launched a series of attacks. We estimate the attackers were a Chinese Communist Forces regiment [some twenty-five hundred soldiers]. The Chinese came in waves and finally entered the trenches, were repelled, but soon overran the outpost in a second attack. Using hand-to-hand combat, the soldiers of King of the 15th again stopped the Chinese and cleared their trenches. We believe about 80 to 90 percent of King Company was killed or wounded." The major's words gave me another sinking sensation.

"Early in the morning of 11 June," he continued, "Easy Company of the 15th Infantry went on Outpost Harry to reinforce King Company. King/15 and Easy/15 finally killed all of the occupying Chinese and successfully defended the hill. Not sure yet how many casualties Easy Company suffered, but I heard they also had a lot. Estimated enemy losses were four hundred killed and nearly a thousand wounded."

Then Major MacLane went on with his briefing. "About 0415 hours last night—that would be 11 June—Baker Company of the 15th Infantry Regiment was ordered to move onto Outpost Harry; relieve elements of Easy Company, Charley Company, and King Company of the 15th Infantry Regiment; and get all American wounded and dead off the hill. 'Be prepared to defend Outpost Harry for the rest of the night of the 12th' was the order to Baker/15. The tremendous Chinese artillery barrages had destroyed many of the bunkers and fighting positions on Outpost Harry. At 2230, Baker/5th RCT attached to the 1st Battalion of the 15th Infantry. Last evening about 2230, the Chinese launched a series of attacks. At that time, Baker of the 15th was defending Harry and had as much trouble on Harry as King of the 15th had received. Baker of the 15th was overrun several times and was in danger of being defeated and losing the outpost."

"We saw the battle. They were really catching hell," I said with growing concern.

As mentioned earlier, infiltration was a technique we used in Korea when one company relieved another. In order to effect the relief, the relieving company would send an advance party to investigate the position of the company to be relieved and then organize the transfer, sending in small groups of soldiers. Infiltration by small groups was a technique to prevent compromising the integrity of the defense. However, because of the high casualty rate and the critical nature of defending Outpost Harry, a normal infiltration transfer was not feasible. The relieving company would simply ask the company being relieved, "Are you with so-and-so Company? If you are, your company has been relieved, so you can move to the rear."

"Well," Major MacLane continued, "the 15th regimental commander, Colonel Akers, decided Baker of the 15th needed some help, so he ordered Baker Company of the 5th RCT to go to the outpost and *reinforce* Baker Company of the 15th. Then he ordered Baker/5th RCT to participate in the defense of the outpost until relieved. An hour or so ago, at about 0255 today, 12 June, Baker Company of the 5th RCT did move onto Outpost Harry.

"Guess what happened," Major MacLane said. "Well, as Baker Company, 5th RCT, moved onto Outpost Harry, soldiers of Baker/15th would ask if they were being *relieved.* Apparently some members of Baker Company, 5th RCT, answered yes, not being sure and presuming a relief was under way. Meaning, of course, the relief would be for Baker Company of the 15th.

"As word of the relief spread, members of Baker/15th, believing they had been relieved, started down the hill. As they were leaving the hill, others would question them about the relief. When Baker/15th soldiers responded 'Baker Company,' the soldier asking the question—who was also a member of a Baker Company, and now believing he had been lawfully relieved—left the hill. Of course, *no one* wanted to stay on Outpost Harry.[6]

"So suddenly the situation on the outpost was a hell of a mess. Mass confusion. Reinforcement suddenly became a disaster. Some members of Baker Company of the 5th, thinking they had been quickly relieved, started back down the hill. All of Baker of the 15th started down the hill.

"Well, as you may guess, Colonel Akers created the confusion as to who belonged on Harry and who should get off. The facts were that everyone wanted off Harry, but no one was supposed to get off Harry. The movement was re-inforcement, not a relief. And the confusion occurred with everyone thinking they had been properly relieved," the major concluded.

Someone in the headquarters tent spoke up and mentioned that a major from the 5th RCT had been at the bottom of the hill, with pistol drawn, interviewing anyone who came off the hill. The major was ordering any nonwounded soldier coming down the hill to return to the top of Outpost Harry. Colonel Akers had made a terrible operational decision in a combat situation. If a soldier from the reinforcing unit were a member of any company other than one with the same name of the reinforced unit, this situation would have never happened. Perhaps the two rifle company officers should have ultimately assumed some responsibility; however, they may not have been briefed properly.

I was beginning to understand that we were in a mess. After my briefing of the situation about the potential loss of the hill, I received orders from the S-3: "Take Able Company, 5th Infantry, 5th RCT, to Outpost Harry immediately." I was to relieve everyone on Outpost Harry, and everyone except Able Company and its attachments was to be off the hill. Then we would restore the position as much as possible. We were to be prepared to defend Outpost Harry the night of 12–13 June. I should expect the Chinese to launch another attack, which would most likely be of regimental strength.

Returning to the Able Company area, I assembled the platoon leaders and senior platoon sergeants and briefed them on what I had learned from Major MacLane. They nodded in approval when I said that we were going into a tough situation but that we could do the job. Then after a few seconds, when everyone in the meeting thought about what we were facing, heads started shaking, but no one was complaining.

Even though we weren't making an infiltration exchange, the first thing we had to do before moving the company was to make a reconnaissance trip to the top of the hill. I had to see what the situation was in order to make the transfer of command, occupy the hill, and defend Outpost Harry. No one had provided me with any information as to the layout of Outpost Harry's trenches, gun emplacements, or enemy positions—nothing. Major MacLane didn't have any information about the situation on Outpost Harry, and the 15th Infantry didn't furnish me with any information. My understanding of the overall configuration of Harry was very important, so the only possible way to find out was to go to the top of Outpost Harry myself and determine what we had to do.

I selected a reconnaissance team of 1LT Del Tolen, Able Company executive officer; 1LT William Bradbury, 2nd Platoon leader; and the company radio operator to go along with me. I instructed those remaining behind to get the company ready for a battle. From the assembly position, the reconnaissance team took a trail for about one hundred yards that led to the jump-off point at the main line of resistance. About 0430 and still dark, the reconnaissance team left the MLR, crossing a small road to a trail leading toward the trench to the top of Outpost Harry. As we started across the road to the trail, we noticed several soldiers milling around a two-wheeled trailer with many mounted tubes. Suddenly rockets started to launch out of the tubes. No one on the recon team had ever before seen rockets ripple off the racks. It was an impressive sight. Of course, we stopped, watched the fireworks, and tracked the rockets heading over Outpost Harry and on their way to "Chinese land."

Once again I realized that the battle we were facing was a heck of a lot bigger than anything I had been involved with at the Punch Bowl. After the rocket show, the recon team continued on the trail to reconnoiter the outpost. From the jump-off point, the distance to the base of the communication trench leading to the top of Outpost Harry was about another three hundred yards. We found a dirt road that served as a supply route for ammunition, water, and food going to the base of the hill and for returning with wounded and dead from the top of it.

Walking along the dirt road, we came to a series of small hills on our left side that we had to go around. As we came closer to the small hills, a full-tracked vehicle came into view. The vehicle looked like an armored personnel carrier (APC).[7] The recon team got out of the way, and the APC rumbled on to the MLR. Adapted from the M18 Hellcat tank destroyer, which was the fastest armored vehicle of World War II, the APC or M39 was an M18 without the gun turret. It was a full-tracked vehicle, with entry for passengers through double-opening rear doors. However, with the removal of the gun turret, none of the roof remained to protect the passengers, even though the driver could button up. Eight to ten soldiers with weapons could ride in each vehicle along with the driver. In Korea the M39s were used to transport anything within a fire zone. The hull of these personnel carriers would provide some protection to the driver and anything else in the vehicle.

One of the ways the M39 vehicle supported the defense of Outpost Harry was to transport the wounded from the mess and medical bunker located at the bottom of Outpost Harry to the aid station operating behind the MLR, a trip of about one thousand yards. Speed and safety were the objectives for moving the wounded to the hospital for treatment. The wounded would be placed inside the APC to provide them some protection for the trip, but as noted above, with the removal of the gun turret from the vehicle, they were still subject to artillery explosions. If no room remained inside the APC because of the number of wounded, any dead American soldiers would be placed on the top of the remaining front hull for transportation to the rear of the MLR. We wanted all wounded and dead UN forces recovered from Outpost Harry.

I was leading the reconnaissance team and walking with my carbine at the ready position as we moved toward Outpost Harry. As we came to the series of small hills on our left side, I noticed that the trail ran close to the hills. I rounded one of the small hills and stopped. On the trail used by the APCs for transportation, I saw what appeared to be an American soldier lying in the center of the trail. The recon team stopped to investigate and determine if the soldier was all right. But he was not all right. The soldier's body had been dismembered.

We surmised that sometime earlier in the night, when the visibility was poor, the APC had been carrying a load of American wounded soldiers from the mess/medical bunker to the ambulance pickup point. The interior of the APC had been full of wounded, so they put one or more American dead on top of the APC. Apparently one of them had fallen off.

From studying the scene, it appeared that the tracked vehicle had run over the soldier several times. The tracks of the APC spread body parts from the man's crushed and mangled torso for several feet. Splattered blood covered several yards. Embedded in the dirt, parts of his spine were visible. I walked over for a closer view and saw the American uniform on the lower half of his body, which was untouched. It was a terrible sight. It appeared that the tracks of the APC had run over the soldier's neck, because the lower half of his skull was crushed and the upper half of his skull had been thrown some six feet from the rest of his body. We looked at what remained of his face but could only determine that he was white.

There was nothing we could do. Realities of combat once again hit home, and we all grasped the awfulness of where we were and what we could expect. The interruption of our trip to Outpost Harry had taken less than a minute. However, the ghastly image of the poor, destroyed soldier will last in our memories forever. What an introduction to Outpost Harry! The crushed, bloody, mangled body of this soldier was a sickening initiation to our new assignment. Ever since I had first learned about Outpost Harry, I imagined it as being bad, but I never envisioned anything quite like the hell we were in.

As the recon team continued walking toward Outpost Harry, we looked at one another and paused for a few seconds. We all looked up to the sky, down to

14. Approximate location of the American body run over by a tank. (Photo courtesy of Jim Jarboe, 3rd Signal Company, 3rd Infantry Division.)

the ground, and slowly shook our heads. I believe each of us for an instant visualized ourselves being in this soldier's condition. We gritted our teeth, took some deep breaths to keep from vomiting, and slowly started to move forward. We did the job we had trained to do. We went to war.

▶ *12 June 0530—Major Connors was designated OP Harry commander to co-ordinate with Baker/15 and Baker/5RCT.*

Going about 350 yards on the trail toward the outpost, we found a bunker at the bottom of the hill that seemed to be in good condition. We looked around for a few minutes to see what was available and decided we were at the medical bunker, as the place was full of wounded soldiers. Some were on stretchers outside the aid station, exposed to any incoming artillery. Most of the wounded men were quiet, probably having received morphine to minimize their pain. I didn't get close enough to see the medical markings used for triage on the soldiers. The wounded were being prepared for the APC trip to the ambulance

15. The trip up to Outpost Harry: (1) dismembered solider; (2) aid station/mess bunker; (3) top of communication trench. (Photo courtesy of Jim Jarboe, 3rd Signal Company, 3rd Infantry Division).

point located behind the MLR. Further evacuation to a hospital from the ambulance point was the next step in providing additional medical care.

We didn't linger long at the medical bunker but proceeded toward the top of Outpost Harry. Just as we left the aid station located at the bottom of the trench leading to the outpost, I noticed that a major with a drawn .45-caliber pistol was interviewing every soldier coming down from the outpost. I didn't recognize him but realized that the story told during Major MacLane's briefing was true. We saluted the major and left him with his problems as we started our climb toward the top.

As we proceeded up the communication trench from the mess bunker, we met soldiers stumbling down the trench—wounded but at least they were moving. I surmised that receiving permission to get off Outpost Harry would be enough motivation to get a body up and moving when otherwise one might be looking for help. In addition to the struggling wounded soldiers, we passed soldiers carrying down two stretchers with the more seriously wounded. All of the soldiers coming off Outpost Harry were bleary-eyed and appeared to be exhausted. Covered in so much dust and dirt, the soldiers' uniforms were hardly recognizable. Our recon team got out of the way of the stumbling soldiers, barely glancing at the wounded, and continued to make our way up the trench. Nearing the top of the communication trench, which ended at the top of the hill, we reached the first of the Outpost Harry bunkers. The Chinese were still firing sporadic artillery. These random shots made us duck, reinforcing our anxiety about where we were and what we were facing.

At this point a trench split from the communication trench toward the right, going about seventy yards. A few fighting bunkers had been constructed along a section of the split trench. Passing the juncture and proceeding forward in the main trench, we reached another bunker, this one with a roof. This roof, covered with rocks, crossed over the trench. We surmised that it was a covered ammunition bunker. The location of the bunker was to facilitate the storage of supplies carried up from the MLR to a protected environment until they could be retrieved. For example, an assistant gunner would go to the ammo bunker, collect various supplies, and return to his fighting bunker.

As we walked through the covered ammo bunker, I noticed the trench had water in the bottom. *Strange, where did that water come from?* I couldn't recall any recent rain. I looked more closely and realized that it wasn't water we were walking through—it was blood. A trench with running blood. As soon as we passed the ammo bunker, we saw that the trench was full of dead Chinese soldiers, destroyed in every conceivable way. These dead were the source of the running blood. To proceed further on the Outpost Harry trench meant we would have to walk on human bodies and body parts.

Some seventy to eighty yards past the ammo bunker the main trench split into two trenches. The left trench ran some thirty to thirty-five yards before it turned to the rear, forming a loop and returning to the starting point.

The space on the top of Outpost Harry where Able Company was to prepare defensive positions was a lot smaller than I had expected. When ordered to defend Outpost Harry, I hadn't received a map, a layout of the trenches, or any other meaningful documentation or description. I didn't even know from which direction the Chinese had attacked the previous two nights. I had no knowledge of the officers or senior enlisted men left on the hill—I'd never met any of them. No one on the hill was available to brief me as to what they had

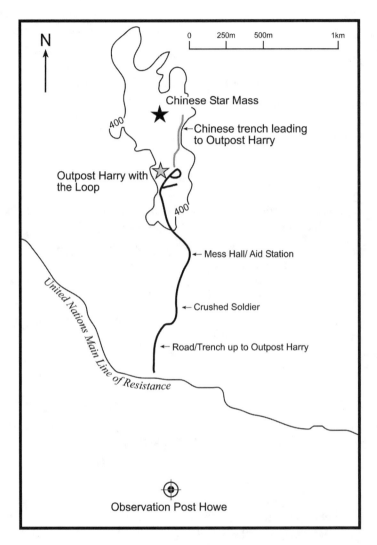

Map 6. Outpost Harry and trench line. The trench runs from the main line of resistance to the top of the ridge where Outpost Harry was located. Artillery observation post Howe was the location from which most of the Outpost Harry pictures were taken. The distance to the outpost from the MLR was approximately 1,425 yards or 1,300 meters.

done to defend Outpost Harry or how their weapons were oriented. I had to analyze and decide upon the defense of the hill without any help whatsoever.

At daybreak the Chinese were still throwing in an artillery round every minute or so, but the incoming was not stopping our review of the hill. However, it did prevent me from standing on top of a bunker on the hill for a good view of the fighting positions, trenches, and bunkers.

The trenches and their condition were a surprise. Compared to the trenches in the Punch Bowl, where I was used to seeing trenches six to eight feet deep and three to five feet wide, the trenches of Outpost Harry looked to be some five to six feet deep and only two to three feet wide—barely enough room to carry a stretcher. In addition, some trenches here were just two to four feet deep. One reason the trenches were so shallow was because in many areas they were almost completely filled with pieces of wooden beams, dirt, rocks, pieces of barbed wire, the metal stakes used to hold up barbed wire, and, of course, dead Chinese. It was truly a horrible sight. Hundreds of destroyed bodies were scattered over the area. Bodies or parts thereof were everywhere.

How could there be so many dead and destroyed humans? The recon team surmised the answer would coincide with what Major MacLane had told us. On the nights of 10 and 11 June, nearly one thousand Chinese soldiers had died while trying to take Outpost Harry. Since the outpost was only one hundred yards long, that meant about ten Chinese bodies for every yard of trench. Many of the Chinese attackers had died before they got to our trenches. However, presuming one-half of the Chinese attackers had died outside the trench, there would still be some five hundred in the trenches. Surely, Baker/15 had thrown numerous bodies out of the trenches and toward the front of Outpost Harry yesterday preparing for the fight last night. Most likely, if they got rid of some two hundred Chinese dead from the trenches, three hundred bodies would still be in them from the previous two nights of fighting. It was no wonder Outpost Harry was one hell of a mess when one considered the amount of artillery that had been fired. Artillery hitting outside the trenches would move the dead and destroyed bodies so that they would fall into the trenches. Lieutenant Tolen and I started trying to calculate the answer to the "how many" question and decided our best guess was just "a lot of dead Chinese."

Some bodies were still in part of their uniforms. Some bodies had been blown out of their uniforms. Body parts covered everything. Bits of human flesh were hanging on the barbed wire, lumped on the top of bunkers, and scattered all over the ground. The smell of burned powder still lingered. The stench of burned flesh from red-hot shrapnel filled the air. The putrid smell of death was everywhere. Some of the bodies were turning black. The stench of eviscerated stomachs and bowels was almost overpowering. Outpost Harry was like a human slaughterhouse in the open.

I couldn't walk without stepping on flesh of some description. As we walked along, bits of human flesh clung to our pants. I couldn't touch anything in the trenches without feeling blood or part of a body. I saw the faces or parts of faces of the dead. I saw the eyes that had not been closed looking directly at me.

The morning of 12 June was the first time I had experienced walking on human bodies. It was a very strange sensation. The partially destroyed bodies gave when I placed my weight on them. By "gave," I mean my foot slid from one side of the body to the other, or the body yielded to my weight and sank, emitting a noise as the air inside was expelled. I imagined the feeling of flesh sliding over the bones was what it might feel like to walk on Jell-O. Or like walking in mud, slipping and carefully placing every step so I wouldn't lose my balance and fall. When I took a step in the trenches, I didn't know whether I was going to slip, slide, fall, or walk.

I had to control myself, choke down the vomit, ignore the horrendous sights, and get ready for my turn in hell. I looked at Lieutenant Tolen, who said, "What in the hell are we doing here? This place is for the dead." He was right.

As Lieutenant Tolen and I walked through the slippery trench, from the outpost entrance for some seventy-five yards and then around the loop, the damage and destruction appeared the same. Most of the bunkers had significant damage. Some of their tops were completely gone. Able Company would have a tremendous rebuilding job to get ready to defend this damn hill. The recon team tried to make a quick inventory of what was usable for protection and what items we should bring up for rebuilding. Sandbags were high on the list. We couldn't get more timbers or use any of the timbers left on the hill. The twelve-foot timbers we had available were just too heavy to move while the Chinese were continuing to shell. We decided we had to salvage any of the logs and timbers that were still in good shape and small enough that we could move them without too much exposure. We couldn't find any drinkable water or usable ammunition on the hill. Any ammo remaining on the site was under the layers of dirt the artillery had thrown into the air. We found several radios, but, as with most hand-operated radios in Korea, none of them worked. One positive result of the ruin, however, was that the incoming artillery had destroyed all of the brushes and bush, leaving clear fields of fire for our machine guns. We wouldn't have to clear brush or other obstructions from the front of the bunkers, because there was nothing left there.

The destruction of many of the bunkers surprised both Lieutenant Tolen and me. However, not all of them were destroyed, as the surrounding damage from the night's shelling might indicate. How could any bunker have missed the barrage? We decided that as viewed by the Chinese, the actual depth of Outpost Harry was relatively narrow. Because of the lack of depth, most shells fired by the Chinese would pass completely over the outpost's trenches or would fall in front of the trenches. Even so, many shells did land on the narrow ridge of the outpost. The scene from the previous night showed thousand of shells hitting the area. Lieutenant Tolen and I decided that our view from the valley had misled us into believing the shells were all landing on top of Outpost Harry, but what we actually saw was the bulk of the artillery fired by our side landing in front of the trenches and on the Chinese position Star Hill. For whatever reason, some of the bunkers remained, but all of the trenches were destroyed.

Strangely, the covered ammunition bunker at the top of the communication trench remained standing with very little damage. Thousands of artillery rounds had hit Outpost Harry in the previous two nights but missed the ammo bunker. The fact that the one tall bunker had avoided disintegration was truly amazing. We had to walk through the covered ammunition bunker to get to the trenches or to leave the outpost. I called the walkway the "Door to Hell." No one questioned the name.

Baker Company, 5th Infantry Regiment, was still defending Outpost Harry as far as could be determined. However, I didn't meet any Baker Company officers and didn't receive a briefing from anyone—officer or enlisted. Additionally, I didn't recognize any 3rd Division troops being present when I was on the outpost at about 0455 on the 12th. In fact, we didn't see many soldiers anywhere on Harry, but they could have been in their bunkers.

What could we do to get Outpost Harry ready? How and where should I place the troops? I finally decided that the answer to the first question was that we would just have to do a lot of work and that even then we may never get our defenses ready for the onslaught. The answer to the second question was that we would need to deploy two rifle platoons on the hill along with part of the weapons platoon. The force would be about 100 soldiers—maybe 110. The weapons platoon of a rifle company consists of .30-caliber light machine guns, 57mm recoilless rifles, and 60mm mortars. The machine guns would fit, and maybe the 60mm mortars. Therefore, I decided the 60mm mortars would be brought up and positioned. An area was located where the 57mm recoil-less rifles would fit. 1LT Robert E. Cole, Infantry, the 4th Platoon (Weapons) leader, was to decide if the 57mm rifles would work, since they had a back blast that was very dangerous.[8] Lieutant Cole would also investigate the location I had selected for the 60mm mortars.

Although I didn't know for certain, I believed Able Company would receive sufficient support from the artillery. I based my belief on what I saw while we were lost and turning around in the valley. And it turned out that my belief was correct.

The official report stated that the 555th Field Artillery Battalion fired more than 56,000 105mm rounds in support of Outpost Harry during the month of June. The 39th FA of the 3rd Infantry Division did about the same. According to official records, the 92nd FA BN track-mounted howitzers (155mm) fired some 32,000 rounds during the battle. We had batteries of rockets firing ripples in our support. In addition, Dog Company, 5th RCT, supported with 75mm recoilless rifles and 81mm mortars. To round out the support, the 3rd Division provided the 4.2 inch Mortar Company and tanks. The big 240mm Long Toms fired in our support also.[9] Ninety percent of the firepower expended during the period of 10 June through 18 June was for the defense of Outpost Harry. Based on estimations, the Chinese fired 86,000 rounds larger than 81mm at us, and we fired 389,000 rounds at them. The HQ IX Corps Command Report for June 1953 reported more rounds fired between 1800 hours June 12 through 1800 hours June 13 than at any time during the entire Korean War.[10]

What I encountered on Outpost Harry as far as having to learn quickly reminded me of training exercises at Elgin Air Force Base in Florida. Imagine that you are a student soldier trying to become an Army Ranger. One of the Ranger training problems was as follows: Elgin Air Force Base, Florida, June 1952. It's about 0200. Your fellow students are very tired, hot, standing or lying in ankle-deep swamp water, and in no mood for games. Everyone's feet are wet, seams in their boots are rotting, and their canteens are filled with warm swamp water that tastes bad because of the pills in them to kill bacteria. The patrol of twenty trainees, who have been in the Florida swamps for two days and are very hungry, needs a new student patrol leader.

The Ranger instructor pats you on the shoulder and says, "The patrol leader has just been killed. You are the new patrol leader. Here is the compass and a map. Get your patrol up and moving!" Since you haven't seen the map for two days, you can't be sure of your location on the map. Since no one wants to start moving again, you aren't sure if you can get them going. Nevertheless, you have to get the patrol moving in the right direction to accomplish its mission. If you can't lead the patrol as ordered, you can't continue in the Ranger program.

This exercise in the swamp was a great way to determine the student's ability to motivate himself and his patrol under extremely adverse conditions. And looking at Outpost Harry with no map or knowledge of the place, standing in a stinking pile of dead bodies, expecting the men to rebuild the position under artillery fire in less than one day and then prepare for a Chinese onslaught certainly reminded me of the Ranger exercise. However, I had to get up and do the job for which I was trained.

Phase one of the overall defensive plan was that if the Chinese overran us, I would make the decision to call in variable-timed fuses (VT, also known as proximity fuses) on my own position. A VT on an artillery shell was set so that the shell's explosion would be roughly one hundred feet above the ground. Able Company VT artillery support was from 105mm howitzers, so the VT shell explosion covered a rather large area. The airburst released many pieces of steel shrapnel in a pattern directed toward the target under the explosion. VT was extremely effective against infantry.

Phase two of the plan was that after the VT shells on our position were "lifted and shifted," Lieutenant Tolen would then lead a counterattack team up the hill to kill those Chinese who remained in the trenches. Not knowing how the previous defenders had positioned their counterattack team—if they even had one—as a major part of my defensive plan for 12–13 June, I decided to place the 3rd Platoon in a counterattack position in the mess bunker. I selected Executive Officer, First Lieutenant Tolen to be the counterattack platoon leader. I selected the mess bunker because the reaction time for the lieutenant would be very important. The mess/medical bunker at the bottom of the hill would be the best place for the counterattack team to stay until needed. Lieutenant Tolen should be able to reach the Chinese in the trenches within ten to fifteen minutes. Starting the counterattack from the main line of resistance would have added twenty to twenty-five minutes to the response time. With the Chinese running all over the top of Outpost Harry, the difference in time for help to arrive could be the difference in saving the hill or all of us dying.

I didn't identify a need for the company first sergeant, Clyde Shinault (better known as "Snake," for some reason) to be on the hill. He would remain at the MLR and make sure we got what we needed. Snake had been a supply sergeant at one time. I selected him to be first sergeant because he had the ability to lead troops and get the job done. From the reconnaissance we had made, I had determined that ammo and water were the most important items that we needed to secure for the night. And if anyone could get them, Sergeant Shinault could.

We had a great deal of work to do before nightfall. Some of the bunkers were beyond repair, but we would have to rebuild those that were repairable. All of the trenches were filled with dirt, timbers, bodies and parts of bodies, barbed wire, and metal stakes and were thus unusable. All of the machine guns needed relaying, and fields of fire would have to be set up. All communication wire had to be relaid. The companies before us had used most of their ammunition, so we had to restock the ammo. No water, food, or medical supplies were on the hill. Sergeant Shinault was going to be very busy.

As the team was finishing its review of Outpost Harry, I decided to take a drink from my canteen. I wore the canteen on my web belt, toward the rear, on my left hip. As I always did, I reached for the canteen with my left hand, and as I touched the canteen cover to remove the canteen, I felt something strange. Quickly pulling my hand back, I realized that in the palm of my hand were small pieces of human flesh. The human flesh had not yet dried. *How did flesh get on my canteen?* I must have bumped into the side of a trench. Pieces of flesh were all over the trenches. These pieces had not turned black yet, so the destruction of the body must have happened just before we arrived on Outpost Harry. I had no idea when or where I had picked up the flesh on my canteen cover.

I looked for a place on the trench wall where I could wipe my hand. I found a spot on the wall that appeared to be dirt, and grabbed a handful. Then I tried to wipe my hand clean by using dirt from the trench wall. But I couldn't wipe my hands clean of the flesh. Working my web belt toward my right side, I positioned my canteen pouch to my front. The canteen cover was smeared with human flesh on one side and on the top. I clenched my teeth and retrieved my canteen from the flesh-spotted protective cover. Bits of flesh clung to the canteen itself. I then unscrewed the top of the canteen, poured the water on my hands, and on the canteen cover. I washed my hands two or three times, using all of my drinking water. But having no water left made no difference to me. I was no longer thirsty.

As the reconnaissance team went back down the hill, we were all shaking our heads and wondering how we could prepare for the upcoming battle. We were shocked at the horror and the human destruction. I noticed that the trenches were now dry as we proceeded on our way down. The blood running

16. Soldiers in trench and the covered ammunition bunker—our Door to Hell. (Photo courtesy of Jim Jarboe, 3rd Signal Company, 3rd Infantry Division.)

in the trench had been absorbed. The dead Chinese bodies and body parts were still in the trenches, and the putrid stench of the dead was still in the air. The horrible mess of human remains would be in the trenches until Able Company cleaned them out.

When we returned to the place where the APC had run over the dead soldier, his dismembered body was gone but signs still remained of a bloody mess. Most likely the morning light had alerted the APC driver to the destruction and he had recovered the body.

Returning to the Able Company area located near the MLR, all officers and senior enlisted who were not on the reconnaissance group assembled. I explained the situation with the trenches and bunkers on Outpost Harry. We discussed the problems we must overcome, especially the fact that we had to accomplish all of our tasks before the Chinese attacked. During the conversation, I encouraged all Able Company leaders to prepare their men to witness a horrible sight, to alert their leaders if they were going to get sick, to try to suppress the vomiting. If they couldn't suppress the gagging, they should try not

17. Aerial side view of the trench line of Outpost Harry. (1) The artillery FO bunker and (2) the company CP as they were positioned on the loop. (3) Air identification panels. (Photo courtesy of 1LT James C. Hafer, 15th Regiment, Tank Company, 3rd Division.)

to vomit in front of others, because if someone saw another person vomit, it might trigger his own vomit reaction.

While the recon team was on Outpost Harry, I made a sketch of the trenches. It wasn't a very good drawing, but I went over what I had with the group. Some of the marks showing bunkers were just marks, since a bunker at the marked position no longer existed—there was just a hole in the ground. Nevertheless, everyone seemed to get a good idea of what to expect. The other recon team members added their ideas about what we had to accomplish on the hill. I told those who were staying to remain on the alert and be prepared to help if I called for them. If we needed help, I would let Sergeant Shinault know we were in trouble and he would lead the men who had stayed behind to help us. I told those who were going with me to prepare for one hell of a tough time. Most important, I again said, they all should write letters home and make their peace with God.

I cleaned up my canteen, canteen cup, canteen holder, and web belt. I tried to brush the bits of flesh still clinging from my clothes. However, I ignored what I missed, because I knew I had to wear the clothes I was wearing anyway. I had no other clothes to change into.

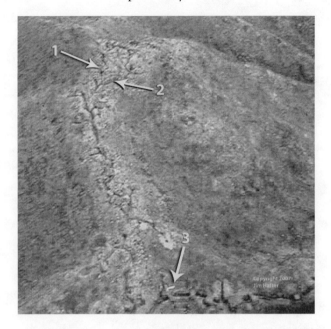

18. Aerial top view of the trench line on Outpost Harry. (1) The artillery FO bunker and (2) the company CP as they were positioned on the loop. (3) Air identification panels. This is an eastward view of Outpost Harry's main trench line with the right spur shown at the bottom. Most enemy attacks were directed toward the loop at the top of the picture. The trench was approximately one hundred yards long from the spur at the bottom to the top of the loop. The dents in the ground are shell craters. (Photo courtesy of 1LT James C. Hafer, 15th Regiment, Tank Company, 3rd Division.)

A runner arrived with a message for me from Major MacLane: "Immediately move Able Company, 5th RCT, and occupy Outpost Harry. Relieve all other units and prepare to defend the outpost until you are properly relieved. You are ordered to hold this outpost at all costs." I made my peace with God and went to work.

10

Occupying the Hill

With Only Twelve Hours to Rebuild and Defend

About 0630 on the morning of 12 June 1953, the soldiers of the 1st and 2nd platoons of Able Company, 5th RCT, assembled. The platoon leaders took a head count and ordered the soldiers to lock and load their weapons. Then the soldiers went to war.

The 3rd Platoon remained at the assembly point under the command of Able Company executive officer 1LT Del Tolen. Lieutenant Tolen was to lead his men to the mess bunker at the bottom of the communication trench in the mid-afternoon and establish the counterattack team. The sun was shining brightly as we left the assembly point. I had been up for twenty-four hours but was not yet tired or sleepy. With our flak vests zipped up tightly and our weapons loaded and ready, we took the same path to the MLR departure position the reconnaissance team had taken earlier in the day. I noticed that someone had removed the rocket launcher we had seen sending up the ripples of rockets. I guessed they had taken the launcher back to refill.

▶ *12 June 0743—Able Company of the 5th RCT departs for Harry.*

We continued to move forward toward the small hills on the left of the path. Just as I led Able Company around one of the first hills (near where I had seen the dead American destroyed by APC treads), a shell exploded with a loud boom very close to us. We all stopped and ducked, looking around to see if we could determine who was shooting at us. The incoming shell seemed to come from somewhere on our right flank. In a few seconds another round hit, followed by several others. Each round was hitting closer. Now I could hear the rounds fired right after the shell hit. As when we were in the trench on the Punch Bowl, the sound of the gunfire didn't travel as fast as the projectile itself. Therefore, the projectile would explode and the sound of the round being fired would catch up a fraction of a second later.

I knew the rounds were from a direct-fire weapon and not a mortar. I was sure the gun had to be either a U.S. 75mm recoilless rifle or a Chinese 76mm. My mind raced as I tried to determine who was firing. The rounds were definitely coming from a hill off our right flank.

If the shots were coming from that direction, then they would have to be from a U.S. position. Why were they shooting at us? I decided we had to move, and move fast, no matter which army was shooting. "Let's go! Go! Go!" I yelled while waving everyone forward. About ninety of us were running, so it took several minutes for everyone to clear the impact zone. Those of us in the front of the group were yelling encouragement to the rest of the company to move fast. The shells continued to hit, but they were off the target. Finally, we all found a safe spot behind another hill. After a short rest we proceeded to the path leading to the mess/medical bunker. Whoever was shooting was not very good. Several rounds were close, but none hit us.

I found out later that the hill from which we were receiving fire was Chinese. I had never had the chance to see a map identifying the Chinese positions, nor ours either. I knew so little about where our position was that I didn't realize the Chinese were close to our right flank. We were lucky. They had a clear shot at anyone going to and from Harry. At the time, I didn't know of or understand the danger (I couldn't have done anything even if I *had* known). I didn't even know where I wanted artillery support to hit if I called for help.

▶ *12 June 0752—3 CCF observed walking on skyline CT508425.[1] Fired on by SA from OP Harry.*

Stopping and crouching while incoming artillery rounds landed close to us, we finally made our way up the communication trench to the top of the hill. A couple of stretchers were coming down the trench. I couldn't tell if the men they were carrying were wounded or dead. Viewing American dead and wounded was the standard introduction to Harry. I'm sure each member of the company watched the stretchers with anticipation.

When we reached the Door to Hell, the odor of death, burned powder, and burned flesh hit us. I stepped aside, allowing the men to pass, and noticed several of them gagging and vomiting as they walked into the trench filled with body parts. Welcome to Outpost Harry.

Once we were in Harry's trenches, we started the process of deploying the two platoons. Any soldier not with Able Company who was found in a bunker by platoon leaders and platoon sergeants had to leave the hill, since Able Company was taking control of Harry. The soldiers who were not with Able Company were battle-weary, and I didn't want them on the hill. If they had any remaining grenades and ammunition, they left it on position and then went down the hill to rejoin their units. It wasn't the best procedure to accomplish relief and transfer of responsibility, but it worked and we completed the occupation of Outpost Harry.

As each squad occupied assigned bunkers and a section of the trench, the men used their entrenching tools to clean out the trench and rebuild their fighting positions. The task was extremely difficult and mentally destructive. Throwing dead Chinese and their body parts out of the trench toward the barbed wire in the front of our position made several men vomit. Everything American was carefully set aside for transportation to the bottom of the hill.

I wasn't sure where the other company commanders had established their command posts while defending Outpost Harry. I couldn't find the company commander for Baker Company, 5th RCT. I presumed whoever was in charge had decided to leave. I would have preferred to meet with the commanders preceding me; however, not seeing anyone was okay. The place was small, I would quickly learn where the Chinese were, and we were already sending anyone not with Able Company off the hill without a debriefing.

I selected a bunker near the split of the trenches at the loop. This would provide me good access to either end of the trench forming the loop. If needed, I could then start in either direction or end up back at the CP. The CP bunker had an offset entrance rather than opening directly into the trench. Whoever had designed the bunker had done a good job. It was larger than most, with room for about six people without being crowded. Interestingly, there were no signs that the bunker had suffered any serious artillery damage. My new command post was within a few yards from the bunker occupied by the artillery forward observer from the 555th Artillery Battalion. The location of these two bunkers would give me quick access to the FO for fire control.

In the command post, our radio operator made contact with battalion, set up the radio nets, and laid the telephone lines to replace all the destroyed lines on the hill. We now had communication via telephone lines to the two platoons. I decided that the hill was under my control, so I radioed battalion that I now had responsibility for Outpost Harry. Our 555th FA forward observer started getting his radio net working and his team in position. This was the time for me to start checking each bunker and machine-gun position throughout the outpost. I wanted to be sure that we were doing everything possible to get ready for the Chinese and that no one remained on the hill except Able Company and its attachments.

▶ *12 June 0810—M-39 returned to BN aid station with friendly casualties and one WIA PW.*

My first interest was the fighting positions on Outpost Harry. As I made my rounds, I met with the platoon leaders for the 1st and 2nd platoons and we checked the fighting positions. I ordered the entrance to the fighting positions closed at dusk using filled sandbags.[2] The only remaining opening or entrance to the bunker would be the aperture from which to fire a weapon. Each bunker would then be like a little pill box.

The idea of sealing up fighting positions with sandbags came from experience. While fighting the NKPA all winter on the northern rim of the Punch Bowl, I became aware of a North Korean tactic that would be fatal for us if the enemy used it on Outpost Harry. When the NKPA soldiers penetrated the barbed wire and other defenses to breach our line, they would jump into the trenches and run down the trench line throwing grenades into each bunker. The tactic was very effective for the North Koreans. With our soldiers firing out of the front of their bunkers, attention would be away from the entrance. Our soldiers wouldn't know if the North Koreans were in the trenches nor would they know what was happening at their backs.[3] It was proven later in the night that without sandbagging the entrances to the bunkers, there was a very good chance that all of us would have been injured or died.

By sealing the back entrance to each fighting bunker, we accomplished two purposes. First, a sealed entrance prevented a grenade or bayonet attack on the person firing in the other direction. Second, if I had to call VT artillery rounds onto our position, then it was unlikely that the shrapnel would penetrate the sealed entrance and injure our own people.

We had a lot of fighting positions with .30-caliber light machine guns. The companies who had been on the outpost earlier had left their machine guns for the next "victims" of Outpost Harry. A lot of the leftover guns were useless, their barrels having been ruined from excessive firing. The continuous firing caused some of the guns' barrels to weld to their frames, ensuring that the barrels were not replaceable. We did repair several weapons, got them into working condition, and ended up with seventeen good .30-caliber light machine guns. Additionally, we had two machine-gun sections of the .30-caliber heavy machine guns from Company D, 5th. This was an awful lot of firepower from two reinforced platoons of infantry.

19. Outpost Harry. In this photograph, the small hole near the bottom of the trench was where the soldier entered to fire the machine gun. This photo, taken in April 1953, two months before the battle for Outpost Harry, illustrates the difficulty of trench warfare. The covered bunker on the left was one of the covered ammunition bunkers. (Photo courtesy of CPT Martin Markley, U.S. Department of Defense photograph.)

▶ *12 June 0825—All wounded have been evacuated from OP Harry.*
▶ *12 June 0850—Heavy shelling (120s) reported by I&R OP on Harry.*

We were surprised that the Chinese would start firing large artillery rounds early in the morning.

Outpost Harry was a narrow strip of land on top of a hill. Although artillery fire would destroy a hilltop over time, precisely landing the shells on a narrow ridge was difficult to do. The impact area for trenches on such a narrow strip was very small for artillery. If the artillery shell were short of the target, it would land on the slope in front of the Outpost Harry trench and would most likely be harmless. If the artillery shell were long, it would pass over the target and land in the valley behind Harry. Mortar rounds had a much better chance of hitting right on a target.

▶ *12 June 0905—Major Byrd will arrive at Harry to survey the damage for Division.*

The effort to clear the trenches was more difficult than initially thought because of continuing incoming artillery from the Chinese. The soldiers would shovel awhile and duck awhile. Some of the fighting bunkers that were covered with dirt and bodies required substantial work before they were usable. Lengths of barbed wire mixed in with the dirt made the effort to clean off the bunkers even more of a challenge. In addition, at mid-morning the summertime sun was warming up the land.

After clearing a section of trench, the next effort was to rebuild those defensive positions. Sandbags sent up by Sergeant Shinault were distributed, filled, and placed. As I watched the men filling the sandbags, I noted that the bags were being filled with something more than just dirt and sand. Finding only sand and dirt was impossible on Outpost Harry. The full shovels I saw going into sandbags were carrying a mixture of dirt, body parts, dried blood, and chunks of drying flesh. The 5th RCT was essentially burying the Chinese soldiers in sandbags.

Wearing a steel helmet and a flak vest, standing knee-deep in human body parts mixed with stinking blood and putrid flesh, and dodging incoming artillery rounds while the bright, hot sun was beating down made for an uncomfortable morning. Nevertheless, the trenches were eventually cleared sufficiently to provide some protection while moving in them.

While dodging incoming artillery, I continued to inspect the progress made to get everybody ready for the night.

▶ *12 June 0950—nine-man screening patrol (friendly) near Harry was dispersed by mortar and artillery fire. One WIA (Katusa named Lee Won Ha).*

As the morning sun moved up in the sky, the day grew hotter. I expected everyone to do his job, and I was in no mood for any laggard, sick from vomiting or otherwise, not working. We were already running short on water. A call to Snake got us some water, ammunition, and rations. Everyone was working hard to prepare his position, knowing we were facing a hell of a night.

As I continued on my bunker checkout, I entered one small sleeping bunker located on the trench that ran along the rear of the outpost. The bunker was approximately six feet wide and some eight feet deep. As with most bunkers, the ceiling was over six feet high. The entrance opened directly into the trench. When entering the bunker, to the right was a double-deck bunk bed made from communication wire strung between two logs, making a place to lie down.

With no springs or mattress, it was nevertheless comfortable if all you had to choose from was a wire bunk or the dirt floor. As usual, large rats roamed the floors looking for food, making tunnels between the bunkers, and feasting on whatever, or whoever, they could find.

On the left side of the bunker was a single communication-wire bunk where two American soldiers were sitting. They were wearing their flak jackets and did not appear to be wounded. They didn't have their helmets on, and their rifles were leaning against the back dirt wall. They were each reading a comic book, looking dazed, and were very quiet.

I was surprised to see them. The sun was getting hot, the little bunker was hot, and everyone else was working except these two. I couldn't recall ever seeing either of these men. I stared for a few seconds and then asked, "You with the 5th RCT?"

At first there was no answer. Then they both slowly shook their heads. I couldn't see their shoulder patches, since all I could see was their right shoulders. I didn't know which unit they were with, but I was sure they were not with Able Company, 5th RCT, because the platoon leaders had reported to me that everyone was present. In addition, I didn't believe an Able Company sergeant would let a couple of his men lounge around a bunker while he and his men were outside in the heat working like crazy. However, I wasn't all that concerned about their unit. I was an officer. I expected enlisted men to rise when I entered a room, even in a bunker.

"Get up," I ordered.

They didn't move. "*Get up*," I ordered a second time. They still didn't move off the communication-wire bed.

I glanced at the upper bunk on the right side of the bunker and noticed someone lying there. When I looked closer, I saw a crossed-rifles badge on his left collar, indicating that he was an infantry officer. On his left shoulder was the blue and white crosshatch of the 3rd Infantry Division (ID). Then I saw why he wasn't moving.

Roofs made from 12-inch-by-12-inch timbers, which were 12 feet long, covered most of the Outpost Harry bunkers. On top of the timbers was some type of tarpaulin material to keep the water out, and then large rocks covered the tarpaulin. Most of these timbers had been hand-carried to the top of Outpost Harry by the Korean Service Corps.

One of the timbers holding up the roof of the bunker had been shattered by an enemy artillery round. The break occurred at about the middle of the timber, and one of the splintered ends had driven itself completely through the chest of the officer, extending out of his back. Apparently, he had died some time ago, as there was no blood running down the splinter. Glancing at the bunk below the officer, I didn't notice any fresh blood on the bunk, either. However, several spots that appeared to be dried blood spattered the lower bunk.

"Get up and get the officer down," I ordered. "I want you to take him down the hill." The soldiers didn't move or respond.

I was in no mood to have one of my orders disobeyed. I repeated my order, but they still didn't move. I pulled my .45-caliber pistol, recharged the chamber so that they could see a round was going in, and aimed the pistol at the soldiers. I told them I would kill them if they didn't move at once. I'm sure I used my command voice as taught at OCS. I may have even raised my voice at them. But I couldn't allow anyone here to not obey me. If I lost command in any manner, I would have lost the hill.

The two men looked at me in disbelief but then realized I was completely serious. They stood up and started to get the officer down. The splinter through his body kept the soldiers from sliding him off the bunk, so I ordered them to take their bayonets and cut the communication wire. Cutting the wire would allow the officer's body to drop to the bunk below, and the splinter could then be extracted. I stood for several minutes, with my pistol drawn, observing their actions to see if they were going to follow my orders. As I continued to watch, they moved faster and seemed to be more alert.

Very likely the officer was a member of a rifle company of the 15th Infantry Regiment. As the soldiers moved about, I saw the same 3rd ID patch on their left shoulders. From what I had heard at the briefing and saw from the valley, the 3rd ID people had really caught hell from the Chinese. No wonder the two soldiers were in shock. We might be in the same condition tomorrow.

"I'm taking your rifles, since you won't need them and we might. You will get off this hill. You will get the officer down and take him with you to the medical bunker at the bottom of the hill," I said. "If I find out you didn't take him, I will track you down and kill you." They looked as if they took me seriously. They should have.

After watching the two soldiers extract the spear from the officer's chest, which took about ten minutes, I said, "I'm leaving you two now. Get the officer down the hill." When I checked back a few minutes later, I saw two soldiers carrying someone toward the trench leading to the communication trench going down the hill. They looked like the men I'd encountered in the bunker. I glanced in the bunker where the dead lieutenant had been lying in the bunk, and he was gone.

Perhaps fright had frozen the two soldiers. Regardless, having to confront an American soldier with death was a very sad situation. Yes, I believe I would have shot them both if I had to. But I have thanked God many times that that wasn't necessary.

Many situations occur during infantry combat that require decisions that if viewed from a long distance (in my case more than fifty years), without stress or fear of death, are sometimes difficult to explain. Perhaps I could have taken other actions to get the desired results. However, I was a twenty-three-year-old soldier facing an attack by enemy Chinese who wanted to destroy my command and me. I will not pretend to explain what happened in that bunker. I just knew that I was responsible for the defense of Outpost Harry and that in order to defend the hill successfully I had to maintain control. I couldn't risk losing control of the company and having many men unnecessarily killed because a couple of soldiers disobeyed my orders. Once a command was cracked, it was very difficult to regain leadership respect.

At 1200 on 12 June we still had a lot of work to do. The work was very trying on the soul, and it was difficult to stay focused. As the temperature rose, the Chinese continued their frequent shelling. In the hot weather everyone was thirsty and drinking a lot, and for the second time since we'd been on Outpost Harry, we were running low on water. Snake got us more.

For some reason, we didn't get a hot meal served on Harry. I think the mess sergeant was afraid of getting bullet holes in his marmite containers. However, Sergeant Shinault had sent up some canned rations earlier. I may have eaten some, but I don't remember eating anything all day.

Another problem we had was the lack of adequate toilet facilities—with or without running water. Someone told me where the regular position for a latrine had been on the top of Harry, which was just behind the front trench. If it had been there once, the facility no longer existed. The latrine had disintegrated. To get to the latrine at the mess/medical bunker was a dangerous trip down and back, so it was best to control our bodily functions. Sometimes fear helped with that. However, if a soldier couldn't control his bodily functions and fear hadn't done the job, he could get a shovel and dig a hole. If he didn't have time for that, he would just have to live with the mess and keep killing the Chinese. All of these problems were entirely their fault anyway.

▶ *12 June 1330—1 CCF sighted CT508426.*

I continued checking out the bunkers. The men of the 5th RCT were making a lot of progress. Soldiers carried the American dead down the hill to the mess/medical bunker. From there, ambulances would carry the deceased to the

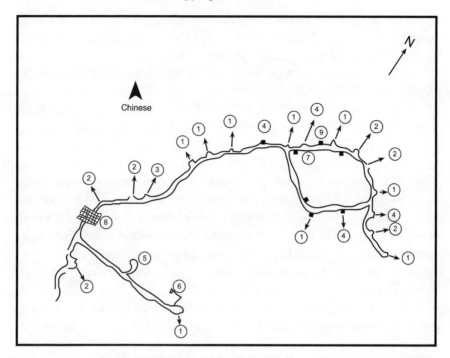

Map 7. Weapon positions at Outpost Harry. The field artillery observation post was on the highest point of the combat outpost. The company CP was just across the trench from the OP. Numerous small bunkers with makeshift coverings were available for the riflemen. Nearly one-half of the riflemen became machine gunners, since we had extra .30-caliber machine guns. Shown are the gun placements along the trench on Outpost Harry; not shown are the fighting positions for some fifty infantrymen. (1) Light .30-caliber machine gun; (2) Heavy .30-caliber machine gun; (3) .50-caliber machine gun; (4) Browning Automatic Rifle; (5) 60mm mortar; (6) 57mm recoilless rifle; (7) Company command post; (8) Covered ammunition bunker; (9) 555th Field Artillery forward observation post.

Graves Registration Division. We continued the practice of throwing any Chinese dead found in the trenches or taken from one of the bunkers over the side of the trenches. Some KSC laborers also carried several dead Chinese off the hill. We didn't have the time or desire to transport them to the bottom of Outpost Harry.

"Lieutenant, sir. I found something in the trench I want to show you." One of our sergeants was at the command post door. "Sir, you have got to see it."

"What is it?" I asked.

"Sir, I can't explain it. You'll just have to see it."

"Where is it?" I replied.

As the sergeant led me out of the command post, we turned right into the trench that curved along the rear of the outpost loop. After going about twenty or thirty feet, the sergeant pointed to the trench floor.

"It's on the bottom on the trench, sir," the sergeant said. "You need to lie down to sec it."

"It" was a hole in the trench wall. The sergeant pointed to the bottom of the right side of the trench. The position of the hole placed its general direction toward the southwest. Looking over the top of the trench in line with the hole gave me a good southwestward view of the Chorwon Valley. The hole appeared to be about two feet wide and one and one-half to two feet high. I lay down on my stomach, scooted forward a little, and peered into it. I couldn't believe what I saw. Inside, cut from solid rock, was a space about five feet by five feet wide and about four feet high. In the wall on the opposite side of the entrance was a small hole through which the sunlight was shining. The floor of the room was about twelve inches below the bottom of the trench in which I was lying. It was a little room.

Inside the little room were two or three devices that looked liked radios. Hanging along the side of the wall were Chinese hand grenades, or what we called "potato mashers." For the first time, I saw unexploded Chinese grenades. They reminded me of the German hand grenades of World War II.

A device that looked like our artillery-spotting scope was lying on the floor. I could barely identify other things in the little room because of the angle of my view. One item looked like a pistol, but I wasn't sure. Another looked like the end of a rifle. Papers, some appearing to be maps, were lying on top of one of the radios. The room was clean and neatly arranged, as if prepared for a new occupant.

My first reaction was to take one or all of the maps and papers. My second reaction was that most likely something in there might be booby-trapped. With caution, I took one slow look around to be sure I was seeing what I thought I was seeing. Then I quickly backed out of the Chinese observation post.

"Sergeant, great job! This has to be a Chinese OP. I'll radio battalion. Don't let anyone crawl into the hole. I bet the room is booby-trapped," I said.

There is no doubt that this Chinese observation post discovered by a 5th RCT sergeant was the reason they wanted Outpost Harry. The Chinese didn't have any air observation capability, so they had to rely on ground positions to direct their artillery fire. I had learned that the Chinese wouldn't shoot artillery if they couldn't see their target. The rumor wasn't true, however, because they couldn't see the pontoon bridge and they certainly shot at that a lot.

The Chinese had recently moved into Korea a new, large-caliber artillery piece. If they could hold on to their observation post here on Outpost Harry, they could easily advance on Seoul. The Chinese had occupied these hills for some time before the United Nations decided the hill was a good location for a combat outpost. So the Chinese had plenty of time to cut their observation post out of solid rock, probably using hand tools, and to stock the room with provisions.

Because of its unique position, the little room wasn't subject to artillery fire. When attacking the OP through the aperture, which faced the southwest, the only way to shoot into it was with a flat-trajectory weapon. Attacking with mortar or artillery fire would never have hit the aperture, since the aperture was on a vertical wall. The only chance we would have of knocking out the Chinese OP would be to fire from a 57mm or 75mm recoilless rifle or tank cannon. And the rounds would have to be a direct hit in a very small hole. Close wouldn't count, because the OP was protected by solid rock.

We were some fifty miles northeast of Seoul, Korea. Had the Chinese been able to take Outpost Harry, they would have had a view of twenty or more miles directly toward Seoul. Even though the terms of the cease-fire negotiations conducted at Panmunjom were almost set, a massive attack down the valley may have delayed, if not completely changed, the cease-fire. Although it seemed inconceivable, the little room was what all of the death and destruction was about—all of the horror just for an excellent observation post that would be difficult to eliminate.

I called our battalion S-2 (Intelligence) section and reported what I had seen. They told me they were going to advise regiment and send someone up to further check out the Chinese OP. However, it was no real surprise to me that no one from S-2 ever came up on Harry to investigate the room. Nor did I ever hear another word from regiment about it. Of course, I don't blame anyone for not wanting to come to the top of Outpost Harry. Nobody I knew ever wanted to be on Outpost Harry.

Most important, until the sergeant for the 5th RCT had discovered the hole in the trench, no one in the UN forces knew about the Chinese OP. Nor did anyone with the UN forces understand its significance on Outpost Harry after the discovery. If only they *had* appreciated its significance, air strikes with five-hundred-pound bombs would have redesigned the hill and eliminated it. Perhaps the Chinese wouldn't have sacrificed so many soldiers for the hill if the OP no longer existed. Moreover, we would have saved many Americans.

Sergeant Shinault had arranged for a steady stream of water, food rations, and all kinds of ammo to be delivered up the hill. A few of the South Korean laborers were working. The soldiers back at the main line of resistance became members of Snake's "pack train." I recall someone saying that the laborers weren't required to enter an active combat zone. So their being there on Outpost Harry didn't make sense to me. I could only conclude that they were loyal to their country, realized how much we were doing for them, and wanted to help. They had helped carry the dead off the outpost, and they had carried most of the timbers used to build the bunkers there.

Even during quiet days, Outpost Harry received fire frequently. Several pieces of the twelve-foot timbers were lying around. I don't recall us using any of these timbers for repairing bunkers. They were too big to handle under the firing we were receiving. In addition, we didn't have anything capable of cutting them. Most of our bunker repairs involved filling sandbags, using small pieces of timbers, and using the metal stakes supporting barbed wire that had blown into the trenches.

During the day, there was a lot of activity from others to protect us and help us defend the hill. The 1st and 2nd Sections of the Machine Gun Platoon from Dog Company, 5th RCT, joined us on Outpost Harry with their .30-caliber water-cooled machine guns. Their appearance was a tremendous help to us. These people were excellent soldiers, superb gunners, and very brave. They joined in preparing everyone's positions and getting ready for the night. I also understood that another group, the 10th Combat Engineers, 3rd Infantry Division, had brought up flamethrowers for us to use. I wasn't aware that flamethrowers were available and believed it was the first time they would be used during the Korean War.

Most of the barbed wire that had been carefully laid by the 15th Infantry Regiment was now practically nonexistent. The 10th Combat Engineers had set out five-gallon cans of napalm in front of the concertina wire that was left and strung barbed wire wherever possible in front of the trenches. All the time they were doing their job, the Chinese were shooting at anyone they could see moving.

▶ *12 June 1700—Casualties reported for B Co. 5th RCT was 126, resulting from action on night of 11–12 June.*

Our communication soldiers got us three working landline telephones and a radio. I didn't expect the landline to work for long once the attack started. I was right. After the first hour, I had only a radio connection to the rear. I had no radio or telephone connection within the company.

▶ *12 June 1815—A Co. 5th RCT passed to operational control of 3d BN, 15th Inf.*

In the early evening, just as darkness was settling on the outpost, I received a message that COL Lester Wheeler, commanding officer of the 5th RCT, was

20. The Outpost Harry trench with open machine-gun positions, March 1953. (Photo courtesy of Robert J. Brandon, 15th infantry regiment, 3rd infantry division.)

21. Barbed wire as seen by the Chinese attacking Outpost Harry. (Photo courtesy of Robert J. Brandon, 15th infantry regiment, 3rd infantry division.)

22. Obstacles awaiting the Chinese attacking the trench near the covered bunker. (Photo courtesy of Robert J. Brandon, 15th infantry regiment, 3rd infantry division.)

23. Machine-gun positions. (Photo courtesy of Robert J. Brandon, 15th infantry regiment, 3rd infantry division.)

at the mess/medical bunker and wanted to talk to me. I went down to the communication trench and met Colonel Wheeler, who was already about three-quarters of the way up to the Door to Hell. He was a tall, lanky fellow, and I believed he was a fine officer.

Colonel Wheeler wanted to know how we were doing and whether we needed anything that he could get for us. I told him that we had enough supplies. We chatted for a while, and then the colonel explained to me how serious the situation was and how extremely important it was for us to hold the hill.

"Lieutenant, you understand that defending Outpost Harry is very important?" Colonel Wheeler said.

"Yes, sir," I responded.

"You will have to hold this hill at all costs. You understand that 'at all costs' means you do not retreat or surrender until everyone is wounded and unable to fight, or dead," the colonel said in a serious tone.

"Yes, sir, I understand," I said. I did understand. I saluted and turned to go.

Colonel Wheeler stopped me. I turned around and he shook my hand, saluted me, and said, "You're doing a great job."

"Thank you, sir," I said, then returned his salute and left.

Colonel Wheeler was the only senior officer I had ever seen even close to Outpost Harry. He would have been in the trenches on top of Harry if I hadn't met him partway up the hill. He didn't have operational control of Able Company when he visited me on Harry. Nevertheless, he still came up while the shelling was going on to help me and give me encouragement. I never saw the battalion commander of the 1st Battalion, 5th RCT, anytime after we left the Happy Valley reserve position. I never saw Colonel Akers, who had operational control of Able Company, or any other 3rd Division officer except a major with the 10th Engineers and the dead lieutenant mentioned earlier. Colonel Wheeler left me with a positive sense that I was capable of doing the job. I was just as glad that none of the other officers had come up and interfered.

I went back up the communication trench finally understanding the situation. I felt the burden and the responsibility. I was twenty-three years old, an Army Ranger, an infantry officer, and a rifle company commander. I was absolutely determined not to lose the outpost—no matter what.

At the thirty-eighth latitude, darkness starts at about 2030 in June, so we weren't expecting an attack until later in the night. The Chinese always attacked at night. I presumed they thought we couldn't see them and that they would have an element of surprise. We had searchlights and flares to overcome the darkness, so the time of their attack wouldn't make much difference.

The Chinese had been attacking at about 2330 on the previous nights. But on the night of 12 June they attacked at about 2130. Able Company was prepared and ready, but we were a little surprised the enemy attacked as early as they did. The early attack stranded some people who were helping us before they could complete the job.

▶ *12 June 2143—100 CCF sighted in front of Harry. SA fired in vicinity of Harry. Co Cdr requests final defensive fire on front and west of Harry.*

The Chinese started their attacks as they had done before. They used whistles either to scare us or to direct the movement of their soldiers. But the whistles didn't scare us, and I don't know if blowing the whistles made any difference to their soldiers. Some Able Company soldiers told me that the Chinese also used horns, but I didn't hear any. Maybe the deep rumble of extremely loud incoming artillery drowned out the bugles.

The enemy artillery and mortars landed just in front of our line and then started in toward us. The noise, dust, and smoke were terrible. I could see only a few feet in front of me. However, we did have the large World War II searchlights aimed at the path used from the Chinese Star Hill located some 379 yards in front of Outpost Harry. They helped.

Just in front of our trench, some fifty yards directly facing the Chinese, was a slight swale in the land that then rose to a small hill about one hundred yards in front of us. The Chinese would leave Star Hill, a much larger hill, and move through their trenches into a position just behind the hill directly in front. They would then charge down into the swale and up through their own artillery fire to attack. After the Chinese artillery barrage, little of our newly laid barbed wire and concertina coil wire remained. Even so, we were happy with what little wire remained, because it did do some good.

Our machine guns opened up and started the slaughter. Our 555th forward observer called in concentrations, and our riflemen started shooting.

▶ *12 June 2145—2 white parachute flares in valley rear of Harry. MG fire from front of Harry. OP George reports 76 and machine-gun fire left and front of Harry.*

▶ *12 June 2149—Final Defensive Fire being laid on the left and front of Harry.*

Some of the Chinese didn't have weapons. The Chinese would sometimes arm one of their platoons in the attack with only concussion grenades. Their game plan was to have the grenades thrown first and then follow up with platoons armed with burp guns.[4] The men who carried only hand grenades would follow and pick up a gun if the armed platoon member was dead. On the other hand, he might get a weapon from an American. This a tough way to fight a war. If the soldiers in the lead didn't die, the followers would hit our trenches with no weapons.

The loop was the "front," since it was closest to the Chinese. The forward observer outpost was on the loop, and most of the fighting started there. In front of the loop there was a shallow approach that evolved into a very steep rise as one moved toward the right rear. The orientation of Outpost Harry was at an angle to the Chinese that allowed the trench to run away from them as it went toward the medical bunker. The Chinese generally attacked from the front, then worked their way around to the right side of the loop and attacked to breach the right flank. Once in position on the right flank, they would try to overwhelm the gun positions and enter into the trenches.

Our turn in hell had started.

11

Chinese Attack

Hand-to-Hand Combat Is the Essence of an Infantryman

The best place to monitor the action around Outpost Harry was from the 555th observation post. From the OP, I watched as the first group of Chinese soldiers started the action for the night. I tracked the CCF as they were moving to our right flank and toward the rear of Harry. The FO and I could see a split group moving toward our left flank.

▶ *12 June 2150—OP Harry reported 100 CCF on their right rear and to their right and left front.*

The Chinese surrounded Outpost Harry, which was an easy task because they were mostly around the base of the hill. However, movement by the Chinese prevented anyone from leaving or resupplying the outpost without a fight.

The artillery observation post was too small to house both the OP and the company CP. I returned to the company CP to be sure our radio operator was relaying the messages about the Chinese movements to the 15th Infantry S-3 as well as our 1st Battalion on the MLR.

A short while later, just before I left the CP and returned to the 555th Field Artillery OP, Major Eldridge H. Cockrell from the 10th Combat Engineer Battalion, 3rd Infantry Division, came into the Able Company command post. As I saluted the major, I wondered what he was doing here, since I thought all of the engineers had left Outpost Harry. The 10th Combat Engineers had worked all afternoon to help fortify the open area in front of the trenches. Someone had started a rumor that the combat engineers were bringing up flamethrowers. According to the major, however, the engineers were bringing up only small antipersonnel mines. Before the attacks started on 10 June, the

24. Trench from the Chinese Star Hill to a few yards in front of Outpost Harry. This picture shows the eastern slope (right flank) of Outpost Harry looking northward toward Star Hill located as the highest hill at the left rear of this photograph. The Chinese Communist trench (on the right side of this photo) started from an intermediate hill between Star Hill and Outpost Harry and is clearly visible in this view. The CCF used this trench to move unobserved from the intermediate hill to an attacking position just in front of Outpost Harry. (Photo courtesy of Americo "Chic" Pelegrini.)

engineers had carried five-gallon barrels filled with napalm to Harry's top.[1] However, on 12 June, because of the incoming artillery being so heavy, placing napalm was impractical, so instead of napalm, the engineers brought up shoe mines. As Ray Anderson, a member of the 10th Engineers, described later, the combat engineers would move to the front of our protective barbed wire, position shoe mines in the ground, and set the triggers. These small antipersonnel mines, which were the size of a wooden matchbox, would remove an enemy soldier's foot or leg, thus disabling him but not necessarily killing him. If all went well, the engineers would place many shoe mines, since they were easy to carry and install.[2]

Major Cockrell explained that the Chinese had attacked earlier in the evening than he had anticipated. Since the Chinese were surrounding the hill, the major and his team couldn't leave without a fight. He thought the 10th Engineers should wait for a while; maybe the Chinese would leave and he could then get his men off the hill without a battle. He acknowledged that I was in command of the outpost and asked if he and his men could be of any help while they waited to leave.

I was surprised that a major would place himself under the command of a first lieutenant. However, Major Cockrell was correct: I *was* responsible for the defense of the outpost and in command. I appreciated his comments and told him that the best thing to do was to get his men under cover. If they were lying in the trenches and I had to call in VT, they were going to get hurt. In addition, incoming artillery required they take cover.

▶ *12 June 2153—100 CCF sighted to front and 50 to right of Harry. Incoming rounds increasing from moderate to moderately heavy. 76 mm and mortar landing on left slope.*

Standing in the FA observation post watching and hearing the incoming enemy artillery, I realized that control of an infantry rifle company in combat disintegrates quickly. The environment for the infantry commander erodes from blinding flashes of light, extremely loud noises, and a dusty atmosphere, which greatly reduces the necessary communication within the company. First the telephone communication goes out. Cutting the telephone wire takes only a few rounds of incoming artillery. Then the dust from the shells hitting the ground and the smoke from the burning powder creates a cloud, making it difficult to see what's going on, much less breathe. Next the noise becomes so extreme that even shouting can't get the message communicated.

Fighting in such difficult conditions is the reason that soldiers in the American army train to do their jobs without direct supervision. Noncommissioned officers, the backbone of the army, make most of the decisions in combat. Our NCOs direct the fire of the soldiers, rally them in battle, and protect them as they maneuver.

In an infantry rifle platoon, one commissioned officer was responsible for forty-four enlisted men. Each of the four infantry squads had a sergeant first class as the squad leader, a sergeant as the assistant squad leader, and the remaining seven men a combination of corporals and privates first class. Normally, one NCO was responsible for two to four enlisted men.[3] Therefore, the weight of a combat command was strictly upon the NCOs. All I could do as company commander with four platoon officers reporting to me was to present the overall plan, be sure everyone was prepared to defend the outpost, coordinate firepower support, and communicate our activities to a higher command. Other than that, I had very little direct supervision. Our success in battle would depend on the leadership of the NCOs and the bravery of the individual infantryman.

The FA forward observer noticed movement on the left front. He adjusted the artillery and pounded the Chinese company that was trying to find a position for an attack on the left flank. The left was a steep approach to Outpost Harry and made attacking from that position difficult. The artillery barrage created another cloud of dust. Apparently the Chinese gave up and started back toward Star Hill, because we couldn't see them when the dust cloud blew out.

▶ *12 June 2201—Enemy attack on left reported broken up by arty fire.*

The incoming artillery quickly cut the communication wires. I went from one area in the trenches to another to see and understand what was really going on. The reports from runners were helpful, but they couldn't give me the feel of battle.

Major Cockrell returned to the CP telling me all of his men were under cover. He again asked what he could do for me. An open case of hand grenades sat near the entrance to the bunker. I told the major that if he wanted to help, the best thing he could do now was to stay in the CP bunker and be ready to start throwing the grenades if the Chinese breached the trench. He positioned himself near the entrance and started to remove the fragmentation grenades from their containers.

From the artillery OP I could see what looked like the Chinese moving into position for an attack. I wasn't sure if they were going to attack from the right flank or the rear. Anyway, I asked the 555th forward observer to place some VT around the hill. He did. The explosions in the air sprayed the ground with shrapnel and slowed the Chinese down. I lost the attackers in the dust, so I presumed they went back to their lines.

The enemy was able to have several men enter the trench around the "loop" on the right. This was the first time I went into the trench to view the battlefield under attack. After spotting the Chinese, I was surprised that they were in the trench. I couldn't call Tolen to counterattack, so I called out riflemen from a couple of the sleeping bunkers where they had waited. With grenades and rifles we made our counterattacking team and eliminated the enemy that had entered the trench. We had caught them by surprise, so the fight was short, with an estimated ten to twelve men killed. I don't recall any of the enemy escaping. Our tactic was the same as in World War I. We used the shell holes for protection, tossing grenades, crawling between trenches, and shooting at everything.

▶ *12 June 2210—Friendly VT around OP Harry*

Major problems in defending Outpost Harry were illumination, communication, resupply, and the restricted area of movement for defense. The problem of illumination arose from the tremendous amount of dirt and burned powder from incoming artillery shells. The explosions created an environment in which seeing was just about impossible. The darkness of night added to the problem. Searchlights, the same ones that had exposed us when we were lost in the valley, illuminated the Chinese Star Hill and the area just in front of it.

Even though the direction of the searchlights was toward the hill, their side illumination provided much-needed light on Outpost Harry.

Another light source was from an airplane that flew around dropping parachute flares to illuminate the area. The 555th Field Artillery 105mm cannons normally supported our flare request. However, the artillery battalions had already expended their supply of flares; therefore, artillery flares were not available. The 81mm mortar also had the ability to shoot flares. Unfortunately, because of the smaller shell size, its flares weren't as bright, didn't remain activated as long, and didn't reach the height of the 105mm flares. The airplane was on position, and I hoped it would remain so all night supporting our fight.

Communication difficulties were blown telephone lines, extreme noise from incoming artillery, and malfunctioning handheld radios. It fell to each officer and enlisted man to be a link in the communication scheme.

Being on a steep hill with no protective cover meant the soldiers bringing up water and ammunition had a very difficult task. Incoming artillery was so intense that stopping and ducking slowed the resupply line. Nevertheless, they did get us our needed supplies.

The restricted area of defense meant that when a soldier met the enemy in the trench, one of the two would die. There was no place to maneuver.

▶ *12 June 2217—OP Harry and I Company receiving heavy mortar and arty fire. I Company say they are 120mm mortars.*

As the rate of incoming increased, the level of fear increased. Everyone sinks as low as possible when very large shells rupture the earth; the concussion penetrates your mind and vibrates through your body. Everyone prays.

▶ *12 June 2220—Large number enemy arty on Harry. Incoming too fast to be counted.*

The pattern the Chinese followed when firing artillery on Outpost Harry reminded me of summer thundershowers—a few sprinkles, a downpour for twenty minutes, and then backing off to a few sprinkles. The enemy artillery never completely stopped. When the shelling reached a downpour, the only thing anyone could do was duck, look up to see if the Chinese were attacking, and duck again if the enemy wasn't firing again. If they were in sight, we would get up and kill them.

As the enemy continued their relentless assault, our bunkers were shaking badly, dirt was falling through the cracks, red-hot chunks of shrapnel were screaming everywhere, and between explosions there was almost total darkness. In the company command post, our light source was a gas-burning lantern along with the occasional flashlight, but its batteries didn't last long. The camp-style lantern used a mantle that would glow from the burning gas but was easily broken by a sudden jar—such as falling off a makeshift table. Our light source went out quickly. The concussions were too many and too strong for the mantles to operate very long. The concussions also prevented us from doing the delicate work of replacing a mantle. Without the flashes from the shelling, the glow from the searchlights, and the flicker from the parachute flares, it was nearly impossible to see. If the dust from the shelling were heavy at the same time, we would be in total darkness.

Somehow one of the artillery battalions that was supporting us had lost their target setting, and we started receiving "short rounds" of friendly fire. I asked the FO to have them shift or cease fire. To determine the size of the short round was difficult, but we guessed the explosions were from a 105mm shell.

▶ *12 June 2223—Arty fire falling left front slope and rear of Harry. Harry requests cease-fire of friendly arty.*

Suddenly the rain of incoming artillery shells increased. The incoming was substantial and had me worried. I surmised that the barrage indicated that the Chinese were starting to make another attack. I wanted to be sure that we had help to stop whatever the Chinese had in mind, so I asked the FO to get all artillery firing.

▶ *12 June 2229—Now Harry requested all defensive fires on both sides and front of OP.*

The second wave of enemy soldiers hit about 2240, and this time they came around the right flank and entered the trenches. Someone started yelling, "Chinese in the trenches! Chinese in the trenches!" I ran to the trench from the command post to see what was happening. Looking toward the right side of Harry, I saw several Chinese soldiers running on the top of the bunkers. They appeared to be injured, because they would fall, jump up, run, and then fall again. I wasn't sure if a machine gun or grenade was being used against them. After I saw two Chinese soldiers fall, I ran back to the CP. I had no idea how many others were already on top of us, but based on the amount of small arms fire, I knew the number was large.

▶ *12 June 2231—Harry receiving hvy MC fire from left front.*

I decided we couldn't kill them all, so I ordered the 555th forward observer to call in VT on our position. We yelled "VT" to alert all who could hear. I was fairly certain that the Chinese didn't understand the term. Our 555th FO came through, and before long, airbursts were going off right over our heads. The airbursts were working, because the Chinese were screaming on top of the bunkers and in the trenches.

Now was the time we needed 1LT Del Tolen and his counterattack team. His

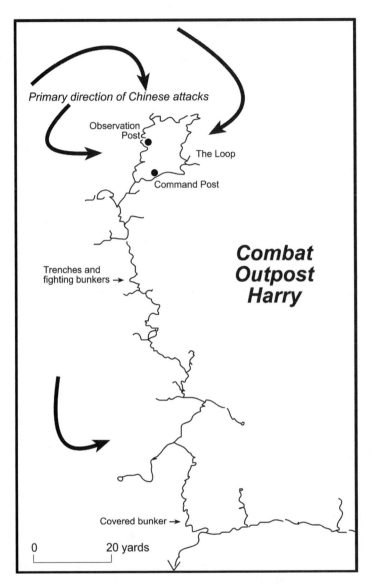

Map 8. Chinese attack lanes. From the covered bunker the trench leads down to the aid station/mess bunker where the counterattack platoon commanded by 1LT Tolen waited until called to attack and repulse the Chinese Communist Forces.

radio was working, and I sent him the message. Lieutenant Tolen said he was on the way. I didn't lift the VT for about five minutes, because I figured he and his men would take five minutes or longer to make their way up the communication trench.

▶ *12 June 2236—Harry complaining about too many short rounds. CCF attacking left front of Harry but have not entered trenches.*

The napalm had been set off, the machine guns had fired constantly, and we still couldn't stop the horde. I really didn't have many choices left.

▶ *12 June 2236—Flare ship is dropping flares 700 yds short of Harry.*

▶ *12 June 2239—Arty relays that CCF is in the trenches.*

The "on position" VT killed some and wounded others, but wasn't killing all of the Chinese.

▶ *12 June 2240—Lt Rockis reports OP Harry receiving intense AW fire from left fronts.*

I previously had told the FO to be prepared to lift and shift the VT away from the communication trench so that Lieutenant Tolen could get up the trench. "Give Tolen about five minutes to get up here, then lift and shift," I added to my instructions. The FO waited a few minutes and sent the message. Immediately the VT explosions lifted and then shifted the VT fire to the east flank. The 555th FA was really a great outfit.

Lieutenant Tolen and his counterattack platoon swept up from the mess/medical bunker, killing all the Chinese who were in their way. The counterattack team met a few enemy soldiers who had advanced as far as to enter the communication trench near the Door to Hell, but killed them before they got to the covered ammo bunker. The counterattack warriors attacked through the Door to Hell into the main trenches and started killing all the Chinese who were still alive.

As the counterattack team fought their way closer to the OP and CP, the three of us left the CP and went out into the trench. I went to several sleeping bunkers to gather riflemen to join us. We were to catch and kill any of the Chinese who were trying to escape from Lieutenant Tolen by running down the trench toward the right side of Harry, which was most likely the way the Chinese entered the trench. Enemy soldiers were both running at us in the trench and jumping toward us along the tops of the bunkers. Fortunately, with the airplane flares and searchlights, we were able to distinguish friend from foe. Lieutenant Tolen knew we would try to trap the Chinese and stopped his attack about halfway up the trench. We opened fire with carbines and M1 rifles before the Chinese realized where we were. I remember firing all of the rounds in my two magazines—some sixty rounds. Our trap caught and killed about fifteen of the enemy. With all of the shooting, I'm not sure how many I killed, but it must have been three or four.

There was one particular soldier on Lieutenant Tolen's counterattack team whose actions I will always remember. I first noticed him when Lieutenant Tolen had the 3rd Platoon and wanted to get this fellow a promotion. According to Lieutenant Tolen, the soldier had been a private for a long time and deserved a promotion to private first class. Perhaps he wouldn't have been selected as a poster boy for the army as he was rather overweight and his head and body were disproportionate, but I liked the way he acted, and I promoted him to PFC. Lieutenant Tolen made him a Browning automatic rifle (BAR) man, and the rifle was just about as tall as this soldier. The BAR used a clip containing twenty .30-caliber bullets, could fire fully automatic, and weighed about fifteen pounds without ammo. Now, being a BAR man, this soldier had a gleam in his eyes.

When the counterattack team came up the trench, this soldier was in front leading the group. He was firing his BAR and killing Chinese. He was fearless—by far one of the meanest men on the hill that night. I recommended him for the Silver Star Medal. The approval cycle for a medal had not yet been completed when I left the regiment, but certainly he deserved the medal if anyone ever did.

Although I can't recall the soldier's name, he taught me that combat soldiers come in all shapes and sizes and that combat soldiers are a different breed, as they have a different attitude and mentality. To be a combat soldier takes someone with the internal fortitude to close down emotions and, from deep within, be able to kill and destroy without regard for oneself. This soldier proved to me that bravery doesn't relate to good looks, a great personality, or wealth. What a man thinks of himself, what he believes he can do even though others do not, what he brings up from the bottom of his soul—this warrior inborn trait makes a combat infantryman. There is no other task in the world that can compare with infantry combat, because if a combat infantryman doesn't have what it takes, he may lose, and losing in combat means never playing the game again. Infantry combat is not a sport—if you lose, you are dead. To be successful you must be vicious and unforgiving of the enemy. You must kill the enemy any way you can. Technique is not important. Killing is what war is all about.

▶ *12 June 2241—3d BN requests supporting fire from Greeks on Hill 478 and to withdraw between 478 and 472.*[4]

To make sure all of the Chinese were dead, Lieutenant Tolen's counterattack team shot each of them in the head. Leaving an enemy alive in the close quarters of a trench is an invitation for a surprise shot in the back. Lieutenant Tolen and his team took any American wounded with them when they returned to the medical bunker during these short lulls.

I tried to stay in either the observation post or the command post as much as I could. If I stayed in the trenches shooting my carbine, then I couldn't help the rest of Able Company and would become just another rifleman, which was not what I should be doing. But even though I had various reports from the platoon leaders, there were times when I had to see for myself what the situation was on Outpost Harry. No runner or telephone could describe what was really happening. I had to see firsthand.

There were two main reasons for me to leave the CP and the OP to run in the trenches. The first was to determine what the situation was and to make sure we were we holding as ordered. The second reason was to give support and encouragement to the men who were fighting so that they would know we were holding. I became good at running in the trenches, hunched over with a carbine loaded and ready. I carried several grenades as well as two banana clips, each with thirty rounds, taped end to end for quick reloading. My bayonet was mounted, and I wore my helmet and flak vest.

It was about this time of night that I received my first injury. While I was out in the trench, a shell hit nearby. I ducked and felt sand hit my right arm. I looked and noticed small holes in my shirtsleeve. I later realized that these small holes were from slivers of shrapnel.

Although I knew the problems of running in the trenches when they were full of dead Chinese, now, at this time of night, I lost any hesitation I had about where or what I stepped on or in. My whole attitude had changed, and I was feeling no guilt or remorse for destroying the enemy in any way. For some reason, however, I couldn't step on the intestines oozing from Chinese soldiers lying in the trench. I could and did step on everything else, but I sidestepped the stomach wounds. A head cut in two was bad, but the image of a stomach blown open was hard for me to take. Sometimes I just had no choice but to step on intestines. I looked up. I kept going. Remembered: The dead Chinese soldier with the stomach problems doesn't care where anyone steps.

▶ *12 June 2247—OP Harry receiving hvy 76 fire from front. OP Harry defensive fires shifted to Mushroom, Bunker Hill area on unknown position.*

The Chinese 76, a version of a Russian-designed weapon used in World War II, is a flat-trajectory weapon. Most likely they were used for trying to get a direct hit on a machine-gun bunker.[5] Whoever was spotting flare drops from the flare plane was not doing a good job. When the flares dropped short, the wind would move the flares off the target (the small hill in front of our trench), and the flares would descend over and behind our position, making us more visible to the enemy.

▶ *12 June 2248—Lt Rockis says flares still dropping short.*

On 12 June, a very heavy artillery barrage broke all circuits to Outpost Harry.

▶ *12 June 2256—OP Harry request more illumination.*

A short time after we had restored the hill and the counterattack team had returned to their mess bunkers, we prepared for another Chinese attack. We restocked the ammo, secured water, tried to get the wounded moving off the hill, and, of course, had a well-deserved smoke.

I was in the command post bunker, and a soldier walked in holding his rifle. His right cheek was blown out. He was calm—maybe in shock. I looked at him and decided the hole in his cheek needed some type of protection. I was amazed at the sight of his injury. This was the first time I had ever looked closely at a face wound. The blood was not dripping at all; it was just oozing. The hole was about the size of a golf ball, and the skin was pointing outward as if it had been ripped open from the inside of his mouth. The ripped skin was about an eighth of an inch thick. I couldn't tell if his mouth was injured, too, but he wasn't talking.

I took the soldier's rifle and looked for his bandage packet. Every soldier is supposed to have with him a special large gauze bandage that is about six inches square, with additional lengths of gauze to use as ties, in case he has a wound to be covered. The bandage is for his own personal use, and no one else's, since each soldier has his own bandage. Being sure every soldier has this basic item of equipment is a commander's responsibility. The wounded soldier before me had a canvas pouch designed to hold a bandage on his web belt, but the pouch didn't contain a bandage.

I didn't recognize the soldier but presumed he was with the 5th RCT—maybe even Able Company. Whatever unit he was with, his commander apparently hadn't checked him for his basic equipment. Part of my responsibility was to ensure that each soldier was properly equipped, so even though I knew I might need my bandage later, I decided I would use the bandage from my pouch to cover his wound. I removed my bandage from the pouch, opened it, covered the wound, and wrapped the ties around his head. Since the man was bleeding only slightly, perhaps it wasn't really necessary to cover the wound, but I did. I had relieved him of his rifle, which he could no longer use. Then I guided him to the bunker entrance and directed him to move down the trench to the aid station in the medical bunker. He should have been able to get to the aid station and safety with no problem, but I never learned if he reached the aid station or not.

I had not seen Major Cockrell from the 10th Engineers for some time because we were all busy. He was to lead all of his soldiers off Harry as soon as there was a break in the incoming artillery and the Chinese had left the area around the trench leading to the aid station. Since I moved through the trench without contacting him, I am reasonably certain that he left the hill with his men.

▶ *12 June 2257—OP Harry requests more illumination. Needs constant illumination. Have 1 WIA.*

I continually tried to get messages to the platoon leaders and NCOs on the hill to keep them informed about the situation we were facing. I didn't need to do much informing, however, because all they had to do was look up and they could see the incoming. If they looked around, they could see all of the Chinese dead filling up the trenches. In addition, they would notice that some bunkers no longer had tops. Harry was only one hundred yards long and about thirty-five yards wide—like a big football field without cheerleaders. I mainly wanted to let everyone know that Able Company, 5th RCT, was still functioning and still holding the hill.

▶ *12 June 2300—Harry receiving heavy 76 fires.*

A telephone line to the platoons started working again, but there was still no wire connection with 1st Battalion. All communication beyond Harry was made via radio. Lieutenant Bradbury called and said he had a prisoner and wanted to know what to do with him. The 2nd Platoon, which Lieutenant Bradbury commanded, was on the eastern half of Outpost Harry. This sector included the loop, which was the primary target of Chinese attacks. I told him I would contact battalion and let them know that a prisoner was on the way down. Lieutenant Bradbury agreed and said he was sending someone to escort the prisoner. Since we killed most of the Chinese we encountered, capturing a prisoner was very important because it gave us the opportunity to interrogate them. Whoever captured a Chinese soldier received a special seven-day R & R trip. I made sure to tell battalion that the lieutenant had captured the prisoner so that he would get the R & R.

The artillery had slackened, so I took a quick tour of the trenches to check things out. Suddenly the incoming artillery got very heavy. While kneeling—crouched—in a trench, hoping the heavy incoming artillery would let up so that I could get back to the CP, I felt some dirt falling on me. That was normal if an incoming round landed close. However, most of these rounds were long. I looked up to see what was causing the dirt to fall and saw a dark shadow looming above me. A Chinese soldier was crawling toward me.

I was still kneeling. My carbine, which I was holding in both hands, pointed skyward. I realized that the son of a bitch was crawling into my trench. My immediate reaction was to shove the carbine upward. I gritted my teeth and lunged upward as hard as I could. I didn't fire, because I had no time. My hand was above the trigger. My bayonet caught the Chinese soldier in the neck just under his cheekbone and continued into his head. As I leaped upward, I lifted him off the ground. My bayonet must have reached his skull, which stopped the bayonet, allowing me to lift him off the ground.

I threw him forward and he fell off my bayonet. He didn't move. I noticed blood running out of the barrel of my carbine. I couldn't allow blood to stay in the barrel. I had once blown the tip off two M1 rifle barrels at Fort Jackson because I had mud in the barrel, so I knew I had a potential problem. I raised the carbine above my head and violently slung the barrel toward the ground. The remaining blood trickled out. I fired a few rounds into the Chinese soldier to be sure that the carbine was working and that the enemy I'd encountered was not. The carbine worked fine.

The machine-gun fire and artillery incoming explosions continued all around me. I kneeled beside the dead man and took a few seconds to regroup. I noticed that his right eye was still wide open. The left side of his face was destroyed. Where in the hell had he come from? All of the Chinese were supposed to be off the hill or dead. Perhaps this soldier had been a straggler, but he wasn't one now. He was very dead. I don't think he ever moved after the bayonet hit his head. I started to search him, but the incoming shells started moving closer. I left for the shelter of the CP and a cigarette.

According to a training maxim, when people are under stress, they react to what they have learned in training. Subconscious combat skills are why teaching a skill correctly is so important. My bayoneting the Chinese soldier was purely reactionary. The hours of army bayonet training I'd had taught me how to parry and thrust. I had needed only the thrust part.

Interestingly, as far as I could determine, the Chinese soldier didn't have a burp gun, club, or any other weapon. Maybe he had been one of the number-two attackers with grenades but no weapon and his number one hadn't lost his burp gun.[6]

▶ *12 June 2301—M 39 on way to Harry to evacuate 2 serious WIAs.*

▶ *12 June 2305—Incoming rounds on Harry have decreased in intensity.*

We were having a problem with getting so many wounded soldiers off Harry. A lull settled on the hill. The lull was interrupted only by the screaming of the wounded, cries for a medic, and men running to get more ammunition. Then a sprinkle of incoming Chinese artillery brought us back to the reality of war.

▶ *12 June 2308—Harry reports 3 WIA. Situation OK. Request constant illumination.*

▶ *12 June 2313—OP Harry rpts supporting fire falling too close. Arty instructed to lift and shift fires. OP requests more illumination. 81s and 60s instructed to fire immediate illumination.*

▶ *12 June 2330—Harry reports receiving 120mm mortar fire. No illumination at all on Harry.*

Recovering from killing with a bayonet, I observed from the Outpost Harry field artillery OP that the lull would be ending soon. I couldn't see very much but had a feeling the Chinese hadn't given up and were just preparing another attack.

▶ *12 June 2332—A/5th RCT wants friendly arty fire lifted because they are getting friendly incoming rounds. Also wants supporting fire on left and right.*

The view of the battlefield from the CP was very restricted. If I was not in the observation post, I had to go out into the trench to track the fighting by looking, ducking, and looking again.

▶ *12 June 2337—Harry reports very poor visibility and very poor illumination.*

▶ *12 June 2339—Firefight on front of Harry.*

I started to the right of the CP, which led me around the loop. As I got close to the end of the curve in the loop where it started back toward the main trench, I heard an incoming shell that I knew would be close. I immediately kneeled, ducked, and the shell did hit close. I felt something hit me on the back of my neck that again reminded me of sand blowing very hard on a beach. I had pulled my head toward my chest. The "sand" hit the back of my neck and the top of my shoulder where it wasn't protected by my flak vest.

▶ *12 June 2343—Flare ship now dropping flares. FO in OP Fox adjusting ship.*

My concerns were correct. The burp guns were popping and some whistles were blowing. The attackers were coming in waves trying to breach the trenches. We were killing them as they approached the barbed wire.

▶ *12 June 2358—Heavy burp gun fire on OP's front.*

I returned to the CP to get a message to battalion about what we were expecting. The back of my neck started itching and I scratched my neck. My hand came back covered with blood. I wiped my neck again and there was more blood. I asked someone to look at my neck. He told me there were many small holes in my neck that were oozing blood. In an attempt to stop the itching, I poured some water from my canteen on my neck and wiped it. The water felt good but didn't stop the itching.

▶ *12 June 2400—SA and AW fire on Harry. Attacking on right front.*

This was the beginning of a major effort by the enemy. Again they entered the trench, this time at the loop. Lieutenant Tolen and his counterattack team were too far away, so I left the OP and rounded up some of the riflemen who were not in a fighting bunker. The loop had the easiest entry to the outpost.

However, the sharp bends in the trench gave us positioning, so we set up a defensive position with bayonets, rifles, and grenades. This fight lasted for some time. We moved a machine gun to the edge of the trench to keep the Chinese down, and then we advanced, throwing grenades and shooting, until we killed them all, probably twenty-five CCF.

▶ *HQ IX Corps Command Report—13 June 0005—A company size of Chinese soldiers attacked but withdrew after a twenty-five-minute firefight.*
This was the third main attack of the night.

▶ *13 June 0008—CCF are jamming airwaves on 81 mm mortar frequency.*
The Chinese were attacking the loop. They had just pulled back from the last attack and started another one. The FO and I continued to converse and speculate about the intentions of the CCF. They were trying to kill us all. We got more artillery east of the loop to try to stop the attack.

▶ *13 June 0015—Harry reports increasing incoming arty.*
The dust and burned powder was hanging right over the top of us, with very little breeze. I could see very little, and my eyes were burning from the dust and smoke from the exploding shells, so I rinsed them with water from my canteen. After several tries, I finally got the dust out of my eyes. Of course, my ears were ringing.

▶ *13 June 0020—Harry is smoked in. Could not make out the outline of Harry.*

▶ *13 June 0025—Harry reports flares still insufficient.*

▶ *13 June 0030—Action on Harry has slackened. Attack was driven off.*
About this time, I went out into the trench to determine what was happening, and an incoming shell hit close to where I was standing. I felt a sharp sting in my right knee. I looked down and saw a rip in my fatigue pants about three inches long. At the same time I felt a trickle of blood running down my right leg. I turned and went back into the CP. Pulling my pant leg up, I found that a piece of shrapnel had sliced my pants and the top of my right knee as a razor would do. The injury appeared to be about two inches long, one-quarter inch wide, deep, and bleeding a lot. Since I had used my bandage on the soldier with the severe cheek wound, I asked someone in the CP to find me a medic. I lit up a cigarette while the medic cleaned my leg, put some medication on the wound, and wrapped my knee with a bandage. The medic thought I should get some stitches. I looked at my knee, and since it wasn't hurting very much, I decided it wasn't bad enough to leave the hill. As I watched the medic and smoked a cigarette, I thought about how lucky I was that the shrapnel hadn't hit an inch lower. The medic agreed with me. An inch lower and most likely my right knee would have been destroyed, maybe gone completely, and who knows what else—perhaps even a good chance of bleeding to death.

▶ *13 June 0032—OP Harry rpts receiving MG fire from left front at range of 300 yards on hill 478. Arty called in.*

▶ *13 June 0040—OP Harry rpts SA from left rear. Arty being placed. 81s ordered to target left rear of Harry.*

A corporal with a 3rd Division patch entered the CP, where I was resting and trying to decide how bad my wound really was. I guessed he was one of the combat engineers who had been working on the hill with the engineer major. I was surprised to see the corporal, since I thought all of the 10th Combat Engineers were off the hill. He was in bad shape. As he staggered in, I saw that his left hand was damaged and covered with a makeshift bandage, and in his right hand he was trying to hold on to an M1 rifle. I took his rifle, since he could neither load nor fire a rifle with only one hand. This warrior was a true fighter. He didn't want to give up his rifle and mumbled something about needing it so that he could keep fighting. I believed he would keep the fight going if he didn't bleed to death first. There was nothing we could do in the CP to help the corporal. I ordered him to get off the hill so that he could get some treatment. He was walking but not talking very much. The last I saw of him, he was moving toward the communication trench to receive the help he very much needed.[7]

▶ *13 June 0050—Incoming rounds on Harry increasing.*

When I returned to the trenches, I ran crouched since I was finding less and less of a trench for cover. The trenches were filling up with mostly dead Chinese—some still identifiable and some just parts. I noted a few Americans dead in the trenches, but we couldn't start to get them down the hill yet because of the fighting.

Word came to the command post that a bunker had received a direct hit and that the left flank was open. As I ran toward the left flank, the strange sensation of slipping and sliding reached my consciousness—the same sensation I'd had when we made the reconnaissance run. I realized that once again it was dead bodies that were giving and slipping.

As I mentioned earlier, when a shell hit close, we would dive onto the bodies and body parts just as we would dive into a strange ditch at night. We would take this action without thinking or caring. *Get down and stay down until the explosion is gone.* Sometimes those explosions were so close and so frequent that I couldn't do anything but stay down. If we could still move, then during a slight pause we would get up and keep moving.

Infantry combat is a very personal thing. It's not at all like nonpersonal combat activities such as flying over the battlefield in an airplane and dropping a few bombs. We didn't care what blood type we were lying in, or even who provided the blood, as long as the blood wasn't our own.

Get up and keep moving. I knew I couldn't avoid the bodies, but I still tried to run without stepping on a corpse. I naturally looked for solid ground, but the trenches were so narrow that it was difficult not to step on the human remains. I kept on moving.

▶ *13 June 0059—Harry reports buildup on their left flank.*

Suddenly, I fell forward, facedown. My right foot had slipped and I went down. As I checked myself out, I found no broken bones. I looked back to see where I had stepped and noticed my right boot was covered in blood. I then realized what had thrown me. As the trenches filled with dismembered bodies, pools of blood would form quickly. Artillery explosions created clouds of dust. Then a layer of dust would form on the pool of blood. In trying to avoid slipping and sliding on the bodies, I looked for clear pieces of ground. I had apparently stepped on something now that looked like dirt, but my boot kept going down and I lost my balance and fell. I got up and looked at my wounded knee. Blood covered the bandage. I couldn't determine if the blood was from the fall or if my knee was bleeding again from my earlier wound. Nevertheless, I kept on going. Bits of flesh, dirt, blood, and mud, all intermingled, were now on much of my uniform.

When I got to the left flank, which was in the curve of the trench, I found a destroyed bunker. A machine gunner from Dog Company had already shifted his position and started shooting at the enemy.[8] Several other soldiers were wounded and moving toward the communication trench. Deciding there was nothing I could do at this location, I turned and started back to the CP.

A rain shower had started, and as I was slipping and sliding in the mud and blood back to the CP, I entered another curve in the trench. Suddenly a Chinese soldier appeared about four paces in front of me. As he walked toward me, he was looking over the top of the trench. He was carrying a burp gun in the port arms position.[9] He turned his head toward me just as I was bringing my carbine up. As he started to swing the burp gun toward me, I fired several rounds before I could shoulder my carbine. The enemy dropped in the trench. I took three or four steps toward him as fast as I could in the slippery trench. Using the carbine again, I shot him once in the head to be sure he wouldn't recover. Even after shooting him in the head, I cautiously approached him and poked him with my bayonet to be absolutely sure he was dead. We could not allow any enemy to live. A live enemy could kill someone, since our fighting was so close. We weren't willing to take a chance and shot any Chinese soldier we thought might still be alive.

The uniform he wore was different from that of any of the other Chinese soldiers I had seen, which was unusual. The Chinese did not wear any rank on their uniforms, since everyone was equal in the Communist world. All uniforms were the same. So I couldn't tell what rank he was, although I never did learn the Chinese ranks anyway. Perhaps he was a political officer. Still, his uniform seemed different—perhaps because of all the dirt and blood—so I decided to search him to see if he had anything important on him. I kneeled in the trench and went through his pockets. The only thing I found on him was a spoon. It was a little longer than one of ours and appeared to be made of solid brass. It looked like the brass from a shell casing. Strange. No pictures, no letters, nothing. No identification at all. This man (he looked Asian) died in a foreign country and none of his loved ones would ever know.[10]

As I was searching the enemy soldier, a very close incoming artillery explosion once again showered me with what felt like blowing sand. This time I could feel it peppering the back of my flak vest and my arms through my fatigue shirt.

▶ *13 June 0100—Harry reports lack of illume—Illume on the way.*

Sometime near 0110, I returned to the CP. I cleaned off some of the flesh and blood I had picked up from my fall in the trench. After searching through my pockets, I found a package of dry cigarettes. I lit up and thought about what had just happened. Trench warfare is sudden and final. Had I been careless, it would have been *my* body in the trench.

I started to pick at the small holes in my fatigue shirt and realized that the sandlike material had penetrated the shirt and entered my arms. Slivers of steel and unburned powder were in my skin. The unburned powder had not penetrated my shirt but had entered the back of my right hand. The tiny black barrels of powder had bounced off the shirt. I guess the powder hadn't been going fast enough to penetrate my fatigue shirt, but the shrapnel slivers had gone right through it.

The buildup on our left flank didn't materialize into an attack. For the last thirty minutes or so, the incoming had slackened. The rain shower I had experienced a short time earlier had started about 0100 the morning of 13 June. The shower blew through and helped to clear the air. With the flares and searchlights, we could finally see to a reasonable degree.

Just as I started to recover my nerves from having killed again, the shower quit and a sergeant came into the command post bunker. He asked me to come outside to help him determine if some people there were Chinese or American. I went with him around to the edge of the trench on the right flank and looked over. We were about 200, maybe 250, feet above the bottom of the outpost hill. The sergeant pointed out a tank that appeared to be aimed toward the Chinese Star Hill, which was a good sign. Several people were moving close to the tank. They were wearing what appeared to be ponchos, which were still glistening from the rain. I didn't believe the Chinese soldiers had ponchos as part of their equipment. After a few minutes of watching, I told the sergeant not to shoot, because I thought they were our people, but to watch them. If they turned the tank around or the people started to climb up and shoot at us, however, he and his men should kill them. My guess was correct. The 15th Infantry Regiment After Action Report for June 1953 identified the tank as being from the 64th Tank Battalion.[11] A platoon of tanks from the 64th plus one platoon of infantry was dispatched east of Outpost Harry and operated successfully as a diversionary force.

Back in the CP, I started getting information that we were running out of water and ammo. The Able Company radio operator sent a message to Snake, who said that water and ammo would be on the way.

I went back out in the trenches to determine how we were holding up and found several soldiers, walking wounded, moving toward the Door to Hell on their way to the aid station. I chatted a few minutes with them, encouraging them to get to the aid station. The trenches were filling up with dead and offering less and less cover. I realized that we would need help soon, since I was losing too many men.

Red-hot shrapnel continued to scream through the night looking for men while thunderous explosions searched for the souls of soldiers. It was a truly horrible place to be—and there was no escape.

▶ *13 June 0130—Unknown number of CCF reported behind Harry. Request flares.*

Just as I was finishing my run through the trench and nearly back to the CP, an incoming shell hit very close to me. In fact, the concussion was so close it lifted me off the ground and threw me backward into the trench. My helmet came off, but I was able to hold on to my carbine. I lay in the trench for a few minutes, and when I finally recovered, I retrieved my helmet and staggered to the CP. My ears were ringing so loud I couldn't understand anyone. My head was hurting, but I couldn't find any wounds except for the one I'd received earlier on my knee, which was beginning to throb. It didn't look as if the knee was bleeding very much, but it was difficult to make sure because of all the mud covering me. I just sat on an ammo box and tried to regain my senses.

▶ *HQ IX Corps—13 June 0130—Estimated enemy battalion attacked the outpost.*

A major attack was starting. This was the beginning of the fourth rush by the Chinese. The shelling was so great that no one could get out of their bunkers or their fighting position.

Although I had rested for only a few minutes or so, I needed to see what was happening, so I went across the trench to the artillery OP. I had recovered some of my hearing, but my ears were still ringing. From the OP I could see that a large number of Chinese were set to start the attack again—much larger than we had seen before. All hell was breaking loose from our machine guns, rifles, and hand grenades. Someone yelled that the Chinese were in our trenches. I decided to call in VT on our position again. The noise level was so great I had to yell at the radio operator to alert Lieutenant Tolen. We would need him soon.

This attack appeared to be an entire battalion coming at us. Our defensive plan repeated itself. Their overwhelming forces again entered the trenches. Again we fought hand to hand in the trenches. Guns fired. Shells exploded. Men screamed as injury and death destroyed humans.

Lieutenant Tolen was moving his counterattack team up the trench again. As soon as the VT lifted, I went back out in the trench to round up riflemen who were under shelter in the sleeping bunkers so that we could start our counterattack from the east end of the trench. Fighting from shell holes and corners of the trench, we were able to divert the attention of the Chinese until Tolen would reach us. There were so many Chinese that I am sure some escaped, but we did kill a lot of them. This was the longest fight we had had so far, and we were all very tired afterward.

The M1 rifle had the firepower to kill at long range, whereas the carbine could not. However, the carbine had sixty rounds—thirty rounds could be fired before a soldier would have to reverse the magazines—so it was a much better weapon for close combat once the Chinese penetrated our defenses. An M1 rifle uses a clip that holds eight rounds. After those rounds have been fired, the clip ejects and the solider must insert another clip to fire his weapon. If the Chinese were too close and the soldier didn't have time to reload, he would have to rely on his bayonet to defend himself. As in World War I, if all else failed, a soldier could use his entrenching tool for close combat.

Again I called for VT, and once again the airbursts scattered shrapnel all over our position and wounded or killed anyone in our trenches.

▶ *13 June 0158—OP Harry Rpts heavy shelling.*
▶ *13 June 0159—M Co reports small arms fire on left side of Harry.*
▶ *13 June 0206—Direction of attack is from front of Harry.*
▶ *13 June 0210—Unknown number of CCF moving in CCF trenches toward Harry.*

The Chinese had a trench from Star Hill running toward Outpost Harry. This meant they could move with some cover to a position where they would start their attack.

▶ *13 June 0212—CCF 100 yds from front of Harry. All available fire being placed.*

A short time earlier we had stopped an attack and cleared the trenches. Now the Chinese were starting again, and I was becoming worried that we wouldn't be able to hold out much longer. This was the fifth major attack.

▶ *13 June 0215—Enemy attack on left flank of Harry. CCF in trenches. Unknown number of enemy on right flank. Reinforcement on way. Request maximum illumination.*

The decision I had made earlier to seal the fighting bunker doors by placing sandbags in the entrance was a good one. The Chinese again breached our defensives and ran freely down the trenches until we could respond. Without the sealed bunker entrances, a grenade launched into each bunker would stop our defense and most likely would have killed everyone before help could arrive.

▶ *13 June 0223—OP reports enemy in trenches in from sector. Request FPF and increased illumination.*

▶ *13 June 0225—OP under heavy barrage. Direct hit.*

After experiencing a very narrow escape when a shell hit within a few feet of the CP, and realizing the number of casualties we were taking, I was becoming increasingly concerned about being able to survive and hold Outpost Harry. Soon I would have no one left to fight the enemy. Apparently the senior officers monitoring the situation decided that help to defend the outpost was necessary. Another company to support Able Company received orders to move forward.

▶ *13 June 0230—2 Platoon, Co L being dispatched to reinforce. Left side is critical. All support fire is maximum.*

We had so many wounded I was told that a second personnel carrier had arrived to help transport the injured from the aid station to the MASH unit. Anyone who could possibly get down to the aid station under his own power used every effort to do so. Stretchers were necessary for the badly wounded. The medics were so busy that the walking wounded warriors volunteered to carry stretchers down the communication trench to the aid station.

▶ *13 June 0240—M39 from 2b Bn dispatched to Harry.*

Lieutenant Tolen and his team of warriors once again swept up the trenches to clean the hill. Every weapon was used in hand-to-hand combat in the trenches—bayonets, rifles as clubs, pistols and entrenching tools—anything that was available to kill the Chinese. The hand-to-hand fighting by the counterattack team cleared the trenches of any live Chinese. As the team moved toward the loop, the Chinese ran from the counterattack team. Again we trapped and killed them. The trenches were filling up again with even more dead Chinese than we had found when we first got on Harry. Our counter-attack plan worked and we restored control.

▶ *13 June 0243—Too much friendly fire in the trenches. Continue with FPF. 3rd platoon, A/5 counterattacks—reinforces Harry.*

All of a sudden all the lights went out. There were no flares or "moonbeams" (searchlights), so only the incoming artillery shells exploding gave any illumination. Along with the hand-to-hand fighting, Dog Company, 5th RCT, was firing all machine guns as fast as possible.

▶ *13 June 0245—Harry reports they are in total darkness.*

For some reason the flares all went out at the same time. The searchlights didn't do a very good job trying to shine through the great amount of dust and smoke on Harry, as they could only penetrate a short distance. The flares, on the other hand, were doing quite well. They weren't great, but they were at least good enough so that we could see and kill an attacking Chinese soldier. So with the flares out, the clouds thick, starlight weak, and moonbeams not doing much good, we were in trouble.

▶ *13 June 0249—1st and 3rd platoon of L Co arrived in the trenches at Harry.*

Company L arrived at the mess bunker some fifteen minutes after Lieutenant Tolen left leading another counterattack. Most of the trench repairs we had made were no longer functional, and several bunkers had been destroyed. The trenches were so full of dead Chinese we could hardly move.

▶ *13 June 0255—Harry requested more arty around right front and left front, more illumination.*

▶ *13 June 0301—Moonbeam ordered to shift to Harry. Harry requests more ammunition. On the way. Request add 300 yds to all concentrations.*

During every break in the action, we tried to get our wounded down the hill to the aid station. Some of the wounded Americans who could move slid down the blood-filled trenches to a place where someone would help them to the medical bunker. Armored personnel carriers picked up the wounded from the medical bunker and transported them to the aid station behind the MLR, where they would be moved on to the MASH facility. The close proximity and skill of the MASH personnel saved many soldiers who otherwise would have died.

I went into the trenches watching our wounded leaving the hill. The trenches were full of dirt, timbers, and a lot of dead soldiers.

▶ *13 June 0302—Flare ship is dropping flares. Is receiving anti-aircraft fire from Hill 478. Harry requests more ammo. On the way.*

▶ *13 June 0305—Harry requests—add 300 yards to all concentrations.*

▶ *13 June 0312—Blue 6 orders 4th platoon, A of the 5th RCT to move out across the MLR at 0330.*

The 3rd Battalion commander of the 15th Infantry Regiment ordered Able Company, 5th RCT, 4th Platoon to move onto Harry. The 60mm mortar squads had already been deployed. The order affected two squads of the 57mm recoilless rifles.

A company-size Chinese unit appeared on the right flank but were unable to get into the trenches. We weren't sure if they had left or were just laying low.

The constant firing of machine guns and rifles created a supply problem. We were getting very low on ammunition and water. I had never thought water would be such a critical need. Everyone had used all of the water in their canteens, and no refill water was available on the hill.

▶ *13 June 0315—1 additional FO team has arrived at Harry.*

▶ *13 June 0318—Reinforcements have arrived on Harry and are moving forward. Want more illumination.*

Sometime during a lull, I received a message that Lieutenant Bradbury was dead. I went to the area he had been defending, ready to find a dead officer. Instead I found the lieutenant leaning against a bunker timber, eating a can of grapefruit. He was out of water and was thirsty, so the K-ration grapefruit did the job. I told him I had received word he was dead and asked him what happened.

Twenty to twenty-five dead Chinese lay in the trench area where Lieutenant Bradbury was standing. He said one of the Chinese lying in the trench wasn't dead and rose up with a burp gun. The lieutenant noticed the movement just as the Chinese soldier fired his burp gun. The soldier missed, and Lieutenant Bradbury returned fire with his carbine, killing the Chinese soldier. At about the same time, an artillery shell hit nearby and knocked Lieutenant Bradbury down. Anyone seeing the sequence of events would have presumed the lieutenant was dead and contacted me. I was very happy to see him alive and well and eating grapefruit. He was an excellent officer.

Lieutenant Bradbury and I used our .45-caliber pistols to be sure no other live Chinese soldiers were lying in the trench. In trench warfare the philosophy of taking care of a wounded enemy doesn't apply. In a trench, the enemy wounded is too close and just waiting to kill you if possible. When the enemy is dead, he can't hurt you.

▶ *13 June 0325—CCF on right, left and front of Harry. Trenches are being cleaned.*

To clean the trenches we would toss all of the dead Chinese over the forward side toward the barbed wire along with any large body parts. The next step was to throw out any boulders and loose timbers. Finally, we would make a quick dig with a trench knife, bayonet, or entrenching tool. We couldn't spend a lot of time working on cleaning the trenches, since the shelling was still incoming.

▶ *13 June 0328—Harry requests have another group bring more ammo. Receiving AW fire from left rear. Also need more illumination.*

I left the CP and went out in the trench to determine the progress of the cleaning effort. My right knee was now hurting so bad when I bent it that I could hardly walk. It must have been worse than I thought. My body was telling me I had a problem—well, just one of many problems.

▶ *13 June 0340—Harry reports CCF still on hill but exact whereabouts unknown.*

▶ *13 June 0345—AW fire from left front, arty notified.*

About 0350 I returned to the command post. A soldier rushed in and told me that some American soldiers were in the trench. I quickly left the CP to find out what was happening. I found some twenty live American soldiers lying facedown in the trench. I will never forget the view—men in clean green fatigues lying on top of body parts and against the dark, blood-soaked ground. I had to jump over some soldiers and step around others to get to the front of the group. I didn't want to step on them, but the trench was narrow and it was difficult *not* to step on them.

I asked who was in charge, and a lieutenant said he was there to help us save the hill. He was ready to take command of Outpost Harry. I became very angry. To paraphrase, I said, "I don't need any goddamn help. I am still commanding this hill. Who in the hell told you to take over my command? I am the commanding officer here."

He said he was with Love Company of the 15th Infantry Regiment and had been ordered to defend the outpost. I said, "Good. Get your men under cover in case I call VT in again. Don't forget, I'm still in command of this hill, and as long as I live on this hill, you will follow my orders."

Able Company had gone through hell for nearly twenty-four hours, and I wasn't about to give up command of Outpost Harry. We had defeated thousands of Chinese, and this was *our* hill. I had told Colonel Wheeler that I would "hold at all costs," and I still had a lot of holding to do.

The lieutenant said he would get his people under cover but that they couldn't leave the hill until daylight. I told him I understood but that he should get his men into fighting positions. If the CCF launched another attack, I wanted everybody under cover. I left them lying in the trench and returned to the command post.

On my way back to the command post I noticed a GI lying in the trench on his stomach with his feet toward me. As I approached, he looked okay. He was still wearing his flak vest, and his uniform didn't look torn up. I kneeled down to see if he was all right or needed some help. I put my hand on his left shoulder and pulled him up. He didn't have a head. I didn't vomit. I was becoming immune—hardened—heartless.

Incoming artillery fire was constant, and our warriors were still shooting back. The flare-dropping airplane was still flying in circles, but it wasn't dropping as many flares as it had before. I guess the pilot could see the daylight from where he was and could see that there were no waves of Chinese coming at us. Apparently he had decided to save his flares for another night. Still, the airplane was flying around and the searchlights were still blazing.

▶ *13 June 0350—Debriefing of wounded man. States that at 0310 there were 200 CCFs on the front slope and in the trenches. That friendly troops were pushing them out.*

▶ *13 June 0352—Forward trenches are secured. No CCF in them.*

▶ *13 June 0356—3d BN requested from 15th Inf. Need translation in Chinese for "I want you to surrender."*

▶ *13 June 0358—All counter battery and counter mortar fire is being directed on the right flank of Harry.*

▶ *13 June 0412 and 0415—More illumination needed.*

▶ *HQ IX Corps, June 1953—Outpost Harry secure at 0420.*

▶ *13 June 0420—Firing outer protective fires for Harry to catch withdrawing CCF.*

▶ *13 June 0425—CCF are withdrawing to Star Hill and Star Ridge, arty and mortar fired.*

▶ *13 June 0450—Harry requests reinforcements, medicine, litters, litter bearers and M39s [an armored utility vehicle]. All CCF off Harry. Co C/5th RCT placed under operational control of Kingpost by Kaiser 5.[12]*

▶ *13 June 0455—Harry is getting heavy arty and mortar fire. Request FPF and counter fire.*

I was surprised that we were receiving so much heavy incoming artillery from the Chinese. The rate was similar to the preamble to their other attacks. Returning to the FA observation post, I realized that the sun was finally bringing first light. However, I also observed that what appeared to be a company-size Chinese unit was making a last attempt to take Harry.

▶ *13 June 0458—CCF attacking OP Harry. OP Harry requests Final Protective fires, Counter-Battery and Counter-Mortar. Arty has complied.*

This was the last attack. The Chinese didn't push this attack and withdrew after the artillery soaked them. I believed that if they tried to attack again, we wouldn't be able to stop them. They would surely overrun us again, and I had no counterattack force left to fight. We had too many wounded, we were out of ammo, and our weapons were burned out. I had to let battalion know of our situation.

▶ *13 June 0501—Harry requests immediate reinforcement. All their weapons are in bad shape.*

A large-caliber machine gun off to our left kept on firing after most of the other enemy guns had begun slowing down. I called in a request to take the gun out. I don't think the artillery could find him, and we couldn't pinpoint his location. A 75mm recoilless rifle remaining on the MLR finally killed the enemy.

▶ *13 June 0502—Arty instructed to revert to normal rate of fire.*
▶ *13 June 0505—1st BN/5th RCT is alerted and ready to move out.*

Finally, the 555th forward artillery observer assigned to Able Company sent the "end of mission" order.

▶ *13 June 0515—Cease fire, end of mission given by OP Harry.*
▶ *13 June 0528—CCF on Bunker Hill [Hill 533] arty laid on.*

Daylight started breaking shortly after the group from Love Company, 15th Infantry, had arrived on site. I'm not sure what happened to them or when they left the hill. The lieutenant never reported his activities to me, but I guessed that by daylight L Company/15th, was ready to leave. I didn't blame them a bit. I was also ready to leave but had not been properly relieved of responsibility for the hill.

▶ *13 June 0602—Lt Summers reports he is wounded and reorganization on OP Harry is very good.*
▶ *13 June 0625—Everything is quiet on Harry.*
▶ *13 June 0632—C/5th RCT had not departed MLR.*
▶ *13 June 0655—One slightly wounded PW on way from Harry to Blue CP.*
▶ *13 June 0756—Two platoons from C Company, 5th RCT close on OP Harry.*
▶ *13 June 0816—Approximately 100 WIA had been processed by 3rd Bn aid station since 2400.*

I knew that Able Company and its attachments had suffered many casualties, but I didn't know the count. We had started the defense with two platoons (aproximately 85 men) from Able Company, two sections from the Dog Company machine-gun platoon, and a headquarter group including the 555th FO team, for a total of 120 men. When Lieutenant Tolen counterattacked, an additional 35 men were on the hill for a short while. Until the Love Company/15th unit arrived, we defended the hill with some 120 to 150 men; afterward nearly 190 men were involved. As reported above, the aid station processed 100 wounded. Most were 5th RCT personnel. Very possibly some of the 100 treated were men from Love Company/15th.

▶ *13 June 0843—All wounded are off Harry.*

▶ *13 June 1300—Estimated enemy force of one reinforced regiment attacked OP Harry during the night 12–13 June. Total incoming rounds [from 1800 on the 12th to 0600 on the 13th] 14,000 mixed mortar and artillery.*

The rate of incoming mortar and artillery fire as reported here for a period of twelve hours is 1,166 rounds per hour, or 19.44 per minute, or one round every 0.32 seconds.

Note: The above description of the battle in the trenches for Outpost Harry does not include several additional combat encounters I experienced. Obviously, in each case I prevailed; however, including descriptions of these additional engagements would add nothing to the historical account of hand-to-hand combat in trench war. For more information on the defense of Outpost Harry, official report excerpts can be found in the "Reports" section at the end of this book.

12

Relief from Hell

Three Days before Operation Ranger

The sun was shining brightly and the heat index was rising. In the early morning of 13 June 1953, an advance team from Charley Company, 5th RCT, came into the command post on Outpost Harry and told me they were starting the relief. I was happy to see them and knew their company commander would soon be on site to relieve me.

"Make your way around the hill, and if you think of anything I can do to help you, just let me know. You can keep all of the machine guns if you want them," I told the advance party.

I could hardly stay awake but was determined to walk off Outpost Harry. A medic cleaned and bandaged my knee wound, which was becoming very sore. The medic said it was looking good even after getting covered with all the mud and blood I had fallen into. I didn't care how my knee looked. It hurt.

When CPT John Porter, the commanding officer of Charley Company, came into the CP about 1230 hours, I was sitting on an ammo box. I rose, saluted, and shook his hand. Captain Porter told me he was to take command of Outpost Harry. We chatted for a few minutes, and then I thanked him and wished him good luck. I saluted the captain, gathered up my carbine and helmet, and looked around to see if there was anything I wanted to take with me, but there was nothing I wanted to take except my radio operator and myself.[1]

However, there were some things I had no choice but to take with me: memories of the horror that I had just experienced. Diving into a trench filled with human body parts. Dirt and blood on my uniform and on my hands and face. The eyes of the Chinese soldiers I had killed. And how could I ever forget the American soldier lying in the trench with no head? These and all the other moments of horror I had just experienced went with me when I left Outpost Harry. Although I didn't realize it at the time, I was taking Outpost Harry and all of its images of hell with me for the rest of my life.

I was extremely tired, but my exhaustion didn't prevent me from leaving the command post, finding my way to the top of the trench leading off the hill, and walking away from the nightmare of Outpost Harry. For the last time, my radio operator and I went slipping and sliding over the human body parts, stepping into or around the pools of blood, smelling the stench of burned flesh from red-hot artillery shrapnel, and seeing bodies already swelling. Once we made our way to the ammo bunker at the top of the communication trench and started down the hill, we began moving faster and faster. Finally, we broke into a full run and got off that hill as fast as we could. I don't even remember my knee hurting as we ran off the "Home of Death."

Walking back on the same road that Able Company had taken some thirty-four hours earlier, we passed the aid station, which was full of wounded and dying Americans. We stopped and looked to see if anyone we knew was there. However, we were so tired that we were numb and didn't recognize anyone. We walked around the series of small hills where we had seen the body of the soldier destroyed by the APC, crossed the trail where the rockets had been firing, and finally reached the dismount area. It seemed as if it had been a long, long time ago that we had first traveled this path to get up to Harry.

As soon as we reached the dismount area, someone told me that Colonel Wheeler, the regimental commander, wanted to see me for a short debriefing. I made my way to the 5th RCT headquarters. Colonel Wheeler greeted me with a warm welcome, and the other staff members were very happy to see me. They asked me a few questions and then dismissed me so that I could get some rest.

As I was leaving, Colonel Wheeler stopped me. He told me he was very proud of me and said he would recommend me for the Distinguished Service Cross. Colonel Wheeler's recommending me for any medal meant a lot. Earning the respect of a soldier who had risked his life to visit and encourage me on Outpost Harry was very important to me.[2] I thanked him, but I was too tired to understand and fully appreciate the significance of his remarks. In fact, when I left the 5th RCT headquarters tent, I was just too tired to go on to our Able Company area. I looked around and found an indentation in the ground. The shallow trench looked like someone had tried to dig a slit trench (foxhole) to use in case of incoming artillery. Whoever had made the effort to dig the foxhole hadn't done a good job, but it was good enough for me. My feet and head would be outside, but the rest of me would fit in the shallow trench. Just as I started to lie down in the trench, a soldier walked over to me. He identified himself as a reporter from the *Stars and Stripes* newspaper and said he wanted to ask me some questions. The reporter asked if I had been on Outpost Harry. I answered in the affirmative. Then he asked if I could describe what had happened on Harry, what the battlefield looked like, and how many Americans were killed. The last thing in the world I wanted right then was to give an interview. Perhaps if I had created a ghastly scene for him, told him about the hundreds of Chinese I had personally killed, and that I was the only one still alive from Able Company he would have written a great story. Maybe the story would have appeared worldwide and I would be famous today. However, I was so tired I could hardly talk. I was very short with him.

"If you want to know what happened and what Harry looks like, climb up the trench and take a look around. You'll have a good view of hell," I said as I lay down in the slit trench and put my helmet over my face to keep the sun out.

The reporter grunted and left. I'm sure he didn't get close to the trench going to the top of Outpost Harry.

I went to sleep. I had been up for fifty-four hours, used every drop of energy in my body, and needed some sleep. Sleep. Anywhere, under any condition. I woke up after an hour or so, because a two-and-a-half-ton truck drove very close to where I was sleeping. The noise and ground shaking broke through my haze. I was hungry and realized I hadn't eaten for some time. In addition, I was sore, every muscle ached, and I was still tired. Slowly, very slowly, I made my way back to Able Company, 5th RCT, looking for some food.

My reunion with Sergeant Shinault, Lieutenant Tolen, and the other survivors was a happy and emotional event. We talked in disbelief about how any of us had gotten off Outpost Harry alive; we were wounded but not seriously. I ate some food, climbed into a bunk, and went to sleep.

On the morning of 14 June, Sergeant Shinault woke me with the message that our replacements had arrived, most likely from the 3rd Division replacement company, where soldiers arriving from the United States were reassigned to units. I got up and went outside to greet the men who would be replacing those we lost while defending Outpost Harry.[3] A formation of about 35 soldiers was standing outside the bunker, and I was very happy to see them. I knew we had lost some men but not how many. Able Company had 17 and Dog Company had 4 enlisted men known to be killed in action and some 100 wounded. Many from both companies had received serious wounds, although

25. Spent shell casings in the defense of Outpost Harry by the 555 Artillery Battalion. (Photo courtesy of U.S. Department of Defense.)

some not so seriously as to require hospitalization. Three officers had been wounded, but none of the officers from Able or Dog Company were killed.

Approximately 125 soldiers (including the counterattack team) from Able Company were on Outpost Harry, of which some 80–90 percent had been killed or wounded. The official IX Corps report for the period of 1200 hours 12 June until 1200 hours 13 June was 24 killed, and 161 wounded.[4] The report included all units involved, such as the 10th Combat Engineers, 3rd Infantry Division; 555th Field Artillery Forward Observers; Love Company, 15th Infantry Division; 3rd Signal Company; and the 15th Infantry Tank Company.

It's typical protocol for the company commander to greet new members to his company—Able Company, in my case—and I did so. I told them they were joining the very best infantry company in the U.S. Army. The men they were joining had just completed a battle like no other and were now considered warriors. I explained that a "soldier" is someone who serves in an army or other military service; a "warrior" is someone who fights or is experienced in warfare. I explained that the men in Able Company were definitely "warriors," not "soldiers," and that they should be extremely proud to be associated with the

26. 1LT James Evans on the morning of 14 June 1953, showing "combat eyes," a swollen face, looking very tired, and aged many years in just 35 hours of combat on Outpost Harry. (Photo courtesy of the author.)

warriors of Able Company, 5th RCT. Suddenly overcome emotionally, I started to choke up and had to quit talking. I ordered Sergeant Shinault to assign the men as needed and get them settled.

Charley Company, 5th RCT, relieved Able Company, 5th RCT, and assumed responsibility for the defense of Outpost Harry on 13 June 1953. The night of 13-14 June, about 0255, enemy artillery and mortar fire preceded a CCF screening action against the outpost for recovering CCF dead. By 0440 the enemy withdrew. Charley Company remained on position until 1530 14 June. At that time, George Company, 15th Infantry Regiment, assumed responsibility for Outpost Harry. During the night of 14–15 June, about 0125, the Chinese, moving through friendly defensive fires, gained the trenches and a hand-to-hand fight ensued. At 0222, friendly forces held the outpost, and at 0345 the enemy withdrew. Able Company, 15th Infantry, replaced George Company of the 15th.

The Graves Registration Office (GRO) asked Lieutenant Tolen to appear at the collection point to identify any 5th RCT KIAs. Lieutenant Tolen would walk through the dead and point out those who had been with us. When asked how he knew the man was from the 5th RCT even when he couldn't see the soldier's face, the lieutenant replied that all 5th RCT soldiers had short haircuts. Outpost Harry survivor Charlie Scott, 15th Infantry Regiment, saw a picture in a newspaper and realized that he was the soldier standing on the left while working for the GRO (see fig. 27). He wrote a letter to the Associated Press in New York requesting a copy of the picture. API sent him a copy along with the following:

KOREAN WAR CHINESE © DEAD
SWEERS STAFFING
WITH THIRD DIVISION ON WESTX CENTRAL FRONT JUNE 12
md Tokyo 13/6/53

GIs of the 3rd Division check over the mass of bodies of dead Chinese at a forward aid station on the west central front after they were killed during an attack on Outpost Harry June 12. A Chinese division trying for three straight nights to win Outpost Harry has lost 3,500 killed and wounded by estimate of the regimental commander fighting them.

WIREPHOTOED FX1 6-13-53

Note the date of 13 June 1953. That was our night on Harry. The photo shows the result of our fight.

Able Company, 5th RCT, devoted 14 and 15 June to determining if anyone still needed medical treatment, rewrapping bandages, and checking for infections. Wounds were festering in my arms, neck, and the tops of my thighs from tiny splinters of steel shrapnel. Neither the medic nor I were able to dig out some of the deeply embedded slivers. The medic told me that they would either work their way to my heart and kill me, or out through the tips of my fingers and toes. I believe most of the slivers came out of my fingers and toes, but many remain in my body.

Unburned powder, which looks like very small black barrels, had hit my fatigue shirt, but penetrated my skin only where my uniform hadn't covered me—the backs of my hands and my neck. I found some fifty of these little holes from which the medic and I dug out the little black barrels.

The two-inch-long cut on my right knee where shrapnel had hit was festering and still sore but didn't require stitches, according to the company medic.

27. Enemy killed the night of 12–13 June 1953 on Outpost Harry. Company A and its attachments defended Harry that night. (Photo courtesy of Charles Scott, Department of Defense photograph.)

The medic said the wound was too wide for stitches and that since the cut was on the top of my knee, it would heal better without stitches. In any case, he said he would watch it closely, and if the healing were not progressing he would send me to MASH for stitches. I guess wallowing around in the mud and blood in the trench neither helped nor hurt my injuries. Our medic took good care of us, cleaning our wounds and putting medication on them to prevent infections.

A major effort undertaken by Able Company was determining which equipment needed repairing, replacing, or cleaning. Sergeant Shinault prepared an after-action report on lost equipment. I recall the list of these losses as being several pages, and I was responsible for all of them. The list included machine guns, rifles, and similar equipment, and I think the list also included a jeep and a tank. I didn't believe those two items would pass the S-4's (the supply officer's) records, but I left them as well as some other questionable losses on the list and signed the combat loss report. The total loss value was approximately eighty-three thousand dollars. I sure was hoping the S-4 would accept the report and not charge me for the losses, and I guess he did accept it, as I never heard anything more about it.[5]

The night of 15–16 June, was quiet on Outpost Harry. The following morning the Greek battalion assumed responsibility for defending the outpost. During the night of 16–17 June, no significant action occurred on the outpost, which permitted engineers to accomplish rebuilding efforts.

On 16 June, three days after Charley Company had relieved Able Company from Outpost Harry, I reported to the 5th RCT 1st Battalion headquarters. I learned that Able Company had another mission, named "Operation Ranger," a plan to send combat engineers from the 10th Combat Engineer Battalion to clear antitank mines from an abandoned railroad track bed.[6] The track bed, which ran through a rice paddy, would provide a safe path that would support tanks. Tanks from the 64th Tank Battalion, 3rd Infantry Division, would then use the cleared track bed to position themselves behind Jackson Heights. From a position in the rear of Jackson Heights, the tanks could fire directly into the enemy artillery positions on Star Hill. Able Company's responsibility would be to protect the combat engineers while they looked for mines.

The Chinese artillery firing positions were located on the reverse slope of a mountain facing us. Imagine a hill with a front and a back. The gun positions were on the side of the hill away from the enemy, which was known as the "back side" of the mountain. Other than an air strike, the only way to destroy the guns positioned in a dugout on this rear slope would be to attack those emplacements with a direct-fire weapon. Therefore, the plan was to use a tank. If the tank was in the proper position, its 90mm cannon could fire a flat-trajectory shell directly into the side of the mountain where the enemy artillery batteries were positioned. By shooting into the rear of Jackson Heights and Star Hill, the tanks could do some real damage to the Chinese artillery. The plan was to check the elevated railroad bed for land mines and other dangers and then have a tank or tanks move directly behind Star Hill. The tanks would have to travel about one and a half to two miles.

I decided to lead the Able Company protection team for the engineer screening operation, and Lieutenant Tolen was to stay behind and take charge of the rest of the company. The lieutenant wanted to go along, but he had to stay and be responsible for the rest of the company. Besides, I never asked a soldier to do anything I wouldn't do. Since screening for engineers was a new type of assignment for us, I thought that my leading the first screening mission would be best.

I determined that a platoon would be the appropriate size for the protection team, and the combat engineers had decided on a platoon-size unit of fifty men for the mine-clearing team, so together we had a force of just over one hundred men. A screening force of some fifty soldiers was bound to make some noise. I instructed our team to do some basic sound reduction, but we didn't have the tape we needed to do a good job.[7] Nevertheless, we left the safety of our trenches—the main line of resistance—at about 2100 hours, dusk, and headed out onto the railroad bed.

I placed one squad to lead the group, one squad to be the rear guard, and one squad on each side of the mine-removal team. The engineers spread out and started down the railroad bed probing with bayonets and waving magnetic disks just above the ground looking for mines. When a mine was located, a marker would show the location and we would continue walking around the engineers who were dismantling the mine. The extracted mines were about twenty-four to twenty-six inches in diameter and twelve inches tall. The combat engineers said they were antitank mines and that if we happened to step on one, it wouldn't explode, as our weight wasn't sufficient to set off the mine. Of course, none of us believed the engineers.

The "find and remove" procedure continued for several hours as the 10th Combat Engineers kept finding mines. Everyone worked as quietly as possible. I was sure the Chinese must have heard us, though, since digging for mines is not a quiet business. We searched the tracks for mines covering over a mile and were nearly across the valley. At approximately 0145 hours, I decided we had to start our return to our trenches or end up in the sunlight, in the middle of the valley, on top of a railroad bed—not a good place to be in the daylight. However, the engineers kept finding more and more mines. They wanted to stay until they found all of them, and I agreed. We might not have a choice.

We set a time limit for finding and clearing the mines—the limit was sunrise. At about 0330 I knew we had to start back even if the engineers found ten more mines. We had no choice. At the rate they were finding mines, the Chinese must have placed scores of them. We decided that enough mines were on the railroad bed to keep us digging for a week. The sun would rise around 0430 and we were a long way from home. Finally, at about 0400 hours, everyone agreed we had to start back whether more mines remained or not. We were so late starting back now that to reach the safety of the trenches before sunrise would be impossible. Regardless, we started back, moving as quickly and as quietly as we could.

Suddenly we heard gunfire! I couldn't tell whether it was coming from the screening team or from a Chinese gun. We all dropped to our knees for a few seconds, but then all was quiet. I guess the Chinese had decided not to pursue us after all. The shots could have been test shots from the Chinese or an accident from one of us. We were dispersed pretty well, so I couldn't be sure. I ordered everyone to get up and moving. We must return to our lines before the sun got too high and too bright. But we were only about halfway back to the relative safety of our trenches when the sun started breaking the night. We still had a long way to go.

However, that day, for the first time I could ever recall, a heavy, dense, picturesque fog had spread over the ground. The sun coming through the fog created a beautiful, shimmering light. The fog dampened all sounds, helping the soldiers to walk silently. No additional shots were fired. All was quiet except for an occasional cough. We kept moving, as quietly and as quickly as we could. What we were seeing was beautiful beyond belief. Our wonderful fog must be a miracle. This was the first fog in the valley for weeks—in fact, I had never before seen one in the valley. We looked at one another and nodded. I'm sure many others were praying with me, thanking God for what he was doing and asking him to keep the fog around for a little longer. We continued walking back toward our trenches hastily while praying we could reach safety without any more shooting or trouble.

We entered the trenches at about 0735, and everyone gave us a big welcome. Well, not really a big welcome. I've never seen a "big welcome" in an infantry line unit. A pat on the back, a handshake, a sincere smile, and a "Glad you got back safely" were the most I've ever seen. Anyway, I felt like we received a big welcome.

Just as we were returning, we could hear the tanks warming up and starting out. The fog eventually lifted at about 1015 hours. We were thankful.

The morning of 17 June found the mess sergeant up and cooking, so we all had a good late breakfast. I dismissed all members of the screening group, and we headed for our bunks for some sleep around 0815. A short time after noon someone woke me and told me that the first tank to go out hadn't done too well. The tank had made it nearly to the point where we had decided to start back, but then it hit a mine, blowing off one of its treads.

I got up, dressed, and learned that Major MacLane was on his way to get me. As I was eating lunch, the major, our operational officer, picked me up in his jeep and told me what we were going to do. As he described the situation, the 64th Tank Battalion had sent out a tank retriever to get the one with the blown treads. But the tank retriever had to stay on the railroad bed, because in the summer the rice paddies on either side of it were several feet deep. I understood that a tank couldn't operate in much mud and water.

Since the tank retriever was unable to move the damaged tank, our 1st Battalion commander, LTC James Richardson, decided to send Able Company back out. We were to return to the area of the damaged tank with a force of two platoons and set up a perimeter of defense around the tank. We would have to stay out all night to keep the Chinese from taking the 90mm cannon, gun sight, and radios as well as all of the ammunition. Battalion scheduled another attempt to save the tank the next morning.

I couldn't believe the plan. As I rode in the jeep with Major MacLane, I spoke as fast as I could to sell him on the idea that Able Company shouldn't be the one to go back out and spend another night on the tracks. Finally, he agreed and said he would get someone else. *Thanks, Lord.* I returned to the Able Company area after Major MacLane dismounted at the 1st Battalion headquarters. Later in the day I learned that a decision had been made to blow the tank's tube (its 90mm gun); take out the gun sight, radios, and ammo; and let the tank remain where it was.

Some forty years later, I found out from CPT John Porter that what I've described here about the tank mission isn't quite what really happened. According to the captain, after Able Company escaped from the tank protection scheme, he learned that Charley Company, 5th RCT, his company, was to be the tank protector. Captain Porter thought everyone involved was crazy, and he refused to take the risk of losing many people for an inert tank. He had been in the army for some time and wasn't as timid as were we first lieutenants. Porter went directly to COL Lester Wheeler, the commanding officer of the 5th RCT, and explained the situation. Captain Porter told me that Lieutenant Colonel Richardson had been relieved of command and that the tank would sit where it was damaged unless someone came along and turned it into scrap.

I recently discovered that both John Porter and I were wrong about some of the tank attack facts. The declassified 3rd Infantry Division Report for June 1953 tells what really happened with Operation Ranger: "The 64th Tank Battalion conducted operation RANGER on 170725I June 53. The mission of this force was to move up the CHORWON Valley to Hill 317 vicinity CT469443 and fire into the rear of the enemy positions. Approximately 800 yards forward of the MBP [main battle position], five tanks were disabled by enemy mines. Recovery work was hindered by continous shelling and additional mines. Two tanks were destroyed and seven damaged."[8] The report doesn't speak well of our screening efforts.

When I returned to the company area after my jeep ride with the S-3, a strange sight greeted me. Outpost Harry was distant, yet visible, from our reserve camp. Something was happening to the top of Harry. A large black column of smoke was rising from the bunker line on the outpost. The Greek battalion was now responsible for the defense of Outpost Harry. A telephone call to battalion revealed the secret.

The defense of Outpost Harry had started on the night of 10–11 June when King Company, 15th Infantry, was defending it. Since then the body parts of more than twelve hundred dead Chinese soldiers were spread all over the top of Outpost Harry, which was only one hundred yards by thirty yards. Seven days in the sun had accelerated the decomposition of the bodies and body parts, and the resulting odor was overwhelming.

The Greek soldiers couldn't live in such an environment, so they had carried heating oil to the top of the outpost. They poured the oil in the trenches, on the bunkers, in front of the trenches on the barbed wire, and anywhere else they found decaying body parts. Then they burned the top of Outpost Harry.

On the night of 17–18 June, Peter Company of the Greek battalion was defending Outpost Harry. The Chinese attacked at about 0052 and the enemy was repelled. At 0240 on 18 June, the Chinese attacked and gained the trenches. Bitter hand-to-hand combat ensued and the enemy was repulsed again. Companies Nan and Oboe of the Greek battalion were committed to reinforce, and the Greeks successfully defended the outpost.

The siege of Outpost Harry ended with the attack of 17–18 June against the Greek battalion. The Chinese only used probes after the eighteenth.[9] On 20 June the 5th RCT received orders to move to the 8th Army Reserve, which had been relocated in an assembly area near Chipo-Ri.

Able Company, 5th Infantry Regiment, 5th RCT, and its attachments had defended Outpost Harry on 12–13 June. A week or so after my experiences on Outpost Harry, I was relieved of my command by CPT Hugh P. Shaw, who was a replacement just arriving in Korea. After Captain Shaw replaced me, the army didn't have a position for me. Knowing that with thirty-six points I would be rotating back to the United States within a few days, the S-1 created a temporary position appointing me as the assistant battalion executive officer.

The men of Able Company would be heading for reserve, where the doctrine was rest, reconstituion, and training. Nearby there happened to be a valley between two ridges that was arranged perfectly for a training exercise on attacking a village. The hills formed a U. I recommended a demonstration of a squad in the attack down the valley. My guess was that 95 percent of the men in the 1st Battalion had already been in defensive (trench) combat. But most likely only 5 percent had even been in an attack. The live-fire demonstration I prepared would show how an attack on a village should be conducted with ap-

Table 1. Action for the Defense of Outpost Harry

	UN Forces		Chinese Forces	
	KIA	WIA	KIA	WIA
10–11 June	9	153	500	1,000
11–12 June	22	186	180	400
12–13 June	**24**	**161**	**500**	**1,000**
13–14 June	0	9	10	90
17–18 June	4	25	120	480

Source: HQ IX Corps Command Report, June 1953.

propriate attack techniques—supporting fire, alternating attack and cover, and so forth.

An old Korean hut was located at the top of the U (the end of the valley), which would be our target. The remaining parts of the battalion positioned themselves along the ridges to observe the action. Arranging two .30-caliber heavy machine guns positioned at the bottom of the U and a 60mm mortar just to the rear, we were ready for the demonstration. To provide some protection to the attacking squad, steel wire posts were placed under the barrels so that the guns couldn't be deflected. Using live mortar rounds, the demonstration started. A squad commanded by 1LT William Bradbury left our simulated MLR and moved down the valley to attack the hut. The two machine guns started firing in support of the attack, and the squad advanced. It was a great show, and Lieutenant Bradbury did a great job leading his squad.

In early July I received orders releasing me from the 5th RCT and ordering me to Inchon, Korea, for a boat ride home. With many good and bad memories, I departed from my home with the 5th Infantry Regiment. I considered extending my tour, because I had a great affection for the 5th RCT—I felt that I was part of it and that it was part of me. However, my overall plan was to become a Regular Army officer, and to do so would require a four-year college degree. If I left Korea in July, I should be able to enroll in a college in September. Thus, my decision to return to the States.

Several days of waiting were required while the tide rose to the correct height so that we could be loaded onto a transport ship for home. After we left Inchon and entered the Pacific Ocean, we learned that the Chinese had just made a major push and overrun a South Korean division. The 5th RCT 555th Field Artillery Battalion (105mm), which was supporting the Republic of Korea 9th Division, had been caught in a trap when the Korean division was unable to stop the Chinese. Firing the 105 howitzers at zero deflection couldn't prevent the Chinese from overrunning the 555th and killing many good men. The loss of life of the 555th Field Artillery Battalion was a terrible event of suffering—two killed in action, twenty missing in action (presumed dead), nineteeen wounded in action, and forty-six taken as prisoners of war. Only two weeks later—27 July 1953—and the war would be over.

The ship's radio kept us advised as to what was happening. Of course, a rumor started that our ship was to return to Inchon and that we would return to our units. The first thing everyone on the ship did each day was to be sure we were still heading toward the sun rising in the east.

San Francisco, California, looked good. We were home and greeted by an eight-piece navy band. No ticker tape. I was proud to have helped the Korean people so that they could live in a free country. They were hardworking and industrious. However, the smell of "home" was a lot better than that of Korea.

13
Coming Home
The Trauma of Returning to Civilian Life

In the preface to this book, I wrote that I would explain how I survived after living through the hell of Outpost Harry. So how did I survive? *By using the wrong approach.*

After leaving the 5th RCT in July 1953, I took a boat trip of fourteen days, and suddenly I was back in the United States. I was welcomed home by my family. The only souvenir I brought home from my combat experiences was the long spoon I had discovered on the Chinese soldier I killed in the trenches on Outpost Harry. I thought the spoon was unique since it was the only item the Chinese soldier had in his possession.

A month later I was in a classroom at Memphis State College, in Memphis, Tennessee. A friend I had known before I went into the service asked me where I had been, saying he hadn't seen me lately. I looked at him and thought, *If you only had any idea where I've been and what I've been doing, you wouldn't ask the question. If I told you what I've done, you wouldn't believe trench warfare. How can I describe hell to you?* But instead I said something similar to "Oh, I went in the army and just got out. Been traveling some but happy to get back home."

I was living at home instead of in the quarters at Memphis State. My family soon recognized that I had problems that I was unaware of. For example, one day my sister, Martha, four years my junior, walked up to me from behind when I was looking into our refrigerator in the kitchen. Suddenly I whirled, hitting her across the room. She was shocked, surprised, and scared. Of course, I apologized and tried to explain that I wasn't used to being out of the army. For an instant it seemed I had been back in the trenches feeling a gun in my

28. Evans showing his parents the spoon taken from the body
of a dead Chinese soldier. (Photo courtesy of the author.)

back. As I had killed with my bayonet, my reaction to protect myself was fast
and beyond my control.

Many more traumatic experiences, some actually dangerous, have occurred
that have required my maximum self-control. For years I have had terrible
dreams that I can't even try to describe. My wonderful wife, Anne, has put up
with all of my behavior in nightmares, including my leaping out of bed, yelling, and destroying lamps. And after experiencing my reaction to her when she
surprised me a few times, she is still very careful to make her presence known
before approaching me when my back is turned.

I had once been a sweet and lovable twenty-year-old Christian man, and
the army had converted me into a one-time warrior. (However, I'm sure that if
they hadn't converted me, I wouldn't be writing this book today.) I had needed
all of my combat leadership, skill, training, and the hand of God to survive

the Punch Bowl and the horror of Outpost Harry. But now I slowly realized that I had to control my feelings and explosive behavior and reduce the terror and images in my life. Otherwise I would do something I would regret forever. My technique, which I don't recommend, was to mentally block out, suppress, and ignore the horrible things I had seen and done. For the next forty years, I didn't discuss the Punch Bowl or Outpost Harry with anyone—not while I was in the Army Reserve or at any military meeting. I knew I had a very strong will and could control any problem as long as I could control the images. I didn't go to VFW or American Legion meetings or visit their bars, because the people I met at these places hadn't seen the kind of combat I had experienced; they hadn't personally faced the enemy and couldn't understand what I lived through. Of course, neither did I understand whatever trauma they had experienced.

Being in a battle zone doesn't necessarily mean the person was in combat. In conversation with some of the veterans I met, as our discussion progressed I would realize that the person I was talking with wasn't really a combat veteran but rather a war zone veteran. The percentage of service personnel who actually participate in combat is relatively small, because so many more people are required to support military actions. My communication with most veterans regarding war participation gradually began to decline. If I were going to discuss combat, I needed to talk with people who had experienced something at least similar to me. If they had not actually experienced close combat, then at least they had seen or understood what I had experienced.

Truthfully, the main reason I avoided these situations of comradeship with fellow veterans was that I didn't want to relive some of my experiences. I had to leave them locked up. So I withdrew. I learned that whenever the images came through, it was best to concentrate on another subject to help the images retreat.

What happened to me since leaving the army is an example of the downside of the conversion from civilian to warrior. I have experienced instances when only with intense, immediate self-control did I avoid doing some terrible things to others. I thank God for intervening and stopping my military reflex. I reacted as trained, but His influence on my inner self stopped me before I destroyed others and myself. Until I started meeting with counselors from the U.S. Department of Veterans Affairs (VA), I didn't understand why I sometimes acted the way I did.

Although I had occasionally hunted rabbits before I went into the army, I have never been hunting since my experiences in Korea. After having tracked humans who would shoot back, tracking a deer in the woods just didn't seem like a very exciting sport to me. If I did hunt and kill, would I lose what civility I have gained since Korea? I'm afraid the feelings, images, and memories that the death, blood, and destruction of the sport would arouse are things I don't want. Although at the time, being a ruthless warrior was what I needed to be to stay alive, I had retrained myself and didn't want to revert.

When I was discharged from the army, no military procedure existed called "counseling" or "debriefing." As I transitioned from Outpost Harry in Korea to the classroom in Memphis, I had no idea that I had suffered a mental injury from the combat in which I had participated. In retrospect, I now realize that I was injured mentally as well as physically. And I am still affected.

Since 1995, when I started counseling and had contact with other combat veterans, I have learned that unexplainable things happen in war. Maybe I could better describe my feelings about what happened on Harry if I could explain some lucky coincidences that had occurred previously. The first time I had this sensation was when I was standing in a bunker door on the Punch Bowl. A couple of soldiers were working on the communication wires (incoming artillery caused most wire destruction), and suddenly I had this great urge to step inside of the bunker. I stepped inside, and a mortar round landed just a few feet from where I had been standing. One soldier suffered wounds. If I hadn't moved, I would have died.

Another time, which I described earlier, was when we were searching a defensive position for some enemy soldiers who may have infiltrated the area. After I had gone some distance to the entry to the trench line, I had a gut feeling and, looking closely, noticed little prongs sticking up through the snow. They were triggers to trip the antipersonnel mines. As I led the men out of the minefield, I had the feeling again and decided to step wherever the sensation took me. I followed my instincts and safely led my company out of the minefield. No one was injured.

These sensations happened to me many times. They happened to me on Harry. I understand that such feelings are referred to as a "sixth sense" of combatants. As I walked the trench on Outpost Harry, checking the battle progress, I would feel the sensation and step inside a bunker for a few seconds. A round would go off very close. When the fight started on the night of 12–13 June, I reacted to close artillery rounds as everyone did: we would drop down in the trench—hunkering down in a bunker. The noise was enough to scare anyone. For some reason, however, I was never afraid of being hurt. I spent a lot of time running around the trenches, but I was never afraid. Of course, having been up for some forty hours, perhaps I was too tired to be afraid. Maybe I didn't have any adrenaline left.

Perhaps the best way to explain how I reacted to control myself is this: I am walking down a road in the middle of a severe thunderstorm. I have to keep going down the road regardless of the circumstances or consequences. I know that lightning could strike me at any time. I also know that it might *not* strike me. In either event, I know that only God can control the bolt, and that I can only follow His desires. I will continue to walk until He decides for me to stop. That is exactly what I did on Outpost Harry.

Numerous slivers of shrapnel and unburned powder hit my hands, arms, neck, and legs while I was on Outpost Harry. A larger piece of shrapnel sliced the top of my right knee. For many years these pieces of steel would find their way to my fingers and toes, where I would extract them. Thank God I didn't receive any serious wounds. I have often wondered, *With so many of my fellow soldiers being seriously wounded and killed all around me, why not me?*

I had participated in hand-to-hand trench combat. I had killed with my hands. I had killed with my bayonet, killed with my carbine, and killed with my pistol. I am hardheaded, hardnosed, and very difficult to persuade. Therefore, I knew I could control my emotions and my mind. I did not need outside help. At least self-control was the front I presented to the world so that I could stay in my shell.

If I told anyone I was afraid of facing the truth—that I had a hard time keeping the mental images under control—I was sure they would think less of me and be wary of my actions. Finally I decided that maybe a discussion with someone who understood my experiences would help me understand why I did what I was doing. Fortunately I found someone with the VA. With his help, I began to understand that I can never cleanse my mind of the deeply hidden images. Fortunately, with understanding my situation now, I can anticipate and control the problems these images have sometimes caused. I wish I had known many years ago.

My experience with the VA began in 1992 when several fellows who had been in the 15th Infantry Regiment, 3rd Infantry Division, placed a notice in the Korean War Veterans Association newspaper looking for Outpost Harry veterans. I was very much surprised that anyone would know anything about the obscure outpost, much less suggest a meeting. I called about the meeting to verify that these people really knew something about Outpost Harry. Convinced that they did, I decided to attend.

The site for the meeting was a motel near Fort Stewart, Georgia. My wife and I were living in Orlando, Florida. The drive to Fort Stewart took about six hours, so I had time to question my decision to take part in the meeting. Were these people combat veterans? Would this be a wasted trip? I discussed my doubts with Anne, the main question being, Did these people actually serve in the battle for Outpost Harry? I wondered who would be at the meeting; I had never met anyone who knew anything about the outpost since leaving Korea in 1953. En route, I just about turned around and headed back home. I knew that whoever these people were, they had not really been on Outpost Harry in June 1953. I was sure my wife and I were going to be disappointed. Nevertheless, we kept driving to Fort Stewart and were very glad we did.

The combat veterans I met really did know about Outpost Harry and had fought there. Finally I had found some men I could communicate with, knowing they knew what had happened there. These warriors had had the same combat experiences I lived through. It was a wonderful and emotional meeting of old combat veterans. In addition, I could easily communicate with the veterans who had not actually been on Outpost Harry but had seen the battle. They understood what I said, and I very much appreciated what they did to support us. While meeting at Fort Stewart, this group of eleven veterans formed an organization called the Outpost Harry Survivors Association (OPHSA). We have met yearly since 1992.

I had never consciously accepted the fact that I had any type of post-Korea problems, but my conversations with other Outpost Harry veterans led me to question myself. Someone asked me if I had ever been to the Veterans Affairs Clinic, and I responded that I had not. They encouraged me to do so, and, of course, I refused to accept their advice. Being hardheaded, I *knew* nothing was wrong with me. However, I began to realize that keeping my memories suppressed was becoming more difficult and my dreams were becoming more disturbing. I decided to investigate what the VA could offer to someone like me. Finally, sometime in 1993 I went to the VA and met a counselor named Bill Sautner in the Orlando Vet Center office. Bill made me face several things. First, he explained that most combat soldiers have some level of post-combat stress and that I am not unusual. However, he said, because of the intense level of combat I experienced, I may have a greater mental injury. The injury had been with me since Korea and would tend to become more dramatic the older I get, he said. Bill also told me that the VA conducts counseling sessions and can explain techniques that would help me cope. He was willing to work with me whenever I wanted his help.

After my meeting with Bill, I couldn't accept his analysis that my experiences in Korea had always been with me and were still with me, affecting my decisions. I didn't meet with him again for about two years. Finally, after a lot of soul searching, I realized that maybe Bill was right. *Why did I survive when others hadn't? Did I do all that I could that night on Harry, or did I miss something? Could I have been a better leader and saved more lives?* These questions have plagued me for years, and I still don't know the answers. And, as Bill said, I never will. Bill Sautner evaluated me, as did three VA physicians, and after consultations, we all concluded that I needed some help. Through Bill's urging, I started to meet with him for individual counseling and with other Korean War veterans in group sessions.

I had been trained not to develop close friends in the army, because if a friend were killed, my effectiveness as an officer would be diminished. Although it may be a good policy for combat, restricting close relationships is not such a good policy in the civilian world. The military training a returning veteran has received may be a reason why he sometimes has trouble making friends. As I reflected with Bill on my professional career after Outpost Harry, I recalled many instances where my subconscious barrier had prevented close professional and personal friendships.

For years, my reluctance to talk about my combat experiences was due to my fear of being misunderstood, misjudged, and allowing the memories to resurface. I was concerned that no one would believe my wild tales of hand-to-hand trench warfare. Not until I met with the fellow veterans of Outpost Harry did I discuss or reveal anything I did in Korea to my wife, Anne. How could I tell her, "Honey, when I was in the trench, I rammed a bayonet through the throat of a Chinese soldier until the bayonet hit his skull." How could I explain any of the other things I had done in combat? How could she or anyone who had not been in hand-to-hand combat understand? Would she be afraid I would go off my rocker? Nevertheless, I finally revealed some of my experiences during a discussion group at an Outpost Harry Survivors Association meeting where she was listening. Thank God, she understood.

As I mentioned above, I have questioned myself many times why, with all the death and destruction around me, I escaped serious wounds or death. I don't understand why, but I believe the hand of God protected me. To those of you who are returning combat warriors, the hand of God has touched you and you are living for a reason. Don't question why you are alive while others are dead. I assure you, those are unanswerable questions.

After many years, I finally decided to express my emotions. Since then I have met many World War II, Korean War, and Vietnam veterans who have had similar post-combat experiences. Imploding emotions, silent suffering, and rejecting friendships are common traits among combat veterans. I discovered that my story was not unique.

Each of us service members had different combat experiences. Some of us were personally involved in combat. Some were involved as bystanders witnessing the horror of combat. Regardless of the level of our activity in combat—whether we were in the U.S. Army, Navy, Marines, Air Force, or other services—

we all experienced similar post-combat trauma when we came home. Thus, my suggestions to the family, friends, and loved ones of a returning warrior are these:

- Recognize that your warrior has experienced things that are beyond your ability to imagine. If he wants to talk about what he has seen and done, let him.
- If he doesn't want to describe what happened to him, let the issue rest. His mind has to absorb images, smells, sounds, and pain before he can separate what he can live with from the unspeakable.
- If he does want to talk, remember that no religious restrictions (or any other kind of restraints) apply in hand-to-hand combat. If you don't win, you're dead. If your warrior is talking to you, be happy, because he won no matter what it took.
- Don't be surprised when he is quietly reflecting on the war. His mind is trying to sort out the horror and replace it with the tender love of his family.
- Recognize that his environment in combat was one of terror, with unbelievable levels of stress. His body and mind responded to that environment, and now he must reset it.
- Never criticize him if he becomes emotional when revealing what he has done. Be gentle. Give him time to recover and continue if he can.
- Most important, DO NOT apply any of your values to his combat actions.
- Remember, your warrior is returning from hell. He is trying to grasp what is happening to him, not realizing that he may have a lifelong burden.

Listed below are the attitudes, desires, and hopes I had when I returned home. I can't speak for every veteran, but the following ideas may also convey a veteran's intent, emotions, and how they desire to be treated. Please understand:

- More than anything, we want to rejoin the life we had before we went into combat; however, we know that turning back the clock is not possible. We will make every effort to adjust.
- We are proud to be Americans even though we have sacrificed a great deal for the rest of our lives. We want the respect we believe we deserve for having served our country.
- We want our families and loved ones to understand that our service was honorable. Destroying the enemy was not something of which we should be ashamed.
- We want our friends and families not to be afraid of us, because we are not

murderers, but soldiers. Our government placed us in a situation where we had to kill or die.

• We all have a deep, if not demonstrable, faith in God and believe that for some unknown reason He protected us and allowed us to live when many others were dying.

• We want to live in peace and allow the horrors of combat to remain locked in our memory, released only when we understand how to control them.

• We want to understand what happened to us mentally and, once we are aware of what happened to us, know that help can be available for us.

• We know that we can never purge our memory of what we have seen and done, but we can live a peaceful life if we understand ourselves.

• We want to love and receive love as normal, rational people.

• We have served our country to the best of our ability, and now we want respect and peace.

When I reflect, I realize that I could have done many things better over the last fifty-some years had I known that the subliminal destructive horror of combat was influencing all of my decisions. But I didn't know, so I suppressed my emotions. By doing so, I missed a great deal of life.

As I said before, I don't recommend the way I survived to anyone else. Don't wait as I did. Receive counseling as soon as possible after leaving combat.

Only recently has the military begun to provide counselors for individuals returning to the United States from a battle zone before they return to civilian life.[1] That is a wonderful procedure, which was not available in 1953. Regardless of service, if you are a combat veteran reading this book and have not yet visited your local Vet Center, I hope you'll do so. The VA counselors really want to help. Take advantage of the chaplain service and VA recommendations for the benefit of yourself and your family. These counselors are sincere, intelligent, compassionate, dedicated practitioners who have the training and expertise to counsel you to a better life. Help is available for today's service members so that they can avoid most of the problems I suffered.

Oh, yes. I will always remember. "Outpost Harry. Outpost Harry." What a place of unspeakable destruction and horror—and of unheralded bravery.

To all service members, wherever you are serving or have served, whatever you are doing or did, I honor and respect you for your service. And I am extremely proud to have served with you.

Epilogue

On 27 July 1953, the fighting stopped in Korea because of a cease-fire agreement between the north and the south. By that time some three million lives had been lost. Each side agreed to move their troops at least two thousand meters from the agreed-upon military demarcation line. This established space between North and South Korea is called the Demilitarized Zone, or DMZ. Because of North Korean governmental regulations, no one is allowed to enter the DMZ or even take pictures of Outpost Harry (although some are taken anyway), which was included in the DMZ. In 2001 Regnard A. Burgess Jr., a member of the 39th Field Artillery, 3rd Infantry Division, promoted converting the Outpost Harry battlefield to an international peace monument for both North and South Koreans. I agree that the strip of ground on which Outpost Harry was fought would be an appropriate memorial.

When I met Mary Anne Talbot in early 1954, our plans were for me to complete my studies for my degree and return to the army seeking a Regular Army commission. I was to be a career soldier. We were married in December 1954, and I graduated from Memphis State College the following June. My short term in college was enjoyable. I became a member of the Kappa Alpha Order, Gamma Gamma Chapter, and participated in their functions. After graduation, I immediately applied for active duty, but the army declined my request because of a severe reduction in force. A trip to Washington, where I visited my congressman and the Pentagon, produced neither a change in the policy nor a waiver for me. I secured employment with the Burroughs Corporation in 1955 and became involved with computer sales in 1958. Assigned to the Redstone

Arsenal in Huntsville, Alabama, I was fortunate to become part of the team in the development of the Saturn space program that flew to and landed on the moon. I remained in Huntsville until 1969, enjoying the leading-edge scientific environment.

On 25 February 1958, the army appointed me a Reserve officer with the rank of captain. I remained in the Army Reserve and completed the infantry advanced army extension course in 1961. I had an opportunity to return to active duty in 1962 but declined, since I now had a wife and two wonderful children. And being involved in the NASA Saturn program was very important to me.

Additionally, it appeared there was a very good chance that this now physically out-of-shape Ranger captain would quickly be sent to Vietnam. My family objected to the idea, but I remained available via the active Army Reserve if the army really needed me. I served a total of sixteen years of active and Reserve service.

My computer career included participating in the development of the first computer operating system and selling large-scale computer systems to federal and state governments.[1] In the late 1970s, I founded a computer software company, developing a computer-assisted property appraisal and taxation system and installing the programs in many counties across the United States.

Anne and I had two children, Carol and William. Our daughter graduated from the University of Florida with a computer science degree, married William Downey, and they have three beautiful children—Elizabeth, Robert, and Anne Talbot. Our son, Lieutenant William Talbot Evans, USN, graduated from the United States Naval Academy, class of 1981, and became a naval aviator, flying the A6 Intruder. Cancer ended his life at the age of thirty-one.

There seems to be mutual respect, comradeship, openness, trust, and forgiveness between soldiers that I have never been able to find in the civilian business world. I have missed the unique bonds of the army and being part of it as a career soldier. Nevertheless, having survived the battle on Outpost Harry, I consider myself extremely fortunate and appreciate the wonderful life that I have enjoyed.

Appendix A: Reports on the Defense of Outpost Harry

The following military reports were filed regarding the June 1953 defense of Outpost Harry.

Report from IX Corps Medical

During the action on Outpost Harry in the 3d US Division sector between 11 and 18 June, the patient load increased so that the normal evacuation methods were inadequate. Normally, all patients requiring immediate surgery are sent to the 44th Surgical Hospital and other patients are evacuated to Rail Holding units for evacuation by train. The number of patients requiring immediate surgery was beyond the capacity of the 44th Surgical Hospital. In order to relieve this situation two new procedures were successfully introduced. First, the most seriously wounded were evacuated to the 44th Surgical Hospital. Those less seriously wounded were evacuated by H-19 cargo helicopters directly to the 121st Evacuation Hospital from division clearing stations. Secondly, when action indicated that the above methods failed to provide enough relief to the 44th Surgical Hospital, the overflow patients were transferred laterally to other surgical hospitals by helicopter.

By this method, best use was made of available medical facilities, and definitive surgery was made available to all cases requiring it. Only one difficulty was encountered in use of the helicopters. No provision has been made by the 6th Transportation Company (Helicopter) for exchange of property such as blankets, litters, and splints. Extensive use of the H-19 helicopter for emergency evacuation would quickly deplete stocks of these items in Surgical Hospitals and Division clearing stations. This deficiency must be corrected before greater use can be made of helicopters under control of Transportation Corps for patient evacuation.[1]

Report from Division Signal Company

On 12 June, all circuits to OP Harry were broken by a very heavy artillery barrage. In an effort to get communication in and working, cable was placed in the personnel communication trench and sandbagged or buried, during the daylight hours. Teams from the wire construction platoon, 3d Signal Company as well as communication personnel from the 15th Infantry Regiment and 5th RCT, under the direct supervision of the Division Signal Officer, worked on the cable project from early morning until late in the evening of the 12th when the cable was completed and working. Project was completed at 2030 hours, and teams left the area. At 2230 the cable was again broken by extremely heavy artillery concentrations. The DSO recommended that additional radio communication be put at the disposal of troops on OP Harry as a means of maintaining communication, this was accomplished. On 16 June a new plan for wire communication to OP Harry was submitted to CG [Commanding General]. This plan recommended a new 6' trench with cable placed in the side of the trench 12 inches from the bottom and sandbagged. This project to be completed as quickly as possible. Project was delayed at that time as the Battalion C.O. on position advised against it due to the continuing heavy enemy artillery falling on and to the rear of the OP constantly.[2]

Heavy Mortar Company, 5th RCT

On 6 June 1953, the Second Platoon, Heavy Mortar Company was attached to the 15th Infantry Regiment. During the period of 11–13 June, the Second Platoon fired a total of 2,914 rounds of high-explosive shells in support of operations in defense of Outpost Harry. The Heavy Mortar Platoon fires the 4.2 inch mortar shell.

555th Field Artillery Battalion

For the entire month of June, the 555th Field Artillery Battalion was engaged in operations against the enemy. During the period, the battalion fired 1,776 missions, consisting of 56,314 rounds of 105mm ammunitions. The majority of the firing was directed toward the enemy attacks on Outpost Harry.

Chinese Artillery

Fifty-thousand incoming rounds from Chinese artillery were reported during the action on Outpost Harry. Incoming was 14,000 81mm mortar or larger rounds from the Chinese reported from 1800 on 12 June until 0600 on 13 June. The CPVA utilized 152mm and 155mm artillery during the second ten days of June 1953. The Chinese fired 222 rounds of 152mm and 49 rounds of 155mm in the Third Division and 9th ROK sectors.

Weather

During the month of June, 17 days in which rain fell were noted. Temperatures ran generally between 65 to 85 degrees with a few variations either way.

Casualties for the Period

Killed in Action	2 Officers, 28 Enlisted Men, 9 Katusa
Wounded in Action	5 Officers, 126 Enlisted Men, 7 Katusa
Missing in Action	1 Enlisted Man

Able Company and attachments had seventeen enlisted men killed in the battle. In addition, Able Company had three officers and eighty enlisted men wounded in action. It is unknown if additional deaths occurred from the wounded.

Approximately 93 men were assigned to Company A on Outpost Harry. That number increased to about 125–150 when the counterattack unit was on the hill.

Based on the above, the killed or wounded on Outpost Harry represent nearly 80 percent of the participants from Able Company.

Note: Unless otherwise specified, the information in this section comes from COL Lester L. Wheeler, "Fifth Regimental Combat Team Command Report" June 1953.

Appendix B: Awards and Decorations Earned for the Defense of Outpost Harry

As noted in the official radio log, there were five major attacks on Outpost Harry (see radio log entries for 12–13 June at 2143, 2240, 0005, 0130, and 0230 hours), plus numerous probes with small penetrations. According to the declassified S2-S3 radio log, fourteen thousand enemy artillery rounds impacted Outpost Harry during the twelve-hour period from 1800 12 June until 0600 13 June 1953. That means that for each and every minute, nineteen and one-half artillery shells struck Outpost Harry, which was one hundred yards long by thirty yards wide, just a little smaller than a football field. For anyone to withstand that level of artillery for twelve hours is astounding. Yet we did it and held all night.

United States Distinguished Unit Citations Awarded

HEADQUARTERS
EIGHTH UNITED STATES ARMY
APO 301, c/o Postmaster
San Francisco, California

GENERAL ORDERS   11 October 1953
NUMBER 923
AWARD OF THE DISTINGUISHED UNIT CITATION

By direction of the President, under the provisions of Executive Order 9396 (Sec I, WD Bul 22, 1943), superseding Executive Order 9075(Sec III, WD Bul

11, 1942), and pursuant to authority in AR 220–315, the following units are cited as public evidence of deserved honor and distinction.

COMPANY A, 5th INFANTRY REGIMENT, 5th REGIMENTAL COMBAT TEAM and the following attached units:

FIRST SECTION, MACHINE GUN PLATOON, COMPANY D, 5th INFANTRY REGIMENT, 5th REGIMENTAL COMBAT TEAM

SECOND SECTION, MACHINE GUN PLATOON, COMPANY D, 5th INFANTRY REGIMENT, 5th REGIMENTAL COMBAT TEAM

FORWARD OBSERVER TEAM, 555th FIELD ARTILLERY BATTALION, 5th REGIMENTAL COMBAT TEAM

distinguished themselves by extraordinary heroism in performance of exceptionally difficult tasks in the vicinity of Songnae-Dong, Korea. On the morning of 12 June 1953, these units relieved other United Nations forces defending a vital outpost and withstood five separate attacks by overwhelming enemy forces during the next twenty-four hours. After earlier mass attacks had been halted by combined defensive fires, the hostile element attacked under a tremendous artillery and mortar barrage during the evening and gained a foothold on the right flank of the position. Refusing to withdraw, the United Nations units closed in hand-to-hand combat and destroyed the enemy force. After an artillery barrage, waves of enemy troops assaulted both the right and the left flanks of the outpost but were again annihilated. In a final effort another onslaught of hostile forces charged against both the front and the flanks of the United Nations forces and again succeeded in entering the trenches. The courageous defenders launched a series of counterattacks, routed the enemy and restored the position. The complete devotion to duty and outstanding courage exhibited by members of COMPANY A and the attached units in hand-to-hand combat were instrumental in the successful defense of the key position. The magnificent fighting spirit of these organizations reflects great credit on themselves and the military service.
BY COMMAND OF GENERAL TAYLOR:
OFFICIAL:
PAUL D. HARKINS
Major General, General Staff
Chief of Staff

OFFICIAL
[signature] R. G. Platt

[typed] R. G. Platt
LtCol, AGC
Asst AG

Orders corrected November 29, 2002, by Department of the Army Military
Awards Branch per letter from Lieutenant Robert L. White, Chief, Military
Awards Branch.

A future Department of the Army General Order change to orders will
amend General Orders Number 1 of January 7, 1954, to reflect the above addition of the 2nd Machine Gun Section.

GENERAL ORDERS NO. 9   DATED 18 November 2005
    XIV—DISTINGUISHED UNIT CITATION—AMENDMENT

So much of Section I, Department of the Army General Order 1, stated
7 January 1954, pertaining to the award of the Distinguished Unit Citation is
amended to add:
2d Squad, 2d Section Machine Gun Platoon
3d Squad, 2d Section Machine Gun Platoon
5th Squad, 2d Section Machine Gun Platoon
7th Squad, 2d Section Machine Gun Platoon
Recoilless Rifle Platoon
Forward Observers, 81mm Mortar Platoon, Company D, 5th Regimental
Combat Team

United States Silver Star Medals Awarded—Partial Listing

HEADQUARTERS
EIGHTH UNITED STATES ARMY
APO 301

GENERAL ORDERS   6 September 1953
NUMBER 819

Section I

AWARD OF THE SILVER STAR

By direction of the President, under the provisions of the Act of Congress
approved 9 July 1918 (WD Bul 43, 1918), and pursuant to authority in AR 600-
45, the Silver Star for gallantry in action is awarded to:

First Lieutenant JAMES W. EVANS, 02028570, Infantry, United States Army. Lieutenant EVANS, a member of an infantry company, distinguished himself by gallantry in action against the enemy in the vicinity of Songnae-dong, Korea. On the morning of 12 June 1953, Lieutenant EVANS, a company commander, led his men to relieve a company on an outpost position where a heavy enemy assault was anticipated. Upon his arrival at the position, Lieutenant EVANS spent the entire day exposed to enemy fire, deploying his men in the most advantageous fighting positions. When the hostile assault was launched that night, the defensive positions of the outpost had been completely rebuilt. The enemy probed the positions for a four-hour period before launching a full-scale attack early on the morning of the 13th. Twice the enemy infantry elements gained footholds in the trenches but they were repulsed both times by bitter hand-to-hand combat under Lieutenant EVANS' directions. Throughout the battle, Lieutenant EVANS remained exposed to hostile fire to call in defensive fire, encourage his men, and coordinate the over-all defense of the outpost. The gallantry exhibited by Lieutenant EVANS on this occasion reflects great credit on himself and the military service. Entered the Federal service from Tennessee.

HEADQUARTERS 3D INFANTRY DIVISION
GENERAL ORDERS   3 July 1953
NUMBER 222

Section II

AWARD OF THE SILVER STAR

By direction of the President, under the provisions of the Act of Congress, approved 9 July 1918 (WD Bul 43, 1918), and pursuant to authority in AR 60-45, the Silver Star for gallantry in action is awarded to the following named officer and enlisted men:

First Lieutenant DELBERT F. TOLEN, 01925370, Infantry, Company Able, 5th Infantry Regiment, 5th Regimental Combat Team, 3d Infantry Division, United States Army. During the early morning hours of 13 June 1953, Lieutenant TOLEN was commanding a platoon supporting the two platoons of his company which were defending outpost "Harry," in the vicinity of Songnae-dong, Korea. Upon receiving word that the situation on the outpost was critical, Lieutenant TOLEN immediately organized his men into an assault group and led them through an intense enemy barrage. Firing his weapon, he made his way through an enemy force attempting to surround the outpost. Upon gaining the crest of the objective, he organized his men and launched a counter attack on the enemy which was entrenched on the right flank for the forward slope. Leading the men down through devastating mortar, artillery and small arms fire, he observed that his counterattacking force was not sufficient. With complete disregard for his personal safety, he again braved the hostile barrage to return to the rear slope. Here, he succeeded in organizing another group and leading it in a final assault that repulsed the attacking enemy force. Lieutenant TOLEN'S outstanding gallantry and devotion to duty reflect great credit upon himself and the military services. Entered the Federal Service from Colorado.

HEADQUARTERS 3D INFANTRY DIVISION
GENERAL ORDERS   8 September 1953
NUMBER 383

Section I

AWARD OF THE SILVER STAR

By direction of the President, under the provisions of the Act of Congress, approved 9 July 1918 (WD Bul 43, 1918), and pursuant to authority in AR 60-45, the Silver Star for gallantry in action is awarded to the following named enlisted men:

Sergeant [then Corporal] JOHN M. ROSS, RA 14456185, Infantry, Company Dog, 5th Infantry Regiment, 5th Regimental Combat Team, Third Infantry Division, Unites States Army. On 12 June and during the early morning hours of 13 June 1953, in the vicinity of Sagimak, Korea, four squads of the Company Dog machine gun platoon were attached to Company Able in defense positions on Outpost "Harry." Sergeant ROSS, a leader of the Company Dog squads, had the additional responsibility of leading two machine gun sections, the leaders of which had been wounded. Through the day, he supervised the evacuation of casualties and the rebuilding of positions damaged by mortar fire. Under his leadership a small attack was repelled that evening. At midnight a second attack was launched during which he effectively kept his weapons functioning. In one instance Sergeant ROSS used cold coffee in the absence of water in a water-cooled machine gun, and successfully turned back this charge. During the early morning hours, a heavy attack was launched, supported by intense enemy artillery and mortar concentrations which disabled and covered with debris three of his squads. Sergeant ROSS dug out and repositioned one gun crew. He then moved to a flank, administered aid to casualties in another squad, repaired their weapon, carried it to the top of a destroyed bunker and personally continued firing on the numerically superior forces. He was an inspiration to those around him and materially aided in the final defeat of the enemy attack. Sergeant ROSS' outstanding gallantry and devotion to duty reflect great credit upon himself and the military services. Entered the Federal Service from Tennessee.

HEADQUARTERS 3D INFANTRY DIVISION
GENERAL ORDERS   3 July 1953
NUMBER 222

Section II

AWARD OF THE SILVER STAR

By direction of the President, under the provisions of the Act of Congress, approved 9 July 1918 (WD Bul 43, 1918), and pursuant to authority in AR 60-45, the Silver Star for gallantry in action is awarded to the following named officer and enlisted men:

Private First Class JOSEPH M. GALLO, US 51173983, Infantry, Company Able, 5th Infantry Regiment, 5th Regimental Combat Team, 3rd Infantry Division, United States Army. During the early morning hours of 13 June 1953, in the vicinity of Sagimak, Korea, Private GALLO was manning his position when his company was attacked by a large enemy force. After his platoon was partially overrun, he refused to leave his position. He remained firing his weapon from the enemy-infested trenches until the friendly forces had formed a counterattack. He then leaped from his trench and joined in the hand-to-hand combat with the enemy until the last position had been retaken. He engaged several of the enemy in bayonet duels and remained at the forefront of the counterattacking forces until the last enemy had been driven from the outpost. Private GALLO'S outstanding gallantry and devotion to duty reflects great credit upon himself and the military service. Entered the Federal Service from New Jersey.

United States Silver Star Medals Awarded—Citations Unavailable

Sergeant Arlie Hall, Able Company, Fifth RCT (official citation not available; information below taken from the 5th RCT newsletter "The Pentagonian" 19 June 1953):

There were many men who showed outstanding courage during the recent days of bitter fighting on Outpost Harry, yet one man deserves mention in particular. He is Sgt Arlie Hall, Able Company. Those that were there described him as a one-man army, when smoke, enemy and death shrouded that vital outpost on the night of 11 June. [This date should be 12 June. No one from Able Company was on the outpost on 11 June].

The Chinese launched three attacks that night, all within the short period of two hours. The first two were light probes into the line, but the last was an enemy horde of 3,000, bent on tearing through the American forces. By sheer weight of numbers the enemy force broke through the line of defense and slowly began pushing the friendly forces off the hill. Realizing the seriousness of the situation, Sgt Hall organized a group of five men and with complete disregard for his own personal safety led a desperate charge through the enemy-infested trenches. Enemy slain and wounded piled high before his deadly accurate rifle fire and grenade throwing. Continually exposing himself to enemy small arms fire, Sgt Hall then succeeded in organizing a perimeter defense. He then proceeded on his precarious mission by distributing ammo to the newly organized defenders who dug in against repeated assaults by the enemy forces—and held.

Sgt Hall's heroic actions are believed a major factor in his Company's defense of the vital outpost, yet typified the spirit of the men of Able Company, who refused to give up, in the face of a numerically superior and determined enemy.

Lieutenant William F. Bradbury Jr., Able Company, Fifth RCT (citation unavailable)

[Of course, many other medals were awarded to soldiers who fought at Outpost Harry.]

United States Bronze Stars with Valor Clasp Awarded

HEADQUARTERS 3D INFANTRY DIVISION
GENERAL ORDERS   27 July 1953
NUMBER 282

AWARD OF THE BRONZE STAR MEDAL

By direction of the President, under the provisions of the Executive Order 9419, 4 February 1949 (Sec II, WD Bul 3, 1944), and pursuant to authority in

AR 600-45, the Bronze Star Medal with the "V" device for heroic achievement in connection with military operations against an enemy of the United States is awarded to the following-named enlisted men:

Private First Class DAVID H. GULBRAA, US56119630, Infantry, Company Dog, 5th Infantry Regiment, 5th Regimental Combat Team, 3rd Infantry Division, United States Army. During the early morning hours of 13 June 1953, in the vicinity of Sagimak, Korea, Private GULBRAA was manning a recoilless rifle in a position that offered little protection. The enemy began a heavy artillery barrage on the outpost with the intent of knocking out the remaining fortifications. Private GULBRAA, at this time, observed a large enemy force advancing around the east ridge of the outpost. Although he was clearly exposed to the artillery fire, he refused to leave his position until his supply of ammunition was exhausted. He remained with his rifle, firing with effective accuracy upon the advancing foe. When he finally did exhaust his supply of ammunition, he and another crew member made their way back to the ammunition supply point. They carried box after box of ammunition through a devastating barrage of mortar and artillery fire. He again returned to his position and set the rifle in action. Private GULBRAA'S outstanding heroism and devotion to duty reflects great credit upon himself and the military service. Entered the Federal Service from Montana.

Private Alonzo Nero, Able Company, Fifth Regimental Combat Team, the Bronze Star with Valor Clasp (citation unavailable).

[An unknown number of Purple Heart Medals were also awarded to warriors for their wounds received on the night of 12/13 June 1953.]

Notes

Chapter 1

1. Kevin Mahoney, *Formidable Enemy: The North Korean and Chinese Soldier in the Korean War* (Novato, CA: Presidio Press, 2001).

2. Michael Slater, *Hills of Sacrifice: The 5th RCT in Korea* (Paducah, KY: Turner Publishing, 2000).

Chapter 2

1. In the army both officers and enlisted men were assigned a unique serial number (SN). For enlisted personnel the "RA" prefix stood for Regular Army, indicating that the person enlisted. A "US" prefix was for enlisted personnel who had been drafted. The "O" prefix was for army officers. My enlisted serial number was RA-14321088; my officer SN is O-2028570.

2. In 1951, the 81mm mortar, with its great range and damage potential, used aiming stakes along with a sighting mechanism that was more sophisticated than that used by the 60mm mortar. The 60mm was so light that it had to be reset after each round fired, which meant a lot of guesswork was required.

3. Dayrooms are rooms set aside to provide soldiers space for writing letters and relaxing, since the barracks are restricted in size.

Chapter 3

1. The full text of this order can be found at the Truman Library Web site at http://www.trumanlibrary.org/9981a.htm (accessed 14 July 2009). Also see Charles C. Moskos and John Sibley Butler, *All That We Can Be: Black Leadership and Racial Integration the Army Way* (New York: Basic Books, 1996).

2. CPT Gustav J. Gillert Jr., quoted in William T. Bowers, William M. Hammond,

and George L. MacGarrigle, *Black Soldier, White Army: The 24th Infantry Regiment in Korea* (Washington, DC: Center of Military History, U.S. Army, 1996), 59.

3. Ibid., 265.

4. Gail Buckley, *American Patriots: The Story of Blacks in the Military from the Revolution to Desert Storm* (New York: Random House, 2001), 335–67.

5. D. F. Ravenscraft, 5th RCT, 5th Infantry Regiment, Company C Morning Report, 13 June 1953.

6. When cartridges are laid one next to another, they form a circle, since the rear of the cartridge is larger than the front with the projectile (slug). Therefore, the container (clip) that contains multiple cartridges must be curved. The clip (magazine), which contains thirty .30-caliber bullets, has to be curved and takes on the shape of a banana. For the .30-caliber carbine, each clip was about twelve inches long. About two inches of the top end (the end where the bullets were loaded) would be inserted into the carbine for shooting. With two of the banana clips we would have sixty bullets to shoot. For speed in reloading another thirty rounds (one clip), we taped one clip to another reversed so that the open end could be quickly inserted into the carbine. We would have to be careful not to let the open end of the taped magazine (now pointing down) get dirt in it, or it would become useless.

7. Gordon Rottman, *U.S. World War II and Korean Field Fortifications, 1941–53* (Oxford, UK: Osprey House, 2004).

8. The normal procedure for exchanging one unit for another is to have an advance party visit the new area. Coordinating with the company to be replaced involves learning about any weapons that may be left, enemy positions, anticipated lanes of attack, and so forth. Most of these transitions occur at night so that the enemy doesn't know if a new unit is responsible for the defense. Under a bright moon, a deep trench from the back to the fighting trench would be necessary to ensure secrecy. Then, in small groups, one squad would relieve another.

Another technique for relieving troops is called "infiltration," where a smaller number of soldiers move in to replace those that are leaving the position. This takes longer but ensures that the movement is made with the least noise.

9. In the summer of 1951, the United Nations and North Korea started talks that by 27 June 1953 resulted in a demilitarized area across Korea. During the two years of negotiations, neither side wanted to give up territory, so an imaginary line was drawn on the map across Korea. As the cease-fire grew closer, the United Nations didn't want to give the Koreans (actually the Chinese) an excuse to stop the agreement. When the Turks moved out on their own, attacking the NKPA and occupying the land, it caused a "bulge" in the line of contact on the map, thereby creating great distress in Washington, D.C. The United Nations had to get the Turks back inside the contact line.

10. For those who have never been on a rifle range, when someone fires a rifle and you're in the dugout pulling and marking the target, the ball (bullet projectile) makes a sharp crack as it passes over your head. Someone told me that what one hears is the sound of the ball breaking the sound barrier. If you listen carefully, you can then hear the sound of the rifle fire a split second after the ball passes over your head. The sound of the rifle firing doesn't travel as fast as the ball. If you have experienced this sound, you know it is unforgettable.

11. COL Lee L. Alfred, 5th RCT, 40th Infantry Division Command Report (hereafter, Alfred, 5th RCT Command Report), November 1952.

Chapter 4

1. Alfred, 5th RCT Command Report, December 1952.

2. Earlier in the Korean War, only leather boots were available (except for Marines, who used waterproof "snow pac" boots), and many warriors ended their tour in Korea with frozen feet.

3. Paddy Griffith, *Fortification of the Western Front, 1914–18* (Oxford, UK: Osprey Publishing, 2004).

Chapter 5

1. Alfred, 5th RCT Command Report, December 1952.

2. COL H. H. Fischer, 5th RCT Command Report (hereafter, Fischer, 5th RCT Command Report), January 1953.

3. Ibid.

4. Patrol leaders could call in a marking shell or a three-round concentration to kill any suspected enemy patrols or to scare the hell out of his own patrol to keep them awake. Staying very still, trying to stay warm, and thinking about home will cause most men to doze. One 105mm artillery shell hitting a few yards in front of the patrol has a great attention-getting effect.

5. As soon as a trip flare or noise in the wire alerts the whole defensive line, chaos ensues. Having senior officers at battalion and upward being awakened and advised about what amounts to a nonaction is not a good thing. No one is happy about a false alarm.

6. A number identifies a position within a unit, such as 6 for commanding officer, 5 for executive officer, and 1 through 4 for the platoon leaders.

7. My comments regarding Puerto Rican soldiers apply only to those soldiers we received from the 65th Infantry Regiment. Other Puerto Ricans and soldiers of Hispanic heritage assigned to the 5th RCT performed as well as anyone.

8. Report taken from LTC Gilberto Villahermosa, "'Honor and Fidelity': The 65th Infantry Regiment in Korea, 1950–1954." Offical U.S. Army Report of the 65th Infantry in the Korean War. U.S. Army Center of Military History, September 2000. Available at http://www.valerosos.com/HonorandFidelity3.html (accessed 16 July 2009).

9. Language differences were, of course, a problem. But the main problem was the culture differences. As with the all-black 24th Infantry, I presume the white officers did not demand as much from the Puerto Rican soldiers as they did from the white soldiers. The 65th Infantry Puerto Rican soldiers' refusal to fight occurred under Puerto Rican officers, so language is no excuse.

10. Review the complete "'Honor and Fidelity'" document from the U.S. Army Center of Military History, for a thorough explanation of the battle plus comprehensive discussions as to the cause of the failures. See note 8.

11. Fischer, 5th RCT Command Report, February 1953.

Chapter 6

1. Fischer, 5th RCT Command Report, February 1953.

2. Ibid.

3. Fischer, 5th RCT Command Report, March 1953.

Chapter 7

1. Fischer, 5th RCT Command Report, March 1953.
2. Sergeant Rewie (correct spelling unknown) was one of the best soldiers I have ever known. He was a World War II veteran, and his leadership inspired us all.
3. COL Lester L. Wheeler, 5th RCT Command Report (hereafter, Wheeler, 5th RCT Command Report), April 1953.
4. Ibid.
5. Ibid.
6. Ibid.
7. Ibid.
8. Ibid.
9. Ibid.
10. COL R. F. Akers, 15th Infantry Regiment Command Report, June 1953.

Chapter 8

1. 15th Infantry Regiment S-3 Radio Log, 31 May–30 June 1953. The original log is stored in the National Archives. Only the log messages for Able Company, 5th RCT, are shown, as to display all of the log messages tracking the action of all units could be rather confusing. An explanation for the message code abbreviations is available in the abbreviations section of this book.
2. "Orange" was the code name for the attached 1st Battalion, 5th RCT.
3. COL Lester L. Wheeler, 1st Battalion, 5th RCT, Operations Plan "Jane," 1000 hours, 10 June 1953.
4. Typically, when assigned to a division, the 5th RCT would put in a beer ration request with the assigned division. However, before the supply channels could get the beer to the 5th RCT, the 5th would transfer to another division. The requested beer would show up at the "old" division to which the 5th RCT had been attached. For some reason, the beer rations would then get lost and never reach the 5th RCT, now assigned to a "new" division. We missed out on a lot of beer.
5. Wheeler, 5th RCT Command Report, June 1953.

Chapter 9

1. Outpost Harry Survivors Association (OPHSA) Web site, http://www.ophsa.org/OPHSA_Intro.htm (accessed 14 July 2009).
2. Akers, 15th Infantry Regiment After Action Report, 29 June 1953.
3. OPHSA Web site.
4. Ibid.
5. Ibid.
6. This was a timing and communication problem. When ordered to provide a backup company, the 1st Battalion, 5th RCT, selected Baker/5th and sent it to the backup position. At that time, apparently the 5th RCT didn't know that Baker/15 was the unit currently defending Harry. When it became critical that Baker/15 receive support, Baker/5th was the only available company. If Colonel Akers realized he was sending one Baker Company to reinforce another Baker Company, he ignored the

fact. Nevertheless, he should have known that the 5th RCT was sending Baker/5th and planned accordingly.

7. The APCs that were used for protected transportation to and from Outpost Harry were from World War II. In fact, with very few exceptions, all of our equipment was from leftover supplies from World War II.

8. Recoil is created by the explosion of a shell inside of a weapon. The projectile goes out the front of the weapon, but the gases created from the explosion cannot escape until the projectile leaves the barrel. Therefore, there is an equal force in the chamber that contained the shell, and the weapon "recoils." Imagine a rifle with the bullet going out one end and the stock going in the opposite direction. With a large-caliber rifle (.30 or larger), the recoil can be very painful to one's shoulder.

A 57mm rifle would be too large to be fired in a conventional manner, so a rifle was developed that would allow the gases created by the explosion to escape. The shell had perforations along its side to allow the gases to escape through the rear of the weapon, thus equalizing the forward and reverse action and making it recoilless. Since the gases would escape from the rear of the rifle, anyone standing behind it would be killed. There are also larger recoilless rifles, 75mm and 106mm, as I recall. The 106mm recoilless rifle was normally mounted on a jeep.

9. The term "Long Toms" originated during World War II. When I was in the army, this term applied to the 155mm and 240mm artillery pieces with an extended barrel that would allow the gases to build up, thereby forcing the projectile farther.

The American 155mm artillery gun was an exceptional artillery weapon of World War II. Well known by its nickname, the Long Tom could fire a 95-pound projectile more than fifteen miles with high accuracy. It could fire more than forty rounds per hour of high-explosive, chemical, smoke, or illuminating shells.

10. Wheeler, 5th RCT Command Report, June 1953; LTG Reuben E. Jenkins, Headquarters, IX Corps Combat Operations Command Report (hereafter, Jenkins, IX Corps Combat Op Command Report), June 1953.

Chapter 10

1. The numbers here are map coordinates. The first three numbers are the longitude and the next three are the latitude. In this example, CT508425, the numbers mean from the 50 grid, go right 80 percent and from the 42 grid go up 50 percent, and you have an exact location.

2. Fighting bunkers have two openings. One is the aperture, facing the enemy. The second is the entrance to the bunker, which is also called the "back entrance" if you're inside the bunker.

3. Soldiers normally would fire out the aperture with their backs facing the entrance to the bunker. With all of the noise in the bunker from machine-gun firing, a soldier couldn't hear anyone running down the trench. If the entrance (which was really just a hole in the ground) was open, the enemy could toss a grenade into the bunker, killing everyone. Figure 19 shows the entrances to the fighting bunker in front of the soldiers in the trench.

4. The name "burp gun" comes from the way the gun sounds when it fires a burst of bullets. It is actually a Chinese submachine gun, which fires rounds from a drum-like magazine.

Chapter 11

1. Richard P. Harman writes that on 12 June 1953 he was assigned as a two-and-a-half-ton-truck driver to the 5th RCT Headquarters and Headquarters Company carrying a load of five-gallon cans full of napalm to Outpost Harry. Because of the hot weather, "the cans were expanding and the gel was popping out all over." Letter from Richard P. Harman to James Evans, 29 June 2009.

2. Ray Anderson, notarized affidavit, 2008. Anderson is the secretary/treasurer for the Society of the 3rd Infantry Division.

3. Donald W. Boose Jr., "Rifle Platoon 1953 T/O&E," illustration, *U.S. Army Forces in the Korean War, 1950–53* (Oxford, UK: Osprey Publishing), 27.

4. This message, from an unknown source, was in the radio log and illustrated the related impact of Outpost Harry.

5. Michael J. Varhola, *Fire and Ice: The Korean War, 1950–1953* (New York: Da Capo Press, 2000).

6. Although a grenade could be considered a weapon, I considered it a supplemental one. Someone attacking a fortified position with two grenades will not likely live very long. I don't recall noticing a grenade on the Chinese soldier. The Chinese used the German potato-masher type of grenade, which is larger than ours. Since he had nothing in his hand, he may have already used his two grenades.

7. Nearly forty-five years later I again met this warrior, Ernie Kramer, 10th Engineer Company, 3rd Division, who now lives in Brooklyn Center, Minnesota.

8. See Silver Star award for Corporal John M. Ross, 2nd Section, Machine Gun Platoon (page 201).

9. In the port arms position, the weapon is held diagonally across the front of the body, with the right hand on the butt of the gun and held in front of the right hip with the barrel up in front of the left shoulder.

10. The spoon is on display in the National Infantry Museum at Fort Benning, Georgia.

11. Akers, 15th Infantry Regiment After Action Report, 29 June 1953.

12. Kingpost was the call identification for the 15th Infantry Regiment commander. Kaiser 5 referred to the assistant division commander in the 3rd Infantry Division.

Chapter 12

1. Years later Captain Porter said I looked as if someone had beaten me. My eyes were blackened, my face sagged, and I looked very tired.

2. In 1997 General John Shalikashvili said the following about Colonel Wheeler: "And just as people are the lifeblood of our Armed Forces, so they have been the joy of my years in uniform. I have worked for and served with the very best—from Sergeant Greiss [phonetic], who taught me how to care for soldiers, to General Lester L. Wheeler, who instilled in me the essence of being an officer, to thousands of others." Office of the White House Press Secretary, "Remarks by the President and General John Shalikashvili in Farewell Cermony," press release, 30 September 1997. I was both surprised and heartened that the same Colonel Wheeler that so impressed me with his bravery and leadership would be recognized and appreciated in such a way by a general of the army.

3. These were men sent to me to replace our wounded and dead. They were as-

signed to Able Company as regular soldiers. No one from Able Company ever returned to Harry.

4. Jenkins, IX Corps Combat Op Command Report, June 1953.

5. Since the combat loss report concerns money and equipment, the S-4 has to review and approve the losses—to make sure no one sold a tank or other expensive piece of military equipment and claimed it as a combat loss.

6. Later, I recalled that I had always thought the name "Operation Ranger" was in my honor. When I joined the 5th RCT, I was the only qualified U.S. Army Ranger on the team. Of course, they called me the "Lone Ranger." The planners remembered I was a Ranger, and Able Company had the mission, thus the operation's name. Most U.S. military operations have similar simple reasons for the selection of an operational name. I never did find out if the name of the operation was for me, but my ego made me believe that it was a possibility.

7. One technique for preparing a quiet operation was to use duct tape to cover anything that might make a sound. We also used white medical tape darkened with mud.

8. Ridings, 3rd Division Command Report, 3rd Infantry Division Report, June 1953.

9. Probes are small groups of soldiers faking an attack to determine the size and fighting capability of the defending force. They involve searching for weakness, looking for prisoners, and distracting the enemy while a full-blown force is attacking at a different location.

Chapter 13

1. Not until the war in the Middle East did the military recognize that there are two types of brain injury: from artillery explosions that shake the brain, and from the visual experiences of combat. The army started to place trained soldiers in combat units to recognize those with trauma and get them help. Nowdays upon release there are counseling opportunities for soldiers. Even so, the fear of being marked as someone who is unstable, a coward because he cannot take it, or someone who is faking trauma to be relieved from combat leads most soldiers to deny that they need help. Our society is not yet able to accept mental illness (mental injury), so the warrior continues to suffer.

Epilogue

1. The first computer operating system was called the Master Control Program, which was written and generated using a compiler named BALGOL. Burroughs had modified the ALGOL compiler and was the first to use a compiler to write an operating system (Burroughs' ALGOL, which is short for ALGOrithmic Language). This was the first multiprogramming system with two processors for simultaneous computing. This control program was installed in the Burroughs B5000 computer, which provided advanced computer capability to the NASA space program.

Appendix A

1. Jenkins, IX Corps Combat Op Command Report, June 1953.

2. MG E. W. Ridings, 3rd Division Command Report, 3rd Infantry Division Report, June 1953.

Bibliography

Akers, R. F. 15th Infantry Regiment After Action Report. 29 June 1953.

———. 15th Infantry Regiment Command Report. U.S. Army. June 1953.

Alfred, Lee L. 5th RCT, 40th Infantry Division Command Report. November 1952.

———. 5th RCT Command Report. December 1952.

Anderson, Ray. Notorized affadavit. 2008.

Boose, Donald W., Jr. "Rifle Platoon 1953 T/O&E." Illustration. *U.S. Army Forces in the Korean War, 1950–53.* Oxford, UK: Osprey Publishing. 27.

Bowers, William T., William M. Hammond, and George L. MacGarrigle. *Black Soldier, White Army: The 24th Infantry Regiment in Korea.* Washington, DC: Center of Military History, U.S. Army, 1996.

Buckley, Gail. *American Patriots: The Story of Blacks in the Military from the Revolution to Desert Storm.* New York: Random House, 2001.

15th Infantry Regiment S-2 Radio Log. 31 May–30 June 1953.

Fischer, H. H. 5th RCT Command Report. January 1953.

———. 5th RCT Command Report. February 1953.

———. 5th RCT Command Report. March 1953.

Griffith, Paddy. *Fortifications of the Western Front, 1914–18.* Oxford, UK: Osprey Publishing, 2004.

Harman, Richard P. Letter to James Evans. 29 June 2009.

Jenkins, Reuben E. Headquarters, IX Corps Combat Operations Command Report. June 1953.

Mahoney, Kevin. *Formidable Enemies: The North Korean and Chinese Soldier in the Korean War.* Novato, CA: Presidio Press, 2001.

Moskos, Charles C., and John Sibley Butler. *All That We Can Be: Black Leadership and Racial Integration the Army Way.* New York: Basic Books, 1996.

Outpost Harry Survivors Association. http://www.ophsa.org.

Ravenscraft, D. F. 5th RCT, 5th Infantry Regiment, Company C Morning Report. 13 June 1953.

Ridings, E. W. 3rd Signal Company, 3rd Division Command Report. June 1953.

Rottman, Gordon. *U.S. World War II and Korean Field Fortifications, 1941–53.* Oxford, UK: Osprey House, 2004.

Office of the White House Press Secretary. "Remarks by the President and General John Shalikashvili in Farewell Cermony." Press release. 30 September 1997. http://clinton6.nara.gov/1997/09/1997-09-30-president-at-gen-shalikashvili-farewell-ceremony.html (accessed 19 July 2009).

Slater, Michael. *Hills of Sacrifice: The 5th RCT in Korea.* Paducah, KY: Turner Publishing, 2000.

Truman Library Web site. "Executive Order 9981." http://www.trumanlibrary.org/9981.htm (accessed 14 July 2009).

Varhola, Michael J. *Fire and Ice: The Korean War, 1950–1953.* New York: Da Capo Press, 2000.

Villahermosa, Gilberto. " 'Honor and Fidelity': The 65th Infantry Regiment in Korea, 1950–1954." Offical U.S. Army Report of the 65th Infantry in the Korean War. U.S. Army Center of Military History, 2000. http://www.valerosos.com/HonorandFidelity3.html (accessed 19 July 2009).

Wheeler, Lester L. 5th RCT Command Report. April 1953.

———. 5th RCT Command Report. May 1953.

———. 5th RCT Command Report. June 1953.

———. 1st Battalion, 5th RCT Operations Plan "Jane," 1000 hours, 10 June 1953.

Index